Obama Green

Environmental Leadership of President Obama

David B. Bancroft

Copyright © 2011 David B. Bancroft

All rights reserved. No part of this book may be reproduced in any form electronic or mechanical form (includes photocopying, recording, or information storage and retrieval) without permission in writing from the author.

Printed in the United States of America

ISBN 13:978-1456599539
ISBN 10:1456599534

CONTENTS

1. Introduction	1
Cabinet Nominations	3
Executive Office of the President Appointees	6
Congress	8
American Public	12
Leadership	14
2. Climate Change	17
Reduce Carbon Emissions	17
House of Representatives	21
Senate	29
Executive Office of the President	39
Environmental Protection Agency	45
Re-Engage with the United Nations	49
3. Green Jobs Creation	57
Create Five Million New Jobs	57
Convert our Manufacturing Centers into Clean Technology Leaders	61
Create a Green Jobs Corps	62
Create a "Clean Vet Initiative"	64
Create New Job Training Programs for Clean Technologies	65
4. Energy Generation	69
Increase Investments in Basic Research and Human Capital	69
Clean Technologies Deployment Venture Capital Fund	74
Production Tax Credit	77
Offshore Drilling	77
Develop and Deploy Clean Coal Technology	79
Safe and Secure Nuclear Energy	83

5. Energy Efficiency	86
Overhaul Federal Appliance Efficiency Standards	86
Make Federal Buildings More Efficient	88
Expand Federal Efficiency Grants	90
Fully Fund LIHEAP and Weatherize	
One Million Homes Annually	92
Invest in a Digital Smart Grid	96
6. Clean Air	99
Clean Air Act	99
Smog and Soot	102
Toxins	103
Mercury	104
7. Clean Water	105
Clean Water State Revolving Fund	105
Drinking Water Standards	106
Major Water Bodies	107
Great Lakes	107
Everglades	109
Chesapeake Bay	110
Gulf Coast	111
Restore the Wetlands	114
8. Healthier Communities	115
Protect Children and Families	
from Toxics Health Hazards	115
Brownfields	120
Control Superfund Sites and Data	122
Protect the Public from Nuclear Materials	124
Strengthen Environmental Justice Programs	126
9. Land and Wildlife	129
Protect National Parks and Forests	129
Conserve New Lands	132
Partner with Landowners	
to Conserve Private Lands	135
Endangered Species	135

10. Transportation	139
Increase Fuel Economy Standards	139
Mandate All New Vehicles	
are Flexible Fuel Vehicles	141
Partner with Domestic Automakers	142
Invest in Developing Advanced Vehicles	145
Reform Federal Transportation Funding	148
Require States to Plan for Energy Conservation	151
11. Agriculture	153
Combat Water Pollution in Rural America	153
Limit EQIP Funding for CAFOs	155
Regulate CAFOs	156
Encourage Farmers at the Cutting Edge of	
Renewable Energy and Energy Efficiency	159
Build Biofuels Distribution Infrastructure	160
Develop the Next Generation of Biofuels	165
Expand Locally-Owned Biofuels Refineries	166
Encourage Organic and Sustainable Agriculture	169
Support Local Family Farms with	
Local Foods and Promote Regional	
Food Systems Policies	170
12. Conclusions	174
Cabinet Secretaries	175
Executive Office of the President Personnel	176
Executive Orders, Memorandums	
and Agreements	179
Rules and Regulations	181
Programs	183
Congress	185
Courts	188
American Public	188
Final Analysis	191
Notes	197
About the Author	225

1.

INTRODUCTION

As president, Barack Obama will make combating global warming a top priority. He will reinvigorate the Environmental Protection Agency (EPA), respecting its professionalism and scientific integrity. And he will protect our children from toxins like lead, be a responsible steward of our natural treasures and reverse the Bush administration's attempts to chip away at our nation's clean air and water standards.

The U.S. Presidential election of 2008 was truly historic, with a pair of major party nominees never before seen in American politics. On the Republican side, Senator John McCain (R-AZ) was not only a veteran of the Vietnam War, but he had suffered cruel detention as a prisoner of war for over five years. McCain handily secured the Republican nomination in the early spring 2008, becoming the oldest first-time candidate ever to become his party's nominee.

McCain watched, as the rest of the nation did, the hotly contested race within the Democratic Party between Senator Hillary Rodham Clinton (D-NY), and Senator Barack Obama (D-IL). Whichever Democratic candidate won, the nation was guaranteed to have either its first female nominee on a major party ticket, in Clinton, or its first African-American nominee, in Obama.

After a very competitive race, Obama eventually won the number of delegates needed to secure the nomination, and he selected Senator Joe Biden (D-DE) as his running mate, during the Democratic Party convention in August. McCain and Obama conducted a very spirited campaign throughout the fall, but on Election Day, November 4, 2008, America overwhelmingly voted in Obama as its first black President.

And he was voted in as America's first green President. Obama had developed a set of environmental proposals that had

never before been seen in a successful Presidential candidate. There had been several multi-page campaign documents issued, covering numerous environmentally related topics, with a myriad of campaign promises. Some the documents included:
- Promoting a Healthy Environment;
- New Energy for America;
- Strengthening America's Transportation Infrastructure;
- Real Leadership for Rural America; and
- Supporting the Rights and Traditions of Sportsmen.

With the campaign over, the environmental community, which had put a lot of effort into the election of Obama, was eager to see him start taking the steps to make all those environmental campaign commitments become reality. A president only has so many tools at his disposal to fulfill his campaign's, and now his administration's, agenda: (1) making cabinet nominations and executive office staff appointments; (2) building relationships with Congress, its leadership, chairs and members; and (3) reaching out to appeal directly to the American people. Let's examine some of the early decisions made by Obama, and the landscape he faced, as his administration began.

Of course, with Biden on the ticket, he already had a vice president. Biden brought over 35 years of experience in the U.S. Senate. He knew the institution and personalities of the Senate well, and would be a key player in helping Obama to move legislation on Capitol Hill. While in the Senate, Biden had focused his time on foreign relations, criminal justice and drug policy. He served on the Senate Foreign Relations Committee, including twice serving as it chair, and on the Committee on the Judiciary, serving as chair for eight years. During the Clinton Administration, he urged action in Kosovo to protect the Serbs, and during the second Bush Administration, supported a partitioning plan to create a stable Iraq.[1]

Obama choose Representative Rahm Emanuel (D-IL) as his chief of staff. Emanuel had a long history in Democratic politics dating back to Senator Paul Simon's (D-IL) 1984 Senate race. In 1988, he served in the Democratic Congressional Campaign

Committee and the following year he joined Richard Daley's campaign for Chicago mayor. Then in 1992, he joined Bill Clinton's presidential campaign and later the Clinton White House as a senior advisor. Emanuel successfully ran for a U.S House seat from Illinois in 2002, where he served on the Ways and Means Committee. Emanuel was later appointed, by then-House Minority Leader Nancy Pelosi, to serve as chairman of the Democratic Congressional Campaign Committee. Under Emanuel's leadership, House Democrats gained 30 seats in the 2006 election giving them the majority.[2] Those who know him do not describe him as a shrinking violet. One of his colleagues said, "He is the rare breed who can engage in a back-alley fight but also understands that there is a time to set aside bare-knuckle fights and attempt to move an agenda. Don't get me wrong. He is a tough as they come."[3] Some in Washington did not know what to make of the appointment of Emanuel as "chief of staff, mixing one of Washington's most combustible temperaments with President-elect Barack Obama's celebrated cool."[3]

David Axelrod, the Obama Campaign's chief strategist was chosen as a senior advisor to the President. Alexrod, who began his career in journalism, jumped into politics in 1984 in running Paul Simon's 1984 Senate race. Shortly thereafter, he started a consulting firm that eventually became known as AKP&D Message and Media. Over the years, Axlerod lent his talents to many Democrat office seekers including: Senators Hillary Clinton, Chris Dodd, and Herb Kohl; Governors Tom Vilsack, Deval Patrick; Representative Rahm Emanuel and Mayor Richard Daley.[4] Axelrod's partner in the firm AKP&D, David Plouffe, who served as the Campaign Manager for the Obama Campaign, declined to join the Obama White House, but served as an outside advisor.[5]

Cabinet Nominations

After Obama made several other key senior-level appointments, and had his White House inner-circle set, it was time to look toward cabinet level nominations. To move his environmental agenda forward, Obama selected a talented a group of individuals bringing a wide range of experience from government, politics, academia and research.

- Secretary of Energy, Steven Chu – Chu is best known as a Nobel Prize winner for his ground breaking research in cooling and trapping atoms using laser light. His findings improved the accuracy of atomic clocks used in space navigation, and the design of lasers to manipulate extremely fine scale electronic circuits. Chu's career has included time at AT&T Bell Laboratories, as head of the quantum electronics research department. He joined the faculty at Stanford University in 1987, but left in 2004 to become director of the U.S. Department of Energy's (DOE) Lawrence Berkeley National Laboratory.[6] Many in the energy community were pleased that a person with such extensive knowledge, and experience, in basic science and energy research, was being placed in a leadership role at the agency. As Frances Beinecke of the Natural Resources Defense Council said, Chu was known to "recognize the grave threat of global warming, but he has devoted himself to developing clean, renewable energy technologies to combat it."[7]
- Administrator of the Environmental Protection Agency, Lisa Jackson – When Jackson was nominated, she was serving as chief of staff to Governor Jon Corzine of New Jersey. She had previously been the commissioner of the New Jersey Department of Environmental Protection, where she advanced the state's efforts to regulate greenhouse gases from cars and other sources.[8] She made New Jersey second only to California, in addressing global climate change.[7] Part of that effort was successfully convincing the governor to support $500 million in energy efficiency improvements in his economic stimulus plan. Jackson was also a leader in the 10-state Northeast Regional Greenhouse Gas Initiative, and was perceived as a thoughtful, and pragmatic leader.[7]
- Secretary of Interior, Kenneth Salazar – Salazar was a colleague of Obama in the Senate, where they both arrived after the 2004 election. Salazar was a farmer,

rancher and an environmental attorney in private practice, who had eleven years experience in water and environmental law. He first entered political life as chief legal counsel for Governor Roy Romer of Colorado, and served as executive director of the Colorado Department of Natural Resources. Winning election in 1994, he became Colorado's attorney general through 2004. He has been quoted saying, "How we improve our energy security……..will determine whether our economic fortunes will hinge on the price of oil that OPEC sets, or whether the U.S. will stand independently, as the world's innovator for clean energy technologies."[9] Not everyone in the environmental community was convinced, like Kieran Suckling of the Center for Biological Diversity, who said "Ken Salazar is very closely tied to ranching and mining and very traditional old time, Western extraction industries. And that is why I'm very concerned about this choice, because we were promised that an Obama presidency would bring change."[10]

- Secretary of Agriculture, Thomas Vilsack – Vilsack was an early rival in the 2008 Democratic presidential primary race, but dropped out and endorsed Obama. Prior to that, he had served as the Governor of Iowa from 1998 to 2006. His political career includes being a state senator, and mayor of the town of Mount Pleasant Iowa. Vilsack, who has been a fierce advocate for agricultural policy, has a vision to revitalize rural areas through renewable energy development. He has been described as having a keen political sense, that would be useful in treading the dangerous waters between the White House in Capitol Hill.[11] Upon his nomination, some in the agricultural and environmental communities were concerned that Vilsack would exclusively take the side of megafarms and agribusiness in any policy discussion, because at one time he had been named "Governor of the Year" by the Biotechnology Industry Organization.[12]

Overall, with a few exceptions, those in the environmental, clean energy and sustainable community were pretty pleased with Obama's cabinet selections, but William Kovacs, vice president of the U.S. Chamber of Commerce said, "What you have got are people who are committed to moving forward with regulation of greenhouse gases under the Clean Air Act, which we believe is a big mistake."[8]

Executive Office of the President Appointees

Cabinet level secretaries work daily managing large agencies that are located some distance from the White House. Every president needs substantive staff within his Executive Office to help move initiatives within agencies, across agencies and in liaison with members, and staff on Capitol Hill. While cabinet secretaries, and many agencies appointees, require Congressional approval, presidential staff are the sole purview of the president. In addition, each president has wide latitude in establishing positions that uniquely fit the times, and the agenda, of the individual presidencies. Obama selected a number of individuals to assist him in moving his green initiatives forward by corralling agency support, coordinating interagency action, negotiating with members and staff of Congress, and providing media messaging. These are some of the senior advisors that President-elect Obama brought on to his White House environmental team.

- Assistant to the President for Energy and Climate Change, Carol Browner – Browner is probably best known as the Administrator of the Environmental Protection Agency during the Clinton Administration from 2993-2001. When appointed by Obama, she was a principal in the Albright Group, former Clinton Administration Secretary of State, Madeleine Albright's global strategy firm. There she worked on environmental protection, climate change and energy conservation, and security. From 1989 to 1991, Browner was Senator Al Gore's senior legislative aide. She also did a stint leading the Florida Department of Environmental Regulation, where she launched the Everglades restoration efforts after setting a lawsuit brought by the federal government against Florida. Kathleen Rogers, president of the Earth Day Network said, "Carol Browner's appointment as a 'climate czar' should signal to the world that the U.S. is taking a new direction on this issue."

- Green Jobs Adviser, Van Jones - Jones was best known as the author of the book *The Green Collar Economy*, which made the New York Times bestseller list shortly after its release. He advanced the idea that as a nation, work, innovation and entrepreneurship in the clean energy sector, would provide the solutions to both our economic and environmental problems. In fact, Jones was instrumental in the passage of America's first "green job training" legislation, the Green Jobs Act, which President Bush signed into law as a part of the 2007 Energy Bill. Prior to his work in Washington, he was a co-founder of three successful nonprofit organizations: the Ella Baker Center for Human Rights; Color of Change; and Green for All. Most of Jones' work had revolved around being an advocate for disadvantaged people and the environment.[14]
- Director, National Economic Council, Larry Summers – Summers had previously been Secretary of the Treasury in the Clinton Administration. He started his career as a professor at MIT, but soon came to Washington, DC in 1983 to work on the President Reagan's Council of Economic Advisors. He later accepted a tenured position at Harvard, but returned to Washington 1991, as chief economist at the World Bank. He joined the Clinton Administration in 1993, working for Treasury Secretary Robert Rubin, whom he later succeeded. After leaving, Treasury in 2001, he became president of Harvard University, but had to resign in 2007, over remarks about whether women may have innate difference to men in understanding math.[15] Summers, Rubin and Federal Reserve Chairman, Alan Greenspan enacted a wide range of economic and bank reforms in the late 1990s. Some have linked those changes with

allowing banks to market derivatives with little oversight, and contributing to the 2008 financial collapse.[16]

- Chair, Council on Environmental Quality, Nancy Sutley – At the time of her appointment, Sutley was the deputy mayor for energy and environment for Los Angeles, California. Since 2005, she represented Los Angeles on the Board of Directors for the Metropolitan Water District of Southern California. Prior to that, she had served on the California State Water Resources Control Board from 2003 to 2005. Sutley also worked for California Governor Gray Davis as energy advisor from 1999 to 2003, managing state and federal regulations, legislative affairs, finances and press relations. She served as deputy secretary for policy and intergovernmental relations in the California EPA from 1999 to 2003, where Sutley worked on water and air pollution policy, and established budget and legislative priorities. During the Clinton Administration, Sutley worked for the EPA as a senior policy advisor to the regional administrator in San Francisco, and special assistant to the Administrator Browner in Washington, D.C.[17]

Congress

Presidents are able to nominate and appoint the people to their cabinet and staff with whom they admire, agree on goals, and are compatible on public policy issues. However, they must work with the Congress that the American people elect. This includes the party that controls each house, the number of members in the majority in each house, and the leadership that each house elects. Obama was given substantial Democratic majorities in both the Senate and House of Representatives of the 111th Congress. The House had 258 Democrats and 177 Republicans. The Senate held 58 Democrats, 40 Republicans, and two independents, who caucused with the Democrats, giving Obama a potentially filibuster proof majority. The Senate and House members elected the their leaders, and the leadership chose the committee chairs.[18]

- Senate Majority Leader, Harry Reid (D-NV) - Reid was first elected to Congress from Nevada in 1982, and served as a Representative for two terms. It was not his first trip to Congress. Decades earlier, while earning his law degree at George Washington University, Reid was a U.S. Capitol police officer. He returned to Nevada working as city attorney, state assemblyman, and chairman of the Nevada Gaming Commission. Then in 1986, Nevada elected him to the Senate in 1986, 1992 and 1998. In 1998, his colleagues voted him to be Assistant Democratic Leader or "Whip". Reid was re-elected in 2004 and unanimously chosen as Senate Minority Leader. He later became Senate Majority Leader, when the Democrats took the Senate in the 2006 election. He is an outdoorsman who championed the creation of Great Basin National Park. Over the years, he has worked to preserve the environment by developing Nevada's solar, wind and geothermal energy sources.[19]
- Senate Minority Leader, Mitch McConnell (R-KY) – McConnell has been Senate Minority Leader since 2007. He also has a long history of Capitol Hill experience serving in the late 1960s and early 1970s as an intern to Senator John Sherman Cooper, and as an assistant to Senator Marlow Cook. During the Ford Administration, he gained executive experience as Deputy Assistant Attorney General. He returned to Kentucky in 1978 as a county judge, before being elected to the Senate in 1984. McConnell became Senate Majority Whip after the 2002 election.[20] The League of Conservation Voters (LCV) for years had given McConnell a zero rating, but in 2008 they also named him to their "Dirty Dozen" list. The LCV stated McConnell had "been the enforcer for Big Oil and other corporate polluters, leading efforts to derail and weaken legislation that would protect our families and keep America's land, air and water clean."[21]

- Speaker of the House, Nancy Pelosi (D-CA) – Pelosi was elected as Speaker of the House after the 2006 election, being the first women in U.S. history to attain that post. This followed her 2002 groundbreaking rise to be the first female House Minority Leader. Pelosi started her political career as a volunteer in the Democratic Party, where she was given more responsibility and became a California representative to the Democratic National Committee in 1976. Eventually, she moved into the position of state chair of the California Democratic Party. That helped her to make the transition to elective office, when in 1987, she won a special election to the eighth district of California, which includes San Francisco. Over the years, Pelosi has been a member of the House Appropriations Committee, and the Permanent Select Committee on Intelligence. She is known as staunch advocate for health care, housing, human rights and environmental initiatives.[22]

- Minority Leader John Boehner (R-OH) – Mr. Boehner who had been elected House Majority Leader upon the resignation of Representative Tom Delay in February 2006, became House Minority leader after the November 2006 election when Democrats took the majority. His rapid rise into Republican House leadership in the 2000s, followed an equally steep decline in 1998. He had been forced out of his leadership in the House Republican Caucus, due to the significant loss of Republican seats in the 1998 election. Boehner first came to the House representing Ohio in 1990. His early career was in sales, and eventually, the president of a packaging and plastic firm in the Cincinnati area. He first entered politics in 1982 as a township trustee, and successfully ran for the Ohio state legislature serving from 1984 to 1990. In the House, he was a key player in drafting the 1994 Contract with America, and was an ally of Newt Gringrich, who became Speaker in 1995 due to their efforts.[23] When asked about global climate change, Boehner said, "The idea that carbon dioxide is a carcinogen that is harmful to our environment is almost comical. Every time we exhale, we exhale carbon dioxide. Every cow in the world, you know, when they do what they do, you have more carbon dioxide."[24]

- Chair, Senate Environment and Public Works Committee (EPW), Barbara Boxer (D-CA) – Boxer became first female chair of the Senate EPW in February 2007. She started her political career winning a county supervisors seat in Marin County, California in 1976, and a House seat from 1982 to 1990. Her big break came in 1992, when California Senator Allen Cranston retired, and Boxer mounted a successful campaign to win his seat. Boxer soon developed a reputation as a liberal with strong feminist, abortion rights and environmental beliefs.[25] Boxer successfully led the 2003 Senate floor battle to block oil drilling in the Arctic National Wildlife Refuge (ANWR), and voted again in 2005 to block oil drilling at ANWR. Boxer was also an original cosponsor of Senator Jeffords' Clean Power Act, reducing power plants emissions of sulfur dioxide, nitrogen oxides, mercury, and carbon dioxide.[26]

- Chair, House Energy and Commerce Committee, Henry Waxman, (D-CA) – Waxman became Chair, House Energy and Commerce Committee in January 2009, beating out Representative John Dingel. Dingel had more seniority, but many believed he was blocking significant environmental legislation. Waxman was first elected to the House in 1975, and had previously been a member of the California State Assembly from 1969 to 1974. During his tenure in the House, he has championed numerous pieces of environmental legislation, including the first bill to address climate change in 1992. He was a primary author of the 1990 Clean Air Amendments, addressing smog, air borne toxics, acid rain, and ozone. In addition, Waxman sponsored the 1986 and 1996 Safe Drinking Water Act

Amendments, 1996 Food Quality Act, the Radon Abatement Act, and the Lead Contamination Control Act.[27]

American Public

The American people were looking for change on Election Day in November 2008. During the previous eight years of the Bush Administration, the public had experienced the tragic attacks of 9/11, killing 3000 of their fellow citizens. They had seen the initiation and the escalation of two wars in Iraq and Afghanistan, which had lasted for too many years. They became disillusioned when they realized that were no weapons of mass destruction hidden in Iraq. In addition, they were living through a decline in the economy that had driven the unemployment rate to 6.7 percent. This was the highest level of unemployment that America had experienced since September 1993, over 15 years earlier. A total of 1.9 million people had lost their jobs over the period December 2007 to November 2008. This brought the nation's total unemployed to 10.3 million.[28] Everyone knew someone who had lost their job, or was about to lose their job, and they were afraid they would be next.

Obama brought soaring rhetoric to the presidential campaign in the language of "hope," "change," "yes, we can," and a vision of an America returning to a better version of itself. America was thirsty for hope and change. And Obama brought an intelligence combined with a gift for language. After eight years of a president who had a hard time expressing himself, when confronted with complicated thoughts, America saw a candidate who was knowledgeable and articulate. Obama communicated a series of policies and plans to take the nation to a better place. In addition, he was young, vital and agile in understanding the pain of America. No time was this more in evidence than on September 15, 2008, when long-time Wall Street giant Lehman Brothers collapsed, and Merrill Lynch was sold to Bank of America. McCain responded by saying that "the fundamentals of the economy are strong."[29] To many people, McCain seemed out of touch and that may have been the day that the election was sealed for Obama.

Election Day, November 2008 was a time for Americans to express their desire for change. They overwhelmingly voted for Obama, giving him 53 percent of the vote to McCain's 46 percent. It was the largest percentage of any first time presidential candidate since Lyndon Johnson's win in 1964. The landslide was impressive in electoral votes as well, with Obama receiving 365 and McCain 173. The final number of votes totaled 131.3 million, showing an increase of 9 million voters in the four years since the 2004 presidential election, indicating greater public enthusiasm and interest in the race. Looking at the percentage of actual voters to potential voters, the 2008 race had a 63 percent turnout rate, the highest since 1960.[30]

It is often said with his good looks, and use of the new medium, that John F. Kennedy ushered in the era of the television presidency in 1960. It could just as easily be said that Obama has ushered in the era of the internet presidency. Obama had perfected the stump speech, and could deliver a public oratory from a teleprompter as well, if not better, than any candidate before him. However, he also deployed the internet, and social marketing networks, to connect with the American people in ways that technology could not do before. During the campaign he had combined video, the internet, and social media sites to recruit and build relationships with volunteers and supporters. This was especially effective with young voters, and those tactics would be instrument in motivating and securing their votes. Supporters were asked to provide their cell phone numbers, and they received regular text message blasts. Videos were uploaded to YouTube, where viewers dedicated 14.5 million hours watching Obama campaign messages, which would have cost the campaign $46 million dollars to air as television ads. Obama's Facebook page had 2.6 million supporters, and his Twitter account had 123,000 followers. From August 2008 through Election Day, Obama was mentioned in 500 million blog posts.[31]

Joe Trippi who had pioneered Howard Dean's groundbreaking internet fund raising efforts during the 2004 presidential race, envisioned Obama using all these social media contacts with supporters to enact his agenda. Trippi said "If the President says 'Here are the members of Congress who stand in the way of us passing health care reform' I would not want to be one of those people. You will have 10 or 15 million networked Americans barging in on the members of Congress telling them to get into line with the program and pass the health care reform bill. That will be a power that no American president has had before. Congress' power will be taken over by the American people."[31] One of the issues that the Obama Administration had to address, was how to utilize the information from the more than 10 million supporters that they had gathered during the campaign. Federal election laws mandate that a president must communicate with all America citizens, and not just with the members of the public who supported him during the election.[32]

Leadership

Obama was not in office long before conservatives, and other right-wing critics, started questioning everything about him. His birth, his citizenship, his allegiance to America, his belief in capitalism, and his religion; everything about his background was on the table for discussion, and up for grabs. For some of his detractors, there were no facts that would end their hyperbolic attempt to convince the American people that Obama was "the other," and "not one of us." Even though he had won the presidency with a landslide 53 percent of the popular vote, greater than even Ronald Reagan did in 1980,[30] day after day you could hear radio and television personalities making millions of dollars by questioning Obama's authenticity. Or you could log into internet blogs dedicated to tearing down Obama, and read the latest piece of gossip or rumor.

Some took the threads of policy ideas from Obama's environmental agenda, and tried to weave them into astonishing conspiracy theories. One opponent said "Implementing this long-sought list of (environmental) policy demands, offered by the larger umbrella of Left-wing activists for decades, in the name of every threat, 'greatest' and otherwise, will simply transfer decisions from individual producers and consumers to the state. It would give them power. It would give them your wealth."[33]

Another critic argues about Obama's climate change agenda, saying, "The bottom line is that any regulatory action that the Obama administration or Congress advocates will be all pain for no measurable climate gain. It will destroy wealth, increase the price of virtually everything, drive industries overseas where they can pollute even more, substantially increase government and greatly restrict personal freedoms."[34]

Not all of Obama's critics were from the right. Some were from the left, who were staunch green economy advocates, and who supported global climate change legislation. They saw chinks in the Obama Administration's armor, structure and tactics, to achieve real and meaningful environmental legislative change. For example, one questioned the commitment of Obama's White House chief of staff to climate change legislation, when he recounts a meeting between the environmental community and Rahm Emanuel, where "they could tell that he didn't much care about climate change. What he cared about was winning – acquiring and maintaining presidential power over an eight-year arc. Climate and energy were agenda items to him, pieces on the legislative chessboard; he was only willing to play them in ways that enhanced Obama's larger objectives. He saw no point in squandering capital on a lost cause. The White House could claim victory if Congress passed a beefy energy bill without a cap."[35]

Others in the environmental community were not satisfied with just questioning Obama's appointments, or legislative priorities, they questioned the environmental commitment of Obama himself. One popular blogger said, "Obama is the first president in history to articulate in stark terms both the why and how of the sustainable clean energy vision. But the question now is whether he really believed what he said."[36]

Who is right? The critics on the conservative right, or the critics on the liberal left? To answer that question, the next ten chapters list Obama's campaign promises by topical area.[37] These chapters examine in detail the strategies and tactics that the Obama Administration has pursued over the first two years in office to fulfill them. The concluding chapter analyzes how Obama has utilized the tools of the presidency – nomination and appointment powers; signings, rules, and programs; relationships with Congress; the courts; and ultimately his appeals to the American people – to assess his environmental leadership in first two years in office. The final analysis will suggest whether he is an under-achieving environmental president, a good environmental president or a transcendent environmental president.

Then, we should have a better idea if Obama has been implementing an unprecedented environmental agenda that is so wide, and so deep, that it will ultimately steal all your power, your freedom, and your wealth. Or, is Obama a charlatan and poseur, carrying out a modern day version of the 1970s movie *Soylent Green*. Where he has ground up the hopes and dreams of the environmental community, and fed them into the political machine in order to achieve power, in a latter day Obama Green.

2.

CLIMATE CHANGE

Reduce Carbon Emissions 80 Percent by 2050: *Barack Obama and Joe Biden support implementation of a market-based cap-and-trade system to reduce carbon emissions by the amount scientists say is necessary: 80 percent below 1990 levels by 2050. They will start reducing emissions immediately in his administration by establishing strong annual reduction targets, and they will also implement a mandate of reducing emissions to 1990 levels by 2020. In addition Barack Obama and Joe Biden will:*

- *require that 100 percent of pollution credits to be auctioned in order to ensures that all large corporate polluters pay for every ton of emissions they release, rather than giving these emission rights away for free to coal and oil companies.*
- *use some of the revenue generated by auctioning allowances to support the development and deployment of clean energy, invest in energy efficiency improvements to help families reduce their energy prices, and to address transition costs, including helping American workers affected by this economic transition and helping lower-income Americans with their energy costs.*
- *establish a National Low Carbon Fuel Standard (LCFS) to speed the introduction of low-carbon, non-petroleum fuels. The standard requires fuels suppliers to reduce the carbon their fuel emits by ten percent by 2020.*
- *establish a 25 percent federal Renewable Portfolio Standard (RPS) to require that 25 percent of electricity consumed in the U.S. is derived from clean, sustainable energy sources, like solar, wind and geothermal by 2025*
- *ensure that at least 30 percent of the federal government's electricity comes from renewable sources by 2020.*

"Each day brings further evidence that the ways we use energy strengthen our adversaries and threaten our planet."[1] Those were some of the first words out of President Obama's mouth in his Inaugural Address, spoken minutes after taking the oath of office. The environmental community across the nation expressed a collective sigh of relief, that after eight years of the Bush Administration, and months of hard work to elect a new president, Obama had not forgotten them, or their issues.

In the weeks prior to inauguration, some leaders in the environmental and business communities, known for supporting climate change legislation, were invited to the Obama transition office. They met with incoming White House energy and climate change advisor Carol Browner and incoming director of the National Council of Economic Advisors, Larry Summers. While the meeting was originally to focus on the proposed American Recovery and Reinvestment Act (Recovery Act) needs, Summers quickly turned to the topic of climate change and cap-and-trade legislation. Summers was not known as a strong climate change advocate. He detailed his views on Recovery Act stimulus funding and cap-and-trade legislation, as interlocking elements, that were both vital to the nation's economic recovery and long-term growth. Summers said, "It's like two blades of a scissors. Stimulus spending is one blade. And a cap-and-trade mechanism will be the other. We need them both. Stimulus alone isn't going to do it."[2]

In the first few week of the Obama Administration, there were daily meetings and conferences of Obama executive agency personnel with member of Congress. They strategized about the path forward in climate change legislation, based on the best science. In addition, Obama' Department of Energy (DOE) Secretary, Steven Chu, did media interviews, where he talked of the dire consequence of ignoring climate change, which included increasing droughts in the western U.S., exacerbating water shortages, and wildfires. He concluded by saying, "I don't think the American public has gripped in its gut what could happen."[3]

A more complete answer to what could happen if the U.S. ignored climate change, came in a study prepared by the United States Global Change Research Program. This was a joint commission of 13 federal agencies, and the White House, which is required to release a report every decade on the effects of natural and human-caused global climate change. The study concluded that climate change would:

- decrease the size of lakes in Alaska, increase the populations of insects in the grain belt of the Midwest, and increase the numbers and intensity of heavy rainstorms in the Northeast:
- impact the economy by affecting snow skiing and sports fishing, damage roads, change electricity demands, and reduce moisture and precipitation across the Southwest and throughout the nation;
- threaten coastlines through sea level rise, submerging the Florida Keys, Cape Canaveral and portions of the Gulf coast, flood wetlands, and destroy six of the nation's ten major shipping ports; and
- challenge agricultural operations by altering growing seasons, especially those that require cold weather chilling, such as cranberries and apples, and impact America's food supply overall.[4]

Obama's Administrator of the National Oceanic and Atmospheric Administration, Jane Lubchenco, commented on the report by saying, "I believe this report is a game changer."[4]

When Obama unveiled his FY2010 budget in February 2009, environmentalists were ecstatic that it included $645 billion in revenues over ten years, from the sale of emissions allowance under climate change legislation. That legislation was assumed by the Obama Administration to be in effect by the new fiscal year, starting in October 2009, just eight month from then. This was further evidence that the Obama Administration was on board to push for climate change legislation, and push for it soon.[5] Also in February, Obama gave his Address to Congress, where he said, "But to truly transform our economy, to protect our security and save our planet from the ravages of climate change, we need to ultimately make clean, renewable energy the profitable kind of energy. So I ask this Congress to send me legislation that places a market-based cap on carbon pollution and drives the production of more renewable energy in America."[6]

The statement was a home run. It had everything the environmental community had been waiting for a president to say. Obama mentioned renewable energy, climate change legislation, and most importantly, a market-based cap. However, to some environmentalists, Obama's call for climate change legislation sounded a little passive with the language, "I ask this Congress to send me legislation." Those in the environmental community agreed with the goal, and were glad that President Obama had made the remarks, but some worried that the passive language meant that he was not going to work hard to champion the cause on Capitol Hill.[7]

The concerns about the Obama Administration's commitment to move out quickly to secure passage of climate change legislation were soon validated, when White House Press Secretary Robert Gibbs stated that the White House would support legislation to reduce carbon emission "whether that is this year or next year."[8] Another clue to the Obama Administration's position was revealed when Council on Environmental Quality, chair, Nancy Sutley, said that U.S. leadership at the December 2009 United Nations' climate change conference in Copenhagen, was not dependent on climate change legislation being passed domestically. Then reports surfaced, after Obama met with the National Governors Association in late February 2009, the timetable he presented for passage of climate change legislation had moved into 2010. Obama was backing away from an aggressive timetable, because of the amount of opposition that his administration had faced from Republicans in passing the Recovery Act.[8] None of this was good news to the environmental community.

Energy Secretary Chu and Environmental Protection Agency (EPA) Administrator, Lisa Jackson, testified on Capitol Hill in April 2009 on behalf of swift action on climate change. Chu endorsed a gradual, market-based cap on carbon, and a renewable electricity standard, saying, "We can neither let our planet get too hot nor let our economy grow too cold. We must get off the sidelines of the clean energy race and play to win."[9] Chu further added that if the U.S. "fails to seize this opportunity to lead, the new clean economy will be created overseas rather than in America."[9] Jackson agreed, telling House members, "Lasting economic recovery will come only when the federal government looks beyond the quick fixes and invests in building the advanced energy industries that will help restore America's economic health over the long term."[9] The Republicans in the hearings were not impressed, and Representative Mike Pence (R-IN) said, "You're talking about legislation that essentially amounts to a declaration of economic war on the Midwest by liberals on Capitol Hill."[9]

Obama's cabinet members were not the only ones to hear scathing skepticism of legislative plans to control global climate change by pricing carbon. Obama heard it directly from some of the members of his own Economic Recovery Advisory Board (ERAB), chaired by former Federal Reserve Bank head, Paul Volker. At the very first meeting of the ERAB, several members including Caterpillar CEO James Owen and AFL-CIO Secretary-Treasurer Richard Trumka warned President Obama about the economic harm that could be done to American business interests, if the U.S. moved unilaterally without similar measures being adopted in international markets, like China. Harvard economist, Martin Feldstein, mentioned his concern that carbon pricing of utilities would be passed on to consumers at a rate of $400 to $1,500 per year. Robert Wolf, CEO of UBS Group Americas, was concerned that new financial markets created to trade carbon offsets, might create similar derivatives issues to those in the housing market, that contributed to the 2008 economic collapse. Obama concluded the ERAB meeting by saying he saw some signs of a return to normalcy in the economy, but "turning to climate change, this is a huge, complicated, difficult issue."[10]

House of Representatives

In late March 2009, the House of Representative took the lead on climate change legislation. Energy and Commerce Committee chair, Henry Waxman (D-CA) and Energy and Environment Subcommittee chair, Ed Markey (D-MA) released a 648-page draft bill calling for the establishment of a cap-and-trade system for greenhouse gases (GHGs), and standards for renewable electricity. This draft bill, known as Waxman-Markey, targeted a 20 percent reduction in GHGs from 2005 levels by 2020. This was more aggressive than the Obama Administration goal of 14 percent over the same period. The bill set a 25 percent renewable electricity standard by 2025. In order to keep the door open for negotiation, the bill avoided specifics when it came to auctioning off, or giving away free, pollution credits, and how any revenue from a cap-and-trade system would be spent. Surprisingly, the U.S. Chamber of Commerce was favorably disposed to some of the bill's energy efficiency and carbon sequestration provisions. The Chamber's vice president for environment, technology and regulatory affairs, William Kovacs, said, "We were expecting the absolute worst, and this is closer to reality than we thought it would be."[11]

Speaker of the House Nancy Pelosi called climate change the flagship issue of her speakership, and indicated that a bill would pass the House in 2009.[12] However, no sooner had the Waxman-Markey bill been released, when House members began wrangling over how the dollars raised from cap-and-trade system would be allocated. The Obama Administration had estimated that a cap-and-trade system would raise $645 billion over the next decade. While the bill was silent on auctioning pollution credits, its sponsors, Waxman and Markey, favored giving the allowances away free to U.S. industry, especially the struggling economic sectors like steel glass and paper. This was also the position of the corporate and environmental group coalition, known as the United States Climate Action Partnership, that had numerous discussions with the House chairmen during the drafting of the legislation. The free allowance would sunset over time, but initially would be provided to firms with heavy international competition, and state regulated electric distribution companies. Obama supported a 100 percent auction of the pollution credits, with the proceeds going to tax credits, energy efficiency projects, and offsets for higher consumer electric bills.[13]

The EPA was asked by Waxman and Markey to perform a preliminary economic analysis of the impacts of their draft legislation. The results showed that:

- The clean energy transformation of the U.S. economy would begin almost immediately with major investments in energy efficiency reducing energy consumption, so that projected 2015 levels, would not reached until the middle of the century.
- Renewable energy commercialization would increase by greater than 150 percent over the next two decades, due to the draft bill's renewable electricity standard.

- Strong demand would be created for a domestic manufacturing market for these next generation energy technologies employing American workers; and
- American economic recovery and job growth would be spurred, including manufacturing wind turbines, developing clean energy from geothermal sources, and engineering coal-fired power plants that do not emit GHGs.[14]

Republicans criticized the EPA analysis on several points, but the one they seemed most concerned about, was the lower economic growth forecast that the EPA used. It tended to reduce the projections for future electric demand and the emissions. Representative Darrell Issa (R-CA) noted that EPA had used a 2.5 percent growth rate for gross domestic product, rather than the 3.3 rate used by Obama, in the development of his proposed FY2010 budget. Issa said that accounted for a $1.2 trillion difference that needed to be addressed, and that the EPA's numbers for offsets did not match Obama Administration's earlier estimates. EPA stated that its analysis was based on a more thorough 600 draft bill, while the White House's earlier numbers were based on a concept. In addition, EPA had the just-released 2009 Energy Information Administration's Annual Energy Outlook to work with, while the White House, a few months back, had only the 2008 report. Issa charged that "This discrepancy is indicative of what may be a disturbing trend by this administration to manipulate facts and figures to justify their cap-and-tax bill."[15]

Republicans were not the only ones concerned about the Waxman-Markey bill. There were several conservative and Bluedog Democrats who did not think the bill was good for their districts, or their prospects for re-election. The Democrats in opposing the bill could be divided regionally, with those from coal dependent areas being concerned that voters would see a steep increase in utility bills, while those from manufacturing districts saw cap-and-trade sending jobs overseas. Representative Jason Altmire (D-PA) said, "Any way you do it, it hurts Pennsylvania, especially Western Pennsylvania. I think cap-and-trade is bad policy."[16]

Waxman said he understood the concerns of Midwestern Democrats. He also believed that those representing the coal-dependent part of the nation, would ultimately come to the table, and help implement a clean energy plan. But in May 2009, Democrats of the House Energy and Commerce Committee were deadlocked over the Waxman-Markey bill. The committee could not come to agreement. Waxman could neither persuade, nor provide enough incentives, to gain the support of Democrats who wanted protections from spiking prices for regional interests, including steel mills, oil refineries and coal plants. Obama met with committee members to urge them to work out differences, but he did not explicitly endorse the Waxman-Markey bill. Waxman said of Obama, "He wants us to try to work out our bill and he is giving us a lot of latitude to do that. He wants us to move. He wants legislation." That meeting, between the Obama and House committee members, resulted from a discussion the prior week on Capitol Hill, between White House senior advisor David Axelrod and energy assistant Carol Browner with key Democratic members of the House.[17]

Waxman continued to work with his fellow Democratic committee members and on May 21, 2009, he was able to pass Waxman-Markey bill out of committee with a 33 to 25 vote. It was mostly party-line vote, with only one Republican Mary Bono Mack (D-CA) voting "yes," and four Democrats voting "no," including John Barrow (D-GA), Jim Matheson (D-UT), Charlie Melancon (D-LA) and Mike Ross (D-AR). The bill passing out of committee had lowered its GHG reduction targets to 17 percent below 2005 levels by 2020, and 80 percent by 2050. Representative Joe Barton (R-TX) the ranking Republican on the committee offered three amendments that were defeated. The first would have eliminated the cap-and-trade provisions from the bill, the second would have stripped EPA of its authority to regulate GHGs, and the third would have spurred more production of oil, gas, coal and nuclear power. Representative John Dingell (D-MI) offered successful amendments that created a new loan guarantee program for clean energy technologies, established a tree planting program, and created a voluntary system of product labeling for carbon content.[18]

Passing the House Energy and Commerce Committee was just the first step in the process. The Waxman-Markey bill had to pass through six more committees before it could reach the House floor. The Ways and Means Committee chair, Charles Rangel (D-NY) wanted to address health care reform first, and two of his committee members John Larson (D-CT) and Chris Van Hollen (D-MD) had substantial amendments to offer. Agriculture Committee chair, Colin Peterson(D-MN) had numerous problems with the bill. He had gathered 26 Democrats poised to vote against the bill, if issues pertaining to the farm community were not addressed.[18] Pelosi stepped in on June 3, giving the six chairmen until June 19 to finish their business, and pass the bill through their respective committees.[19]

In the end, Rangel and his committee had very few issues with the Waxman-Markey bill, it was Peterson's committee that proved to be more challenging. Peterson had multiple concerns including: (1) farmers would see higher oil and gas prices affecting the prices they pay for feed, fertilizer and fuel; (2) a carbon market would give Wall Street a greater hand in affecting energy prices; (3) the definition of biomass under the renewable fuel standard was too narrow; (4) farmers wanted agricultural offsets created, so that they could get credit for changing tillage practices to increase soil carbon; (5) electric cooperatives were short changed in favor of large utilities; and (6) EPA has established an "indirect land use' element under the renewable fuels standard that penalized ethanol production.[20]

The indirect land use issue, was not part of the Waxman-Markey bill, but was a provision of the 2007 Energy Information and Security Act. As part of EPA calculation of the carbon content of renewable fuels, the agency was to consider land change internationally, based on decisions that farmers make domestically. For example, if a farmer decided to plant corn for ethanol, rather than soybeans for the food market, EPA needed to consider the fact that the need for soybeans may increase, spurring a farmer in South America to clear rain forest for soybean production. The loss of the carbon sequestered in the rainforest, would have to be included in the carbon calculation for ethanol.[21]

With the climate change bill stalled in negotiations between Waxman and Peterson over the agricultural issues, the Republicans seized the opportunity to introduce their own energy bill, The American Energy Act. The bill, announced by House Minority

Leader John Boehner, had three basic thrusts, which were to increase domestic energy production, deploy more renewable energy sources, and adopt more energy efficiency practices and technologies. Republicans saw a great abundance of untapped energy in the Outer Continental Shelf estimated to contain 86 billion barrels of oil, and 420 trillion cubic feet of natural gas. The bill would accelerate current leasing plans, and expand the Outer Continental Shelf to 12 miles from state shorelines. Some of the revenues from these leases would fund renewable energy programs. Nuclear energy was another part of the bill, with a plan to bring online 100 new reactors in the next 20 years. Additionally, the Republican plan would provide tax incentives for residential and business investments in energy efficiency.[22]

Two new studies were released in June 2009 that had positive impacts on Waxman-Markey congressional discussion. A Center American Progress report was published that indicated that $150 billion investments in renewable energy would create a net gain of 1.7 million jobs. The second analysis, performed by the Congressional Budget Office, showed that climate change bill would cost the nation about $22 billion per year by 2022. This would translate into $175 per home, or as some Democrats said, one postage stamp a day.[23]

Waxman and Peterson came to agreement in late June 2009 on a set of provisions that would allow the agricultural coalition, which was blocking the Waxman-Markey bill, to come on board. Some of the major parts of the package included the provision that U.S. Department of Agriculture USDA) would oversee a program of agricultural carbon offsets for the farm community. EPA's role in those agricultural offsets would be determined at later date. In addition, EPA would back off the "indirect land use" requirement that farmers engaging in sales of corn for ethanol must set aside land to replace international land losses.[23]

It was at this time that former Vice President Al Gore scheduled a meeting with Obama White House chief of staff Rahm Emanuel. The purpose of the meeting was to discuss increased White House engagement in the upcoming House vote over Waxman-Markey.[24] Gore and Emanuel knew each other well from their days working in the Clinton White House, and respected each other's political judgment. More involvement from Obama on House climate change legislation was a tactic that the environmental community had been urging, and expecting for long-time. While everyone appreciated the behind the scenes work of Axelrod, Browner, Chu and Jackson, the environmentalists were frustrated that Obama was not out in public, making statements in support of the Waxman-Markey bill.[23] When Gore sat down with Emanuel, they went over House voting lists name by name, and before Gore left the White House that day, Emanuel had agreed to put Obama's weight behind the bill.[24]

Emanuel called Pelosi, Waxman, Markey and other House members to tell them that the White House was fully on board. Obama began making calls to members who were on the fence or leaning toward voting "no". The next day, Obama, responding to a question on climate change during a press conference, called on House members to pass the Waxman-Markey bill.[25] Later in the week, Obama made a statement in the Rose Garden to pressure House members to support the climate change legislation. He told the members of the House, and the nation, "Make no mistake: This is a jobs bill. This legislation will finally make clean energy the profitable kind of energy."[26]

While Obama's direct involvement in securing votes for passage made the process easier, that does not mean it made passage easy. Pelosi and her leadership team, including Majority Whip James Clyburn (D-SC) who had primary responsible for counting votes, still did not have enough support for passage on the day of the vote in late June 2009. Business on the bill started with five and a half hours of debate, including Boehner speaking for an hour, by reading from a 300 page amendment to the bill that had just been released at 3:00 am that morning.[27] Then the House went into an extended period for voting, where Pelosi posted one of the taller members of her party, Representative Jay Inslee (DF-WA) at the door to lobby, and instructor her caucus not to leave the House chamber until the vote was over. Pelosi told them she wanted the bill to pass, and she might need some of them to change their votes to make that happen.[28]

As the voting began, Pelosi set her sights on lobbying four members specifically. Two of the members Lloyd Doggett (D-TX) and Bob Filner (D-CA) were going to vote "no," because they thought the bill was not tough enough. The other two members Ciro Rodriguez (D-TX) and Joe Baca (D-CA) were concerned about how voting "yes" would affect their re-elections. Pelosi was seen having nose-to-nose discussion with each of them, lasting as long as a half hour. All four eventually were persuaded by Pelosi to vote for the bill. However, when called, Rodriguez voted, "no," and quickly left the chamber with Representative Anthony Weiner (D-NY) in hot pursuit yelling, "Rodriguez, Rodriguez." A confused group of news reporters watched the action, not knowing what had just happened.[28] The Waxman-Markey bill passed the House with 219 to 212 vote tally, giving Obama and Pelosi a major victory.[27]

The final Waxman-Markey bill that passed contained 1,300 pages and was designed to lower GHG emissions to 17 percent below 2005 levels by 2020, and 83 percent below 2005 levels by 2050. The cap would apply to electric utility generators, manufacturing plants, and oil refineries. It would allow the regulated industries to buy and sell emissions credits to help meet the cap. The bill would provide 85 percent of the pollution allowances to the regulated industries for free, but this practice would be phased out over a 10 to 20 year period. In addition, the bill contained a provision for a renewable electricity standard, for those utilities selling over 4 million megawatt hours of electricity annually, which would require 20 percent of their power to be derived from renewable sources. However, governors could request that the federal government allow utilities in their states to use documented electricity savings from energy efficiency technologies for up to two-fifths of their renewable electricity obligation.[29]

The passage of Waxman-Markey did not end the discussion of the bill's advantages and failings. The Energy Information Agency (EIA) of the DOE released a report, later in the summer of 2009, which indicated that costs of the climate change bill would be modest in the short-term. The EIA projected that the bill would only increase electricity rates three to four percent by 2020, and gasoline prices would increase 23 percent by 2020, and 36 percent by 2030.[30] A study sponsored by the National Association of Manufacturers, however, painted a bleaker picture, stating that

Waxman-Markey would reduce economic growth by 2.4 percent and reduce employment by 2 million by 2030.[31]

Senate

The Senate was a little slower in moving forward on climate change legislation than was the House. As George Washington famously said, "The Senate is the saucer into which we pour legislation too cool." Our first President was absolutely right, but even he would be surprised to see the slow pace of the 111th Congress, with 136 cloture votes being filed. This Senate procedure then requires 60 votes to put a time limit on consideration of the bill, prevent a filibuster, and proceed to voting. There has been a steady rise in threatened filibusters requiring cloture votes over the past 50 years. In the 1960s cloture filings were in the single digits, during the 1970s and 1980s they jumped to an average of about 40, the 1990s saw them peak at 82.[32] The 110th and 111th Congresses with 139 and 136 cloture votes respectively, reflected an unprecedented rise in legislative obstructionism.

Even before a Senate bill climate bill was introduced or even drafted, forces in opposition were expressing their displeasure toward any proposed legislation. Senator Debbie Stabenow (D-MI) had formed a coalition of 16 members, from coal-producing and industrial Midwest states, to blunt any negative economic impacts, or job reductions, that might be included any proposed legislative package. Senator Arlen Specter (R-PA) and Judd Gregg (R-NH), who had been supporters of a climate change bill in the previous Congress, stated that they were opposed to Obama's proposal. Senator Bob Corker (R-TN) voiced his opposition, believing that any cap-and-trade legislation would be a tax increase.[33]

Browner floated the idea that climate change legislation could be passed in the Senate using budget reconciliation, that would only require 51 votes, not the 60 needed to invoke cloture. Senator Barbara Boxer (D-CA), chair of the Senate Environment and Public Works Committee, who would be drafting the climate change legislation, said she would be open to using that procedure. However, members of her own party like Senator Kent Conrad (D-ND), and members of the Republican Party, like moderate Senator Susan Collins (R-ME), advised against that route.[33]

Members of the Senate were not the only ones to voice their concerns regarding future Senate climate change legislation. Labor groups began warning the Senate leadership that the strong trade protections, included in the House Waxman-Markey bill, were essential in any Senate bill. The Blue Green Alliance (BGA), a coalition of labor and environmental organizations, had provided support to House members in voting for the Waxman-Markey bill. However, BGA threatened that it would turn quickly against Senate legislation, if it did not have key trade protections that would shield domestic industry from inexpensive foreign goods. Otherwise, BGA believed, a bill without those protections, would create incentives for energy-intensive U.S. industries to export jobs to nations without similar laws and costs.[34]

Agricultural groups had concerns as well, and some did not feel that the deal struck in the House by Peterson, to help pass the Waxman-Markey bill, was favorable enough for the farm community. The American Farm Bureau Federal believed the House legislation was not a good model for the Senate, because it did not address whether international agricultural competitors, such as Russia or China, would be forced to make similar commitments on climate change emission reductions. The National Cotton Council agreed, and said their members did not have the opportunities for till farming, or biomass production, and they viewed climate change legislation as just a driver for increase fuel costs. On the other hand, the National Farmers Union and the American Farmland Trust were supportive of legislative efforts, while the National Corn Growers and National Milk Producers were neutral.[35]

After the House passed the Waxman-Markey bill, Axelrod said he thought the bill "ameliorated some of the hard edge that people were worried about, and I think that will carry the day in the Senate."[36] He further added, "There is a growing awareness that we need to move on energy. We've been waiting for decades. And this bill will create millions of clean-energy jobs. It will deal with....our dependence on foreign oil and we have to deal with that. And it deals with this deadly pollution and global warming that we have to move on."[36]

The White House, possibility buoyed by the win in the House, or by the criticism from the environmental community that it was late to the effort in the House, leaked a full-court-press strategy for climate change legislation in the Senate. Part of the strategy was pairing Senators who were leaning against climate change legislation, with an Obama Administration official. The White House developed an approach to best match each wavering member of the Senate, with an administration official with the personality and substance to convince them to support the bill. For example, the State Department's special envoy for climate change Todd Stern was paired with Midwestern Senators Sherrod Brown (D-OH) and Claire McCaskill (D-MO), who were concerned about job exports. Chu was tapped to work with Senator Mary Landrieu (D-LA), who was interested in more domestic oil production in the Gulf of Mexico, and an increased reliance on nuclear power. At the same time, Browner and Sutley were regularly dispatched to Capitol Hill.[37]

Senate Majority Leader Harry Reid announced that his strategy for climate change legislation was to melt two different bills, from the Energy and Natural Resources Committee and the Environment and Public Works Committee, into a bipartisan compromise bill that would move through the Senate in the fall 2009. Senator Bingaman, chair of the Energy and Natural Resources Committee had already passed bill out of committee that required utilities to generate 15 percent of their electric power from renewables by 2021. In addition, it mandated an inventory of outer continental shelf oil and natural gas, and would allow for offshore drilling in the Gulf of Mexico near Florida.[38] Boxer said that she anticipated marking up a climate bill in committee before the August 2009 recess, and to move a bill to the full Senate in the fall 2009. In addition, while the Waxman-Markey bill had set a cap for GHG reductions from a 2005 baseline at 17 percent by 2020, and 83 percent by 2050, Boxer said that "You might see a little bit of a stronger bill come out of committee."[39]

By early July 2009, right after the House passed Waxman Markey, Reid could only identify 40 to 45 Senators willing to sign on to any climate change package.[40] Reid not only knew that he needed 51 votes to pass the legislation, but he would need 60 votes to file for cloture to avoid a filibuster. At the same time, he was having a similar problem in finding to votes for health care reform. Reid, with White House approval, prioritized health care a head of climate change. He pushed back Boxer's committee work saying that the Senate would be busy with health care reform at least through October, and that by adding climate change, the schedule might get too crowded.[41] This was in direct opposition what Obama said a year earlier, when on the campaign trail, he argued that climate change was the key element to his national strategy. In a debate with Senator McCain (R-AZ), Obama said, "Energy we have to deal with today. Health care is priority number two."[42]

One observer concluded, "Indeed, the president has made no concrete demands of the Senate, preferring to let Majority Leader Harry Reid direct the bill – a hands off approach that is unlikely to produce a measure of any substance."[43] A top congressional aide said, "You have two camps right now in the Senate. One is the camp of 'Let's put something together, put it out there, whip it really hard to get 60.' And then you have the Harry Reid model, which is 'Let's wait until we know we have 60 votes.'"[43] An environmental advocate noted, "But despite having a climate bill in hand (Waxman-Markey) the White House decided to put its muscle into passing health care reform. Emanuel promised climate advocates that the administration would return to global warming in early 2010."[43]

Emanuel and Reid seemed to be on the same page after the August 2009 recess, when Reid indicated that the Senate was bogged down in health care negotiations, and he was also looking to pass financial reforms. A less than favorable Treasury Department analysis was published at same time that indicated a cap-and-trade program would cost the nation $200 billion. That, of course, did not increase the support in the Senate to proceed immediately with climate change legislation. Reid concluded, "We are going to have a busy, busy time the rest of the year. And of course, nothing terminates at the end of the year. We still have next year to complete things if we have to."[44]

Boxer had been increasingly working with Senator Kerry (D-MA) in drafting the Senate bill to build a more bipartisan base of support. In September, the first draft of the Kerry-Boxer bill was released. However, the two Senators continued working with their colleagues, including those across the aisle, like Senator Lindsey Graham (R-SC), and released another draft totaling 923 pages in late October.[45] The revised Kerry Boxer bill set a more stringent 20 percent reduction in the GHG target from 2005 levels in 2020, than the 17 percent reduction in the Waxman-Markey bill. The other targets were the same including a 3 percent reduction in GHG from 2005 levels in 2012; 42 percent reduction in 2030; and an 83 percent reduction in 2050.[46]

The regulated entities covered by Kerry-Boxer, included large stationary sources emitting greater than 25,000 tons per year of greenhouse gases, producers and importers of petroleum fuels, distributors of natural gas, producers of hydrofluorocarbon gases, and other large sources. Similar to the Waxman-Markey bill, GHG emissions allowances were allocated with 35 percent going to electricity generators, nine percent to natural gas local distribution companies and states for home heating oil, and 1.5 percent to states to use benefit residential, commercial and industrial consumers. The balance of the allowances were proved free to refineries and to energy-intensive, trade-exposed industries.[46]

Boxer set mark up on the bill for early November 2009 in the Environment and Public Works Committee (EPW). However, Senator Voinovich (R-OH) requested a more thorough EPA review and analysis of the bill, which would take about five weeks. He asked for a postponement of the mark up, until the EPA review was completed. Boxer refused saying that EPA had done a very thorough review of Waxman-Markey, and because the Kerry-Boxer bill was so similar, there was no reason for delay. That caused Voinovich and Senator Alexander (R-TN,) both moderate Republicans, to announce a total Republican boycott of the committee mark up. The Republicans contended that Senate rules do not allow Boxer to hold the committee meeting without two members of the opposition party in attendance. Boxer said she would use all the tools available to her as chair, and move forward with the mark up.[47]

The ranking Republican minority leaders on six other Senate committees, with jurisdiction over climate change legislation, sent a letter to Boxer asking her to postpone the hearing, and not to proceed under the Republican boycott of the mark up. The Republicans warned that Boxer's push to move the bill out of committee could backfire, because when it reached the Senate floor it would need Republican support to overcome a filibuster. The letter said, "As the Ranking Members of the six committees that have jurisdiction over a great deal of the matters addressed by S. 1733 (Kerry-Boxer), we felt it important to let you know that we are deeply troubled by the failure to accommodate a request from Senator Voinovich and other Republicans for a complete analysis of the bill's projected impacts on the nation."[48]

Boxer delayed the mark up of the Kerry-Boxer bill for two days, in order give her Republican colleagues more time to gather information from EPA, but she would not postpone the EPW committee meeting for five weeks. With no Republicans in attendance at the mark up, the only path forward for Boxer, according to Senate rules, was to pass the bill out of committee without any amendments. And that is what she did, with seven empty Republican seats, 11 Democrats approved the measure. Only Senator Max Baucus (D-MT), who chairs Senate Finance Committee voted against the bill saying he wanted a bill with a 17 percent reduction of GHG emission by 2020, and only if other countries passed similar measures would it trigger an increase to 20 percent. The bill passed out of committee, but the partisan battle over the vote made the bill a non-starter for the rest of the Senate.[49]

Reid, after the EPW vote, signaled more delays for climate change legislation, indicating that a job recovery bill may have to come first. Other moderate Democrats echoed his call in a closed door meeting, saying that jobs were more important to Americans than cap-and-trade. Baucus who had voted against the Kerry-Boxer bill in the EPW mark up said, "While we must always be mindful of the cost of legislation, that's particularly true in today's economy."[50] Other moderate Democrats thought the Senate should take up a bill with strong energy production provisions, like the Bingaman bill, and leave cap-and-trade for a time when the economy was stronger. Republican Graham concurred with that view, saying, "If environmental policy is not good business policy, you'll never get 60 votes."[50]

While Senator Kerry was instrumental in developing the Kerry-Boxer bill, it was not the only Senate climate bill he was riding. In August 2009 through Senate staff contacts, Kerry started working with Graham on climate change. Eventually, they jointly wrote a climate change Op-Ed for the *New York Times*, that promoted expansion of oil drilling, more nuclear reactors and limiting EPA authority to regulate GHGs. While Kerry was concerned about the proposal they espoused in the editorial of reining in EPA, and whether he had gone too far right, Graham was concerned that Kerry was pushing him too far left. So Graham called in Senator Joe Lieberman (I-CT) to be a moderating force in the group.[42]

Kerry, Graham and Lieberman (KGL) decided that they would build their bill around an aggressive greenhouse gas reduction goal, but would negotiate away any of the provisions of Waxman-Markey or Kerry-Boxer, that were keeping Republicans from joining the effort Senators Murkowski (R-AK) and Snowe (R-ME) were the first approached to come on board, but Murkowski's demands were too much, and Snowe had a never ending list of provisions she wanted in the bill, but would never commit to being a partner if they were fulfilled. In the interim, Senators Maria Cantwell (D-WA) and Susan Collins (R-ME) developed their own Cantwell-Collins climate bill, that eliminated the open carbon markets, and restricted trading to regulated industries.[51] Then Senators Jim Webb (D-VA) and Lamar Alexander (R-TN) introduced legislation that would double nuclear power over the a 20 year period.[52] KGL was willing to adopt any, or all these all these ideas, for a commitment of support for their bill, but they had no takers.[42]

So KGL developed another strategy. If they could not convince any Republican Senators to come on board with their legislation directly, they would bring on business, oil and electric utility interests, and indirectly attract Republican support. It was a classic, "build it and they will come" strategy. KGL first met with Tom Donahue president of the U.S. Chamber of Commerce. Kerry told him they planned to pre-empt EPA from regulating carbon under the Clean Air Act and wanted to know if the

Chamber would come to the table. Donahue replied. "We'll start working with you guys right now."[42]

KGL also wanted the oil companies with them so they met with representatives of Shell, BP and Conoco who did not want to pay for permits to pollute in an open exchange, but wanted a "linked fee" to be in the bill. This is where the fee the company pays for carbon is based the amount of gasoline sold, linked to the price of carbon over the previous three months. KGL agreed, even though the public might perceive this as a gas tax. So in exchange, the oil firms had to agree to a public relations cease fire over the climate change bill, from the time the draft legislation was released, and until the EPA economic analysis was released. The "linked fee" agreement within weeks was changed by KGL and their oil industry partners to an off market permit, that government would sell at a stable price. However, talk of their linked "fee" agreement was circulating widely among Washington DC political circles.[42]

The last deal KLG struck was with Tom Kuhn president of the Edison Electric Institute (EEI), representing the electric utility industry. Most of what Kuhn wanted was already in the bill, but he requested an additional billion dollars in free allowances, and a start date for capping emissions that would begin in 2015, rather than 2012. KLG readily agreed. While the KLG bill had not yet been drafted, with all the deals that were made with big business, the oil industry and electric utility sector, it was far different climate bill than either the House Waxman-Markey or the Senate Kerry-Boxer.[42]

The draft KGL bill, released in late March 2010, would put an economy wide cap on GHG emissions with targets of a 17 percent reduction below 2005 levels by 2020, and an 80 percent reduction below 2005 by 2050. The caps would be different depending on the sector, with both utilities and industry being able to buy pollution allowance from the government. There would be a "hard collar" on the extent of the price fluctuations for carbon, with the bottom being $10 per ton, and when the price exceeded $30 per ton, the government could provide excess supply from a strategic reserve of 4 billion credits. The prices would be indexed to inflation. However the language prohibited derivatives, and it limited permit auctions only to regulated emitters covered in the legislation. There would also be renewable electricity and energy efficiency standards, and consumer rebates. The KGL bill would promote offshore and natural gas drilling, encourage enhanced oil recovery, and enact a fuel fee to support transportation funding.[53]

KLG then set up a meeting with White House officials, Axelrod, Emanuel and Browner. Emanuel wasted no time and asked, "How many Republicans did you bring on?" Kerry said in addition to Graham who was in the room, and Collins and Snowe who they had spoken with earlier, they had secured Scott Brown (R-MA) and George LeMieux (R-FL). With those five Republicans, getting to 60 votes would be achievable.[42]

Finally the White House was on board. But during the course of KLG negotiations to bring on Republican Senators and business leaders, there were four Obama Administration missteps and miscommunications that almost sabotaged deal:

- Announcing the opening of offshore drilling, giving away a key bargaining point;
- Increasing the nuclear loan guarantees in the proposed FY2011, giving away another negotiating point;
- Agreeing to delay the implementation of any EPA actions to regulate, giving away a third negotiating point; and
- Leaking to the press that Senator Graham's support of the "link fee" in the KGL climate bill was his endorsement of a gas tax.[42]

KGL scheduled a press conference in late April in order to announce all their partners and to put on a final push for passage of their bill. Then Reid made a surprise announcement that an immigration reform bill, which had not been drafted and no one had seen, would take priority over climate change. That was the final straw for Graham, who wanted to be part of an immigration bill, but knew that both immigration and climate change were long, involved pieces of legislation, that could not be accomplished by December 2010.[42]

The statement released by Graham on a Saturday said, "I want to bring to your attention to what appears to be a decision by the Obama administration and Senate Democratic leadership to move immigration instead of energy. Unless their plan substantially changes this weekend, I will be unable to move forward on energy independence legislation at this time. I will not allow our hard work to be rolled out in a manner that has no chance of success."[54] Graham ultimately withdrew from the KGL climate change effort and the press conference was canceled.

While White House would not say so publicly, behind closed doors senior aides seemed to indicate that Reid made the decision unilaterally. The bill was moving along smoothly, then Reid went before the camera and announced immigration was going first. A White House aide said, "News to us! It was kind of like, 'Whoa, what do we do now? Where did that come from?'"[42] Without the support from Graham, everyone knew the effort to pass a climate bill in the Senate would flounder, and not gain the Republican backing necessary to pass.

In late April 2010, Reid tried resolve the situation by agreeing that the climate bill was "much further down the road in terms of product" and said, "The energy bill is ready. We will move that more quickly than a bill we do not have."[55] Later, Reid added, "Immigration and energy are equally vital to our economic and national security and we have ignored them for far too long. I'm committed to doing both this session of Congress."[55] On substance, Graham did not believe that the Senate could do both bills. Personally, he felt burned one too many times by the White House, and Reid, so he kept to his original position and stayed out of the formal climate discussions.[42]

Kerry and Lieberman eventually held a press conference on their bill in May 2010 to garner more support for the bill. While Graham was not in attendance, several environmental groups were there along with Tom Kuhn of EEI. BP, Shell and Conoco were true to their word, and did not disparage the bill, in fact Shell issued a statement praising the Kerry-Lieberman draft.[56] When that effort failed to garner the support necessary, Kerry and Lieberman dropped the provisions in their bill to regulate GHGs from the oil industry and manufacturing, concentrating solely on the electric utility sector.[42]

There was very little further movement in the Senate on climate change, until late July 2010, when Democrats conceded the effort was dead. Reid concluded, "It is easy to count to 60. I could it by the time I was in the eighth grade. My point is, we know where we are. We know we do not have the votes (for a bill capping emission). This is a step forward."[57] Reid's comments came just weeks after Browner said, "What is abundantly clear is that the economy-wide program, which the president has talked about for years now, is not doable in the Senate."[43]

There was no further action on climate change in the Senate of the 111th Congress when in finished business in December 2010. Interestingly, the immigration bill that Reid viewed as priority legislation over climate change, never surfaced.

Executive Office of the President

"Energy we have to deal with today. Health care is priority number two" was the prioritization of the issues for Obama when he was campaigning for the presidency.[42] The challenge for Obama was how to translate that direction from the campaign, into policy action at the White House level.

Jason Grumet served as Obama's senior advisor on energy and the environment during the 2008 presidential election, but Grumet's full-time job was president of the Bipartisan Policy Center (BPC). BPC is a nonprofit policy organization, primarily focused on energy, agriculture and health care issues, that Grumet founded with former Senators Bob Dole (R-KS), Howard Baker (R-TN), George Mitchell (D-ME) and Tom Daschle (D-SD). In the Obama campaign, Grumet served as chief spokesperson on energy and environmental matters and was known for saying "the hardest part of energy policy is the environmental side, and the hardest part of environmental policy is the energy side."[58]

Grumet also headed up the Energy and Environment Working Group (E&E Work Group), a brain trust of 500 experts from across the nation that could help the campaign address any technical or policy issue that may arise. The E&E Work Group was broken down into five functional areas: (1) outreach to key states; (2) outreach with policy resources and surrogates; (3) policy development and rapid response; (4) policy development and analysis; and (5) general communications.[58]

Grumet worked on the Obama campaign since its inception, knew all the issues, knew all the players, and was well respected in the Washington, DC energy and environmental community. However, after the campaign, Obama was not able to secure Grumet as an administration official to provide energy and environmental advice on critical issues such as climate change. Grumet's recent lobbying work was a bit of barrier, because Obama had made numerous public statements about not hiring lobbyists. In addition, Grumet had young children, and a high-level Obama Administration position would not only necessitate long hours away from his family, but also a substantial decrease in compensation from his BPC salary.[59] Without Grumet in a leadership position advising the Obama Administration on energy and environmental matters, there was a significant break in continuity from the campaign into governing.

Carol Browner was brought into the Obama White House as assistant on energy and climate change. Browner had been the administrator of the EPA during the Clinton Administration and had a passion for seeing climate change legislation pass. (For more on Browner, see Chapter 1. Introduction, Section, Executive Office of the President Appointees.) Browner was not part of the original Obama campaign team, and some believe that affected her level of influence in the West Wing.[42] However, Browner was able bring on to her staff, Heather Zichal, as deputy assistant for energy and climate change. Zichal had been a legislative director for Senator John Kerry. More importantly, Zichal had worked very closely with Jason Grumet, and with the Obama campaign staff in Chicago, so she brought relationships and continuity from the campaign to the White House.[58]

Some have noted that Browner has been charged with the president's number one priority; to create a clean energy American economy and reduce the nation's carbon foot print. However, Browner was only provide with three assistants to do so. One observer noted, "Hey, change the entire economy, and here are three staffers to do it. It's a bit of a joke."[42] To be fair, while Browner was selected to be the Obama White House's tip of the spear, in moving forward the climate change agenda, Obama also appointed staunch and passionate climate change advocates across numerous federal agencies, such DOE Secretary Chu, EPA administrator Jackson, USDA Secretary Vilsack, Interior Secretary Salazar, Council on Environmental Quality Chair, Sutley and National Oceanic and Atmospheric Administration director, Lubchenco. While there may have been resources to double, or triple, Browner's staff, White House budgets are typically relatively small compared to agency budgets. Having climate change allies across multiple agencies, and being able to tap those budgets for personnel and resources, as necessary, appears to have been part of the Obama's climate change strategy.

Browner and her staff, as well as all the pertinent cabinet secretaries, were frequently on Capitol Hill testifying, and providing closed door briefings on climate change for members of Congress. The environmental community, however, could not help but notice, that the Obama Administration was being much more high profile in its efforts to support health care reform. Cabinet secretaries and administration officials were appearing daily on the cable news networks to advance health care reform, as well as, the Sunday network talk shows, but a similar level of efforts was not being put into climate change. They saw Obama on the news giving a major speech on health care reform at the American Medical Association, while on that same day, he was meeting behind closed doors with member of the House on climate change.[23]

The environmental community viewed Obama as conspicuously absent from public messages about climate change, and noted that he had not used the bully pulpit to engender more support for climate change on Capitol Hill. Some began to think that climate change was the 'neglected middle-child"[23] or the "stepchild"[42] in the Obama Administration's agenda.

If not for Gore using his personal relationship with Emanuel to secure a White House meeting to talk about climate strategy, many believe Obama would not have gotten directly engaged in the House vote on the Waxman-Markey bill.[24] That meeting was also key in motivating Obama to express his direct support for the Waxman-Markey bill at a press conference, and make a public announcement in the Rose Garden, to highlight the importance of the vote.[25]

The Waxman-Markey win in the House, along with the criticism from the environmental community that the White House lacked a high-level, climate change public effort, spurred the Obama Administration to develop a strategy to move climate change legislation forward in the Senate.[37] The clearness of the vision set out in that strategy seems to have fallen apart when Reid delayed climate change legislation in the summer of 2009, and prioritized health care ahead of it. That would have been a time for Obama to have exercised leadership on his number one goal.[43] Instead a White House spokesman said "The administration is continuing to work with the Senate to pass comprehensive energy legislation and believes it's on track."[41]

A very telling insight into the White House strategy, regarding the prioritization of climate change and health care, came from a senior Obama Administration official who said, "The plan was to throw two things against the wall, and see which one looks more promising."[42] There maybe some merit in that statement because the Obama Administration went back into a behind-the-scenes mode for much of the Senate discussions on climate change. It did not have much of a public or private strategy for success, other than to leave the Senate and Reid to move forward in whatever fashion would work. The Obama Administration meetings with Senators Kerry, Graham and Lieberman in late 2009 exemplify that lack of a strategy, when they were described as "It's kind of like a drum circle. They come by, 'How are you feeling? Where do you think the votes are? What do you think we should do?' It is never 'Here's the plan, here's what we're doing.'"[42]

Browner, in early 2010, told the press that the White House was not thinking about scaling back its climate change legislative expectations, even though they had just finished a contentious health care debate, and lost the filibuster proof majority in the Senate. She concluded by stating, "I think predictions about when something is going to happen in the legislative process are very, very hard to make, you just have to continue working at it. We're encouraged by what we are seeing, and are going to continue working at it."[60]

Obama hosted a White House climate change meeting in March with Senators Kerry, Graham, and Lieberman, as well as,

Sherrod Brown (D-OH), Judd Gregg (R-NH), Lisa Murkowski (R-AK) and Dick Lugar (R-IN). White House press secretary Robert Gibbs said the purpose of the meeting was to get "an update from bipartisan lawmakers on a series of proposals and get an idea of where those are."[61] Gibbs added that Obama "strongly believes that we need to get something done" on climate change.[61] This was another behind-the-scenes type of meeting, but when asked about whether the Obama Administration would spend political capital on climate change, Brown said , "It is too early to tell. My guess is they will, but we have got things bigger than that now – we've got the healthcare bill and the focus on jobs."[61] Shortly after, Emanuel called Reid and suggested that the cap-and-trade bill be abandoned for a smaller piece of legislation that required utilities to generate more power from renewable sources. He was backed up by Axerod who said, "Fuck whatever Congress wants, we're not for them." [42]

On Earth Day 2010, Browner was interviewed, and was asked about Obama's engagement in the Senate legislative process to move climate change. Browner replied, "We're not at the nitty-gritty level; that would not be appropriate right now, but that does not mean we're not having conversations. I spent a lot of time on the Hill with members. We did have a bipartisan meeting there, about six Democrats, five Republicans who sat with the President to talk about the concepts broadly. The next step in the process is for the legislative language to be put forward, and then we can engage."[62]

Two explosions occurred that week that tested Obama's commitment to global climate change legislation. The first was Reid's announcement in late April 2010, that immigration reform would take precedence in the Senate, over the KGL climate change bill. That caused the only Republican willing to put his name on a climate change bill, Graham, to bow out of a leadership role, and blocked Republican cooperation in moving forward the legislation. It is unclear whether the Obama White House knew of Reid's decision before hand, but it is clear Obama did not do enough after the announcement to placate Graham, and bring him back into the fold.

The second explosion was that of the deep-water Horizon drilling rig in the Gulf of Mexico, which caused eleven deaths and was the largest environmental disaster in U.S. history. The human and environmental tragedy in the Gulf consumed much of Obama's time during May, June and July 2010. The consequences of the Gulf Oil Spill were so severe, that Obama decided, after 18 months in office, to deliver his first prime time speech from the Oval Office. There was much anticipation in the days leading up to the speech, about what the president would say about cap-and-trade global climate change legislation. Senate Minority Leader Mitch McConnell (R-KY) said, on the floor of the Senate, that he could see no connection between the Gulf Oil Spill and cap and trade climate legislation.[63]

The night of the Obama's Oval Office speech, the environmental community was waiting in anticipation of what endorsement the president would give to Senate climate change legislation. During the speech, Obama did not say the word "carbon" or the word 'greenhouse gases" or the word 'global warming" or the word "cap-and-trade." While he mentioned the fact that climate legislation passed the House, there was no acknowledgement of any Senate climate change action. He spoke favorably of draft legislation with renewable electricity standards, like Bingaman's bill, and those with strong energy efficiency standards, like Lugar's bill. He told the nation that it must break its "addition to fossil fuels," he was "happy to look at other ideas and approaches from either party," but concluded that "we don't yet know precisely how to get there."[64] He did not call for the Senate to pass cap-and-trade legislation. One member of Congress who spoke anonymously concluded, "He knows if he mentioned a carbon cap, his success or failure would be measured by his ability to get it."[65]

The environmental community was livid. One commentator said, "Disasters drive sweeping legislation, and the precedent was on the side of a great leap of forward in environmental progress. In 1969, an oil spill in Santa Barbara California – of only 10,000 barrels, less than the two-day output of the BP (Gulf) gusher – prompted Richard Nixon to create the EPA and sign the Clean Air Act. ...But the Obama Administration let the opportunity slip away. ...It was a terrible teachable moment, one in which (President Obama) could have connected the dots between the oil spewing in the Gulf and the planet-killing CO2 we spew everyday into the atmosphere."[43]

Then, one month after Browner had said that climate legislation "is not doable in the Senate,"[43] and three weeks after Obama failed to mention Senate cap-and-trade legislation in his Oval Office speech, Browner said that Obama has not accepted defeat on climate change legislation. She stated that in September 2010, "the Congress is coming back and we will continue to see if we can get legislation. We passed it in the House and we will continue to work in the Senate."[66] When asked about whether climate change could pass in a lame duck session she says, "Potentially."[66]

In a late September 2010, President Obama was talking about his priorities for 2011, and about climate change, and he stated, "We may end up having to do it in chunks as opposed to some sort of comprehensive omnibus legislation."[67] One environmentalist said, "Not exactly a climate hawk anymore – not exactly someone who sounds like he is going to the mat on this issue in 2013 even if he were re-elected in a landslide that flips the House. No, he is more like a climate woodpecker, banging his head against the tree over and over and over and over again, in the hope of digging out a tiny morsel.[68]

Environmental Protection Agency

The Obama Administration advanced on a two track system for the regulation of GHGs. The first track, and the most preferable, was new legislation passed through Congress. The second was moving through the regulatory of process of EPA, using the authority of the Clean Air Act, and recent U.S. Supreme Court rulings. However, the Obama Administration could not wait for progress from Congress, and began the EPA regulatory process in early 2009.

Jackson issued a preliminary finding in April 2009 that GHGs threaten the public health and welfare. The finding was issued after thorough examination of the scientific evidence, which determined that GHGs are a primary contributor to global climate change. While the preliminary findings did not impose propose any regulatory requirements, they did establish the legal basis for future

EPA regulations of GHG emissions. EPA regulation of GHG emissions was triggered by a 2007 U.S. Supreme Court decision, which held that greenhouse gases fit the definition of "air pollutant" under the Clean Air Act (CAA). EPA was obligated to act to regulate GHG emissions from new motor vehicles, unless it found that the GHGs do not endanger public health or welfare.[69]

Under the Bush Administration, EPA had also made the same preliminary findings on GHGs, but Vice President Cheney refused to sign off on them.[69] As a preliminary ruling, EPA held two public hearings and a 60 day comment period, where it received 380,000 comments.[70] The final finding was issued in December 2009, and EPA issued several other GHG rules.

- EPA issued a rule in September 2009 that required the reporting of GHG emissions from every sector of the economy. However unlike the other EPA regulatory actions addressing GHG emissions, it was not dependent on the Supreme Court ruling. The authorization for the reporting rule was part of the FT2008 Omnibus Appropriations Bill.
- A "Subject to Regulation" memo was issued by EPA in April 2010, confirming that GHGs would become "subject to regulation" on January 2, 2011
- A "Tailoring Rule" was issued in May 2010, to phase in the application of GHG permitting requirements to new, and modified stationary sources.
- EPA issued a rule in May 2010 for a GHGs standard to apply to passenger cars, light-duty trucks, and medium-duty passenger vehicles, covering model years 2012 through 2016.
- EPA announced in December 2010 a proposed settlement agreement with states and environmental organizations, in which it agreed to regulate GHGs from fossil-fuel fired power plants and refineries under the Clean Air Act. EPA said it would propose standards for power plants in July 2011, and for refineries in December 2011, with final standards to be issued in May 2012 and November 2012, respectively.[71]

Many in Congress were not pleased with the Obama Administration and EPA beginning the regulatory process on GHGs before Congress acted. Senator Ben Nelson (D-NE) said, "I am very concerned about their unilaterally moving forward. If alphabet agencies can do what they want without regard to what Congress believes, there is something wrong with the system."[72]

Murkowski was so upset over the Obama Administration's decision to move forward with GHG regulations, she decided to employ a relatively unknown provision, the Congressional Review Act, to stop it. Under this law, any Senator may submit a "disapproval resolution' of any action taken by a federal agency or department. That resolution is sent to the Senate Committee with jurisdiction over the agency. If the committee does not report the resolution out in 20 calendar days, it can be brought to the floor with 30 Senators in agreement. In the case of EPA, Boxer's Environment and Public Works Committee had the jurisdiction. Murkowski said, "Congress is being threatened in a misguided attempt to move a climate bill forward. But this strategy is highly flawed because it assumes Congress will pass economically damaging legislation in order to stave off economically damaging regulations. This is a false choice and it should be rejected outright."[73]

The Senate rejected Mukowski's resolution by a vote of 47 to 53 with six Democrats joining the Republican caucus to express their disapproval of EPA GHG regulatory actions.[74] However, that vote was not the end of Senate action. Senator Rockefeller (D-VW) had introduced a bill that would delay any EPA GHG rules by two years. Rockefeller said he drafted the legislation to safeguard jobs, the coal industry and the entire economy. Reid promised Rockefeller that the bill would hit the floor in the fall 2010, then during the lame duck session, but it was never acted on when the Senate adjourned in December 2010.[75]

The House also tried to prevent EPA from regulating GHGs. The leadership in the House introduced a resolution very similar to Murkoski's. Boehner was concerned that with the nation in a recession, climate regulation would only be a new tax. The bill never came up for consideration in the Democratic led House. Representative Blackburn (R-TN) expressed her frustration saying,

"The EPA has not only moved from its mission of being the Environmental Protection Agency, now they are the Economic Punishment Agency."[76]

The business community was just as opposed to the EPA regulation of greenhouse gases, and questioned its endangerment finding. The Chamber of Commerce believed that EPA had based its findings on unrepresentative data, and that it was further skewed by the agency's personnel. The Chamber stated, "We are not denying that CO2 (emissions) are rising…(but) the EPA has to make the link between CO2 and health and welfare and they haven't made the link. There is no evidence that CO2 has an impact on health and welfare."[77] To make its point, the Chamber requested that EPA hold a formal on-the-record hearing, before a neutral arbitrator. That would provide an opportunity for the Chamber, and other interested parties, to ask questions and examine the data that EPA used for its finding. EPA declined that request, so the Chamber submitted a formal petition to EPA detailing their concerns.

Jackson responded to the Chamber petition in the summer 2010. The Chamber had questioned the EPA conclusions, because they were based on data from the International Panel on Climate Change. The Chamber alleged the scientists had doctored the climate data. A series of emails had been leaked to the press from scientific community that, the Chamber said in its petition, indicated collusion by the scientist to hide contradictory data. The Chamber further alleged that the scientists covered up the inconsistent data, so it would not expose flaws in global climate change theories. Jackson said in her reply to the Chamber, that no uncertain terms its petition lacked merit. She further stated, "These petitions – based as they are on selectively edited, out-of-context data and a manufactured controversy – provide no evidence to undermine our determination."[78]

The Obama Administration began regulating GHGs, using EPA authority under the Clean Air Act, on January 2, 2011. More than 150 lawsuits have been brought against EPA over its regulations of GHG emissions, but the courts have refused to stay the EPA rules. Plaintiffs in these cases include businesses, advocacy groups, trade associations and government entities, including the states of Alabama, Florida, Indiana, South Carolina, Texas, and Virginia. All of the suits have been consolidated into three major cases challenging the endangerment finding, the tailoring rule, and the light duty vehicle rule.[71]

If the courts overturn the endangerment finding, all of the EPA GHG regulations would be voided, because that finding provides EPA with the legal basis for its GHG regulations. However, the plaintiffs are challenging the fact that EPA based it finding on outside data, from International Panel on Climate Change. EPA regularly uses outside review panel data, and the courts have sided with EPA on these types of issues in the past. The tailoring suit contends the rule does not apply the thresholds as explicitly stated in the statute. If that rule is struck down, a larger number of stationary sources would be come under regulation. If the light duty vehicle rule is voided, EPA would have to redraft the regulation, but underlying legal authority would not be removed.[71]

Re-Engage with the U.N. Framework Convention on Climate Change (UNFCCC): *Barack Obama and Joe Biden will re-engage with the U.N. Framework Convention on Climate Change (UNFCCC). The UNFCCC process is the main international forum dedicated to addressing the climate change problem and an Obama administration will work constructively within it. In addition they will:*

- *create a Global Energy Forum – based on the G8+5, which includes all G-8 members plus Brazil, China, India, Mexico and South Africa – comprised of the largest energy consuming nations from both the developed and developing world, which would focus exclusively on global energy and environmental issues. This Global Energy Forum will complement – and ultimately merge with – the much larger negotiation process underway at the UN to develop a post-Kyoto framework.*
- *create a Technology Transfer Program within the Department of Energy dedicated to exporting climate-friendly technologies, including green buildings, clean coal and advanced automobiles, to developing countries to help them combat climate change.*
- *develop a comprehensive strategy to combat global warming must address tropical deforestation which accounts for approximately 20 percent of global greenhouse gas emissions. By offering incentives to*

> *maintain forests and manage them sustainably, the United States can play a leadership role in dealing with climate change.*

One of the driving forces behind the Obama Administration's, and the environmental community's efforts, to pass global climate change legislation in 2009, was the United Nations Framework Convention on Climate Change (UNFCCC) was being held in Copenhagen, Denmark in December of that year. It would be the first opportunity for the Obama Administration to lead the U.S. re-engagement in UNFCCC agreement writing, since the Clinton Administration participated in the negotiations of the Kyoto Protocol in the 1990s. The Senate had rejected the Kyoto treaty, and the Bush Administration said they would not abide by its precepts.

The Kyoto Protocol had set binding targets for 37 countries to reduce GHG emissions. The amount of the GHG reduction targeted, averaged five percent of the 1990 levels over the five-year period 2008-2012. In anticipation of the end of the first commitment period of the Kyoto Protocol in 2012, a new international framework would be negotiated and ratified in Copenhagen Denmark in 2009.[79]

Secretary of State Hillary Clinton would be leading the U.S. negotiations at Copenhagen. Of course, Clinton had been First Lady during the Clinton Administration, and had won a Senate seat from New York in the 2000 election. She was long thought of as the front runner in the 2008 Democratic primary for president. It was quite a stroke of genius, and a coup, for Obama to recruit her to serve as his Secretary of State. Clinton selected Todd Stern to be her special envoy for climate change. Stern had served in the Clinton Administration as staff secretary to the president managing every detail of presidential paperwork. Then he was tapped to be the senior Clinton White House negotiator, for both the Kyoto and Buenos Aires climate change conferences.[80] Clinton and Stern immediately started preparing for the end of the year UNFCCC Copenhagen meeting. However, there were several international events where climate change would be front and center prior to that.

Obama attended the G-8 Summit in July 2009, and used that meeting as a platform to create momentum for the

Copenhagen meeting. At the Summit, he admitted that the U.S. track record in climate negotiation may not have been the best, saying. "I know that in the past, the United State has sometimes fallen short of meeting our responsibilities. So, let me be clear: Those days are over. One of my highest priorities as president is to drive a clean energy transformation of our economy, and over the next six months, the United States has taken steps toward that goal."[81]

There were two incremental climate change outcomes of the G-8 Summit. The first was that the G-8 developed nations pledged to reduce carbon emission by 80 percent by 2050. That included Russia, Canada and the U.S. They also endorsed a 50 percent global reduction goal by that same year, but would not set any 2020 targets because Obama was concerned about preempting Congress.[83] The second outcome was that 17 industrialized and developing nations, reached an agreement to limit global warming temperature rise to 3.6 degrees Fahrenheit. That is the limit of temperature rise that many climate scientists say the earth can sustain, without damaging impacts on weather, shorelines and farming. It was the first time that India, China and the U.S. have agreed to a goal. Stern addressed the vagueness of the commitments by saying, "Look these are all principles that are getting articulated, so none of this is exactly binding on either side right now. But it sets up measures that would go into an ultimate agreement. They have never done that. That's a quite significant undertaking."[82]

The United Nations Climate Change Summit was held in New York City in September 2009, where Chinese President Hu Jintao committed his nation to "'mandatory national targets' for reducing energy use that leads to heavy emissions, as well as for growing forests."[84] Obama outlined the steps the House had made in passing the Waxman-Markey bill, but did not mention that the Senate would not take up climate change until 2010. The point was not lost on John Bruton, the European Union ambassador to the U.S. who said that the Senate is "acting as though it is the only deliberative body in the world, and that we should all wait until it gets healthcare passed."[84] Senator McCain (R-AZ) was asked about

Bruns comment, and McCain replied, "Well, I do not think there are ten Americans that know who he is."[84]

United Nations Secretary General Ban Ki-Moon in early November 2009 requested action by the U.S. Senate on climate change legislation, prior to UNFCCC Copenhagen meeting. He recognized that expectations for the conference were beginning to diminish. The concept of a political agreement being signed by the major leaders of world, rather than a legally binding treaty, was starting to look like a more realistic outcome. Ban urged the Senate to pass at least a resolution containing broad principles, which would include reductions of GHG and other emissions reductions strategies. Ban said, "I would sincerely hope that the Senate will take the necessary action as soon as possible."[85]

The UNFCCC Copenhagen meeting was not far off when President Obama attended the Asia-Pacific Economic Cooperation (APEC) Summit in November 2009. The declaration at the end of the APEC meeting echoed Ban's assessment, that a political agreement was the likely outcome of Copenhagen. All nineteen nations, including China, signed an APEC declaration, that restated the overall commitment to address global climate change, but emphasized that technology transfer, and financial assistance to developing nations, were equally important. Rather than set more stringent emission levels at Copenhagen, the APEC declaration stated that setting new deadlines for emissions targets, and securing increased levels of funding, should be the focus of the conference. In addition, the nations did not endorse the 50 percent reduction of GHG by 2050, set at the G-8 meeting.[86]

From Singapore, Obama made a brief stop in China for direct talks with Hu. Obama said at a press conference, "We agreed that each of us would take significant mitigation actions and stand behind these commitments."[87] However, when Obama arrived back in the US, some in the environmental community were livid over the APEC meeting agreement. Greenpeace called it "sop to President Barack Obama's political vulnerabilities" and "complicit in a US so-called deal which would put Obama's political difficulties ahead of the survival of the world's most vulnerable countries."[88]

The negative comments from some environmentalists moved the White House to invite the press in for a climate change briefing, and to put the UNFCCC Copenhagen meeting on the president's calendar. Obama would attend some of the earlier sessions, but leave before most of the other world leaders would arrive, because he was coordinating the trip with his acceptance of the Nobel Peace Prize. He intended to propose at Copenhagen a "US emissions reduction target, in the range of 17 percent below 2005 levels in 2020 and ultimately in line with final U.S. energy and climate legislation. In light of the president's goal to reduce emissions by 83 percent by 2050, the expected pathway set forth in this pending legislation would entail a 30 percent reduction below 2005 levels in 2025 and a 42 percent reduction below 2005 in 2030."[89]

In addition to Clinton and Stern, the Obama Administration dispatched several members of the cabinet and White House staff for the entire Copenhagen meeting, including Chu, Jackson, Sutley and Browner, as well as, Interior Secretary Salazar, Agriculture Secretary Vilsack, and Commerce Secretary Locke.[89]

Obama changed his schedule as the Copenhagen meeting approached, so he would be there at the same time as other world leaders. In addition, the Obama Administration indicated that the U.S. would be willing to paying "its fair share" of a $10 billion annual payment to less developed countries.[90] Some Republicans were concerned about the level of commitments that Obama was making, not only regarding U.S. emissions reductions, but also financially. Senate Minority Whip John Kyle (R-AZ) held a press conference saying the Obama Administration had "raised some concerns on our part that the president may believe that he has the authority to bind the United States to some kind of international agreement without action by the United States Senate."[91] Senator Inhofe (R-OK) was so concerned about Obama's plans for Copenhagen, that he decided to attended the meeting in Denmark as well as, to serve as a "truth squad."[92]

The UNFCCC Copenhagen meeting opened with greatly diminished expectations. Everyone appreciated the fact the U.S. had finally returned to the negotiating table in good faith, but they knew Obama was arriving without a solid commitment for GHG reductions endorsed by Congress. All eyes were China, because it was the other major GHG contributor. Early in the session China informed Western negotiators that it would not be able to make an operational type agreement that Obama was seeking. It would, however, be open to short, nonbinding collective statement.[93]

Clinton arrived at the meeting pledging U.S. support for a $100 billion multinational fund to assist developing nations. Clinton hoped that would sway the Chinese into a quantifiable and verifiable agreement. When Chinese negotiators hesitated, Clinton reminded them of Hu's commitment to Obama on his recent trip to their country. Clinton said, "All major economies (must) stand behind meaningful mitigation actions and provide full transparency as to their implementation." She added that China's reluctance on that front was a "deal breaker."[94]

When Obama arrived in Copenhagen, he had a private meeting scheduled with Chinese Premier Wen Jiabo. At the scheduled time for the meeting with Wen, the Chinese leader was in a session with officials from India, South Africa and Brazil. Obama barged into that meeting, and told the leaders that unless a deal was struck, he was leaving. That forced their hand, and Obama was able to pull together the final stages of a deal.[95]

The Copenhagen Accord set a goal of keeping global temperature rise to 3.6 degrees Fahrenheit, and each nation would list their domestic pledges to reduce GHGs to meet that goal. The nations agreed to three overarching components: transparency, mitigation and finance. Jointly the signatories agreed to raise $100 billion, from both public and private sources, to aid developing nations. In order to negotiate the deal, Obama had to give up his goal of a global GHG emissions reduction by 2050, and agreed to provide $3.6 billion during the 2010-12 time period.[96] Obama said about the commitments, "We know that they will not be by themselves sufficient to get to where we need to get by 2050. But I want to be very clear that ultimately this issue is going to be dictated by the science, and the science indicates that we're going to have to take more aggressive steps in the future."[95] By the time the Copenhagen meeting was over, few people had much enthusiasm for the Cancun talks scheduled for December 2010.

Weeks before the Copenhagen meeting, approximately 1000 emails were leaked from the website of the UN International Panel on Climate Change (IPCC). Those emails provided evidence for climate change skeptics to question the quality of the science that the UNFCCC was using in Copenhagen to make major policy decisions.[97] In some cases, the emails seemed to indicate that scientists were manipulating scientific data to reach the conclusions they wanted. In particular one email said, "I've just completed Mike's Nature (the science journal) trick of adding in the real temps to each series for the last 20 years (ie, from 1981 onwards) and from 1961 for Keith's to hide the decline." Many readers were concerned about the words "trick" and "hide."[98] Bob Ward director of policy and communications at the Grantham Research Institute on Climate Change and the Environment at the London School of Economics, said, "You can't tell what they are talking about. Scientists say 'trick' not just to mean deception. They mean it as a clever way of doing something – a short cut can be a trick."[98]

A full independent investigation of IPCC practices was initiated, and a report was issued in August 2010. The report found the IPCC "has been a success and has served society well."[99] However, it also found that the IPCC needed to revise the way it manages its climate change assessments. This included having its scientists be more open to alternative views, more transparent about conflicts of interest, and not so quick to endorse public policy recommendations.[100] A particularly troublesome issues was a 2007 IPCC policy report, that said it had a high confidence that by 2020, climate change could reduce yields from African farms by 50 percent. The investigation concluded that the IPCC did not account for the uncertainty of the data in those projections. It was also recommended that the IPCC institute a conflict of interest policy, and change leadership more often.[99]

The UNFCCC Cancun meeting convened in December 2010, and its expectations were significantly scaled down from the Copenhagen meeting. At Cancun, approximately 193 counties adopted a formalization of the 2009 Copenhagen Accords, which committed each country to continue to implement its own programs to cut GHG over the next decade, in order to avoid exceeding the 3.6 degree Fahrenheit worldwide temperature increase. The meeting also advanced increase transparency in those programs. In addition, it established a set of principles for monitoring, reporting and verification to measure whether each countries programs are meeting their stated goals.

The agreement also created a "Green Fund" which provides a mechanism for funding developing countries in their adaptation and mitigation programs. The Green Fund reiterates the Copenhagen pledge of $100 billion over ten years, as well as, a "fast start" finance provision that make $30 billion of that available in 2012. The United Nation's program of reducing emissions from deforestation and land degradation (REDD) was also adopted. Lastly, two other boards were created to assist developing countries with climate change adaptation and clean energy technologies.[101] State Department special envoy for climate change Stern said, "This package obviously is not going to solve climate change by itself, but it is a very good step and a step that's very much consistent with U.S. interests and will help move the path – the world down a path toward a broader global response to changing – to stopping climate change."[102]

3.

GREEN JOB CREATION

Create Five Million New Jobs: *Barack Obama and Joe Biden will help create five million new jobs by strategically investing $150 billion over the next ten years to catalyze private efforts to build a clean energy future.*

President Obama inherited an economy in the middle of deep recession, and a rising unemployment rate. During his 2009 Inaugural Address, he said, "The state of our economy calls for action: bold and swift. And we will act not only to create new jobs, but lay a new foundation for growth. We will build the roads and bridges, the electrical grids and digital lines that feed our commerce and bind us together. We will restore science to its rightful place...We will harness the sun and the winds and the soil to fuel our cars and run our factories."[1]

Obama, as well as his White House environmental and economic advisors, saw the American Recovery and Reinvestment Act (Recovery Act) as the down payment on the creation of a new clean, green economy, providing jobs for millions. It was the first of a two part plan. The Recovery Act would make basic investments in green infrastructure generating jobs, while later, climate change legislation would establish a long-term demand for clean energy technologies, and build a truly sustainable American economy. As described by Obama's director of the National Council of Economic Advisors, Larry Summers, "It's like two blades of a scissors. Stimulus spending is one blade. And a cap-and-trade mechanism will be the other. We need them both. Stimulus alone isn't going to do it."[2]

Democratic leaders in Congress began working with Obama in January 2009 to develop a recovery bill, and to determine the size and scope of the spending plans, including the tax cuts it would contain. Former Vice President Al Gore also engaged in the discussion. Gore pushed for a recovery package that would provide an unprecedented investment in energy efficiency, renewable energy technologies, smart grid and clean cars. He told Congress that these investments would "create millions of new jobs and hasten our economic recovery – while strengthening our national security and beginning to solve the climate crisis."[3]

The $787 billion Recovery Act passed in mid-February 2009, with a House vote of 246 to 183, with only seven Democrats voting against the legislation. In the Senate, three moderate Republicans joined 55 Democrats and two independents to vote in favor of the bill 60 to 38. Speaker Nancy Pelosi was elated with the victory and passed out candy bars to House committee chairs that had an image of the Capitol and the words, "A stimulus package we can all sink our teeth into." Minority Leader John Boehner had a different assessment saying, "The president made clear when we started this process that this was all about jobs. Jobs, jobs, jobs. And what it's turned into is nothing more than spending, spending and more spending."[4]

Overall, the Recovery Act included $507 billion in spending programs and $282 billion in tax relief.[5] In the legislative package, there was about $80 billion dedicated to green technology and smart grid development, and $20 billion in clean energy tax incentives. Some the spending included $6.3 billion in energy efficiency grants in residential and commercial buildings, $4.5 billion in federal green buildings programs, $16.4 billion for transit and high speed rail and $5 billion for low income weatherization. There was also $20 billion in clean energy tax incentives, such as an extension of the Production Tax Credit for solar, wind and other renewable energy investments. All of this was touted as good news for the economy, and the clean energy industry. An analysis by an environmental think tank indicated that for every $1 billion spent on clean energy programs, 5,000 more jobs were created than with tradition infrastructure spending.[6]

Obama thanked Congress for its swift approval of the Recovery Act, when during his February 2009 Address to Congress he said, "As soon as I took office, I asked this Congress to send me a recovery plan by President's Day that would put people back to work and put money in their pockets, not because I believe in bigger government – I don't – not because I'm not mindful of the massive debt we've inherited – I am. ….Over – over the next two years, this plan will save or create 3.5 million jobs. More than 90 percent of these jobs will be in the private sector, jobs rebuilding our roads, and bridges, constructing wind turbines and solar panels, laying broadband and expanding mass transit."[7]

Like all new presidents, Obama faced the challenge of filling appointments in his cabinet, and across the agencies of the federal bureaucracy. He had the additional burden of a brand new $787 billion spending package passed to stimulate the economy, but he did not have his personnel in place to quickly enact the legislation. After a month in office, three cabinet positions remained unfilled, only two of fifteen agencies had confirmed deputy secretaries, and a large percent of lower-level position were vacant. Due to some earlier missteps and scandals, the Obama Administration added more layers to its vetting process. The length and depth of the review process by both the Obama Administration and Congress, caused some candidates to abandon their nominations or appointments.[8]

There were even issues surrounding the identification of qualified candidates. While an application process had been promoted by the Obama Campaign, Obama Transition Office, and White House website, many talented individuals never heard from the Office of Presidential Personnel. Jason Grumet, Obama's senior advisor on energy and the environment during the 2008 presidential election, said that the situation was "a mess" and that "there is no process."[9] So the agencies were filled with career civil servants, and former Bush Administration appointees who had burrowed into the bureaucracy. Terry Sullivan, associate professor at the University of North Carolina and executive director of the White House Transition project said, These "guys who are filling these chairs are not going to switch these policies. They're going to be carrying out the policies of the last guy standing, and the last guy standing was Bush."[8]

To try to address the slow expenditure of Recovery Act funding, Rahm Emanuel, White House chief of staff, and Peter Orzag, director of the Office of Management and Budget, sent out a 50-page memo outlining how the Recovery Act dollars should be spent. The memo gave the agencies daily, weekly and monthly reporting requirements, and requested detailed spending plans.

Some agencies, like the Department of Energy (DOE), put together their Recovery Act funding plans very quickly, and initially seemed to be moving forward at a rapid pace.[10] However, the Obama Administration soon learned, there was no substitute for having your own people in the agencies, and the DOE was still fielding questions on its slow granting process in mid-2010.[11] As the Environmental Protection Agency (EPA) Administrator Lisa Jackson said, "In an ideal world, on Day 1, everyone starts, but I know that is not how the confirmation process works."[8]

Later in 2009, President Obama outlined his vision of the Recovery Act, and how it fit into a much larger context saying, it was "the largest investment in clean energy in history, not just to help the end this recession, but to lay a new foundation for lasting prosperity. The Recovery Act includes $80 billion to put tens of thousands of Americans to work developing new battery technologies for hybrid vehicles; modernizing the electric grid; making our homes and businesses more energy efficient; doubling our capacity to generate renewable electricity. These are creating private sector jobs weatherizing homes; manufacturing cars and trucks; upgrading to smart grid electric meters; installing solar panels; assembling wind turbines; building new facilities and laboratories all across America.[12]

The Council of Economic Advisors released a report in July 2010 that provided data showing that the Recovery Act was responsible for 2.5 to 3.6 million jobs. The study indicated that for every Recovery Act dollar spent, it leveraged three times that amount in outside private investment. In addition, the report indicated clean energy was one of the areas generating the highest volume of outside investment. With $46 billion in Recovery Act expenditures, partners contributed $107 billion, supporting over $150 billion in energy efficiency, renewable energy generation and other green technologies.[13]

While the Recovery Act may have created two to three million jobs, employment statistics at the end of 2010, showed that the nation had lost two million jobs over the previous two years, with a net job savings of only 150,000. The Obama Administration had promised the nation that unemployment would not rise above 8.5 percent, if the Recovery Act was passed. With joblessness hovering close to 10 percent at the end of 2010, many in the public, and in political circles, were skeptical if the Recovery Act had lived up to Obama's expectations.[5]

Convert our Manufacturing Centers into Clean Technology Leaders: *Barack Obama and Joe Biden believe that America companies and workers should build the high-demand technologies of the future, and he will help nurture America's success in clean technology manufacturing by establishing a federal investment program to help manufacturing centers modernize and help Americans learn new skills to produce green products. This investment will help provide the critical up-front capital needed by small and mid-size manufacturers to produce these innovative new technologies. Along with an increased federal investment in the research, development and deployment of advanced technologies, this $1 billion per year investment will help spur sustainable economic growth in communities across the country.*

Obama requested and received from Congress $2.3 billion in Recovery Act funds in 2009 to provide Advanced Energy Manufacturing Tax Credits, for firms engaged in clean energy manufacturing across the U.S.[14] In January 2010, after a thorough review of over $7.6 billion in applications,[15] the Obama Administration selected 183 projects in 43 states. The manufacturers receiving the monies were involved in domestic production of clean energy technologies, such as solar, wind, energy efficiency and energy management technologies. It was estimated that these federal grants would leverage more than $5 billion in private sector investments, catapulting the U.S. into a leadership role in the clean energy arena, and create over 17,000 jobs in the fastest growing sector of the U.S. economy.

Some of the major Advanced Energy Manufacturing Tax Credits that were awarded included:
- Miasole was the recipient of $91 million to manufacture solar PV cells based on an innovative thin-film production technology in order to drive down costs for renewable energy generation.
- United Technologies Inc. was granted $110 million to re-equipped their existing manufacturing facility to build a new jet engine, increasing energy efficiency.

- Wacker Polysilicon North America LLC received $128 million to produce 10 metric tons of pure polysilicon annually for photovoltaic solar cell markets.[15]

In July 2010, Obama called on Congress to approve an additional $5 billion in clean energy manufacturing tax credits to stimulate new jobs. He added that the federal credits dedicated to clean energy businesses would spur over $12 billion in private investment,[16] leading to the creation of 90,000 green jobs.[17] Obama was even more bullish in August 2010, when he said that the clean energy manufacturing tax credit, coupled with other administration initiatives, would generate 800,000 jobs in the following two years.[18]

Create a Green Job Corps: *Barack Obama and Joe Biden will create an energy-focused youth jobs program for disconnected and disadvantaged youth. This program will provide participants with service opportunities to improve energy conservation and efficiency of homes and buildings in their communities, while also providing practical experience in important career fields of expected high-growth employment. It will also engage private sector employers and unions to provide apprenticeship opportunities. The program will also work closely with Barack Obama and Joe Biden's proposed Clean Energy Corps to help participants find additional service opportunities after they complete the Green Job Corps.*

In the early day of the Obama Administration, the primary environmental training initiatives for youth were the existing programs of the National Park Service (NPS). The NPS over the years had established programs with the Youth Conservation Corps, Public Lands Corps, Student Conservation Corps and Corps Network. These are wonderful programs that are tied in with more than 25 state groups, and are great for youth to get experience doing construction work on trails and campsites, removing exotic plants, doing wildlife research, and conducting environmental education. The established programs provided a clear pathway for young people from all economic backgrounds, as well as rural or urban roots, to develop the skills to pursue natural resources careers with the NPS.[19]

However after Obama was elected president, more than 80 labor, environmental, civic, and policy organizations drafted a broader proposal for a Clean Energy Corps. This program was designed to train urban and rural youth in new energy technologies, and help to secure America's economic recovery.[19] In April 2009, Obama signed the Edward M. Kennedy Serve America Act, which incorporated the Clean Energy Corps (CEC). The Corporation for National and Community Service was designated as the agency that would manage the program and CEC would be funded out of its $1.1 billion budget.[20]

The vision for CEC was that it would provide pathways to prosperity for low-income young men and women. It would enable under-educated, under-served young people to gain the skills, work experience, and credentials needed to enter the green jobs pipeline. Young people would begin with low-skilled tasks, such as installing foam insulation or performing home energy audits. Then, through a specially-designed career path, these youth would move through apprenticeships, industry-recognized credentialing, additional educational opportunities and management positions. Ultimately, some of them would be on the career path to being small business owners. The CEC would meet local needs, and take a five-pronged approach to help create a green economy:

- Efficiency - reduce energy use through weatherization, retrofits and energy-efficient upgrades, water savings, and the repair and improvement of our transportation infrastructure.
- Waste Reduction - help communities minimize waste; for example, in local or regional recycling programs.
- Renewable Energy - install and maintain solar panels, wind turbines, and other new and emerging technologies
- Public Lands - plant trees, restore wetlands and streams, conserve water, landscape, and serve in our public lands, enhancing, rehabilitating, and repairing trails
- Education/Community Awareness – assist others by working with community based organizations or other local stakeholders to raise awareness about ways to reduce home energy use and improve the environment.[21]

It was anticipated that CEC could install energy-efficient measures in over 15 million existing buildings, ranging from adding insulation to replacing inefficient boilers. By retrofitting millions of structures, CEC would create at least 600,000 jobs in green industries, and train young people to successfully fill them. This would provide one of the essential building blocks for a greener American economy.[19]

The Department of Education held the *National Sustainability Education Summit: Citizenship and Pathways for a Green Economy* in September 2010. It brought together representatives of all the major players that have a significant role to play in preparing American youth for jobs in a clean, green economy; federal agencies, state agencies, higher education, career and technical school, community colleges, K-12education, business and environmental groups. The Secretary of Education, Arne Duncan, said that his agency had "been mostly absent from the movement to educate our children to be steward of our environment" and had not "been doing enough in the sustainability movement."[22] But he promised the Department of Education would "be a committed partner in the national effort to build a more environmentally literate and responsible society."[22]

Create a "Green Vet Initiative": *Barack Obama and Joe Biden will ensure that more of our veterans can enter the new energy economy. They will create a new "Green Vet Initiative" that will have two missions: first it will offer counseling and job placement to help veterans gain the skills to enter this rapidly growing field; second, it will work with industry partners to create career pathways and educational programs.*

The Obama Department of Labor (DOL) reworked an existing program, the Veterans Workforce Investment Program (VWIP), to include a green jobs component and increased the budget request for VWIP. The DOL says "The intent of VWIP is to provide support for employment and training services through grants and contracts that assist eligible veterans with reintegration into meaningful employment within the labor force and stimulates the development of effective service delivery systems that will address their complex employment problems. Eligible participants in VWIP must be veterans with service-connected disabilities, veterans who have significant barriers to employment, veterans who served on active duty in the armed forces during a war or in a campaign or expedition for which a campaign badge was authorized, and recently separated veterans within 48 months of discharge (under conditions other than dishonorable). Veterans who received a "dishonorable" discharge are ineligible for VWIP services. Projects that, support the President's commitment to 'Green Energy Jobs,' and propose clear strategies for training and employment in the renewable energy economy, are unique and innovative, will receive priority consideration."[23] The VWIP requested a budget of $9.6 million in FY2010 to provide services to approximately 4,600 veterans.[24]

Create New Job Training Programs for Clean Technologies:
The Barack Obama and Joe Biden plan will increase funding for federal workforce training programs and direct these programs to incorporate green technologies training, such as advanced manufacturing and weatherization training, into their efforts to help Americans find and retain stable, high-paying jobs.

    The Obama Administration provided $500 million from Recovery Act funding for job training, giving workers the skills and expertise for careers in the energy efficiency and renewable energy industries.[25] The funds were allocated through competitive grants to states and nonprofits to support programs of training and placement of workers in green sector jobs. It also included $100 million for training and hiring workers in the utility and electrical manufacturing sectors, to advance the construction and implementation of the smart grid.[26] The Obama Administration touted green jobs as paying 10 to 20 percent higher than traditional jobs, and the installation of energy efficiency and renewable energy technologies domestically were not positions that could be exported.[26]

    The Bureau of Labor Statistics (BLS) developed a definition of green jobs to be used in gathering statistics for its Quarterly Census of Employment and Wages, and Occupational Employment Statistics programs. According to the BLS definition, green jobs are:

- "Jobs in businesses that produce goods or provide services that benefit the environment or conserve natural resources; or
- Jobs in which workers' duties involve making their establishment's production processes more environmentally friendly or use fewer natural resources."[27]

The training funds from the Recovery Act were allocated through grants by the Department of Labor's Employment and Training Administration and were distributed in five different funding streams:

- State Labor Market Information Improvement Grants:
- Energy Training Partnership Grants;
- Pathways Out of Poverty Grants;
- State Sector Training Grants; and
- Green Capacity Building Grants.

Some funds in the Energy Training Grants and State Sector Training Grants were held back to address the needs of middle-class autoworkers and auto-related worker in pursuing green employment.[28]

One of the soap operas of the Obama Administration revolved around the appointment and resignation in September 2009 of Van Jones, as the Obama's "Green Jobs Czar." Jones came to the White House with an impressive background in the fundamentals of clean energy job creation having written the 2008 book, "The Green Collar Economy: How One Solution Can Fix Our Two Biggest Problems." He was well known in Democratic Party circles, having worked at the Center for American Progress, run by former Clinton Administration official, John Podesta.[29] Then, in the summer of 2009, other aspects of Jones' past began coming to light. This included a 1990s association with the group Standing Together to Organize a Revolutionary Movement, which opened him to charges that he had communist leanings. Jones had also had let his name be attached to a "truther" letter, calling for an investigation into whether President Bush had allowed the September 11 attacks to occur, in order to engage the U.S. in a war. Lastly, Jones was known for occasionally using impolite language in reference to Republicans. His associations became nightly fare on Glenn Beck's Fox News show, and powerful Senate Republicans began calling for hearings on Jones' affiliations. Jones resigned his position as Green Jobs Czar in the early hours of Sunday, September 6th, Labor Day weekend.[30] No one else in the Obama Administration possessed his poetry and passion for green jobs. It is unclear whether Jones' departure slowed down the Obama Administration's green jobs agenda, but his past associations certainly did not help the public relations surrounding green jobs.

The Council of Economic Advisors (CEA), in early 2010, released a report examining the clean energy investments of the Recovery Act, and determined that they were not only creating jobs now, but were projected to do so in the future. The CEA estimated that the Recovery Act expenditures saved or created 63,000 jobs, and that 700,000 more were expected by 2012. The type of jobs the CEA was referring to included "skilled laborers who can install efficient heating and cooling systems and windows, who can retrofit homes to save electricity, who can build and install solar panels, wind turbines and other clean energy technologies."[31]

The FY2011 budget that Obama presented in early 2010 allocated $85 million to green energy jobs training, as well as, $170 million for bioenergy research and $300 million for other renewable energy initiatives.[32] While the Obama Administration was confident in its green jobs and clean energy initiatives to help stimulate the economy, by creating "800,000 jobs in the next two years,"[18] others were not so sure. Andrew Morriss, a professor of economics at the University of Illinois wrote a report critical of the Obama approach to economic recovery, and stated "Before governments act on the scale that green jobs proponents propose, we need evidence that the action at least won't hurt the economy. I'd give an "F" mark to all of the major studies supporting green jobs programmes if a student turned them in for an undergraduate economics class."[33]

As 2010 marched on, and the unemployment rate continued to go up, reaching 9.8 percent rather than going down, many people started to wonder if Professor Morriss might be right. Reports started to surface about long-term unemployed people who had gone though green jobs training, but still could not find a job. A case in point is Laurance Anton a former construction worker from

Ocala, Florida, who had participated in a green jobs training course to learn how to solder components to a circuit board. After 200 job applications, he remained unemployed. The green jobs were just not there, due to a sagging green energy industry that was not experiencing growing demand.[34]

The renewable energy industry was disappointed that federal mandates for renewable electricity, and caps on carbon emissions, had not been passed by Congress. Both of those would have really spur demand for their products, and increased the need for hiring some of the unemployed who had been trained. Samuel Sherraden a policy analyst at the New America Foundation has said about the Obama Administration's green jobs strategy, "It was a little too ambitious given the size and depth of the recession and small size of the renewable energy industry."[34] While the Obama Administration claims the investments in green energy and job training have saved or created 225,000 jobs, that is a small percentage of the 7.5 million jobs lost since the recession began in 2007.[34]

4.

ENERGY GENERATION

Increase Investment in Basic Research and Human Capital::
Barack Obama and Joe Biden will double federal science and research funding for clean energy projects.

The history of U.S. government funding for R&D in renewable energy is not a positive one, when compared to the level of support other energy technologies have received. An examination of the 60-year period from FY1948 to FY2007, indicates that nuclear energy received $85.1 billion or 53 percent of federal R&D funds; coal, oil and gas received 39.6 billion or 25 percent; and renewables received $16.96 billion or 10.7 percent. The equity distribution has changed for the better in more recent years, with the renewables share in the period FY1998 to FY2007 increasing almost seven points to 17.4 percent.[1]

The federal government also provides subsidies for energy resource development beyond R&D, such as tax credits and insurance liability limitation. A look at federal subsidies (excluding hydropower) from FY1943 to FY1999 shows that the nuclear industry received $145.4 billion or 96 percent of all funds, while solar received $4.4 billion and wind received $1.3 billion.[2]

Another challenge for renewable energy development is that historically, the amount federal funding requested by presidential administrations, and appropriated by Congress, roller coasters based on rises in gasoline prices and other factors. That has created inefficiencies in scaling up and scaling down projects, the loss of information gained from one cycle to the other, and exodus of talented personnel to other more stable job sectors.[3]

President Obama brought a fresh perspective to federal involvement in renewable energy research, development and deployment. In addition to committing to double the resources for clean energy, Obama set a goal of doubling U.S. renewable energy generation capacity from wind, solar, and geothermal by 2012. This would install as much renewables in the next three years, as the U.S. had in the previous 30 years. More specifically, the Obama goal was to double the existing 2008 renewable energy capacity from the 28.8 gigawatts (GW) of solar, wind, and geothermal generation, to 57.6 GW by the end of 2011.[4]

In February 2010, Obama unveiled the U.S. Department of Energy (DOE), Office of Energy Efficiency and Renewable Energy (EERE) proposed budget for FY2011. The Obama Administration budget proposal, included significant increases for many EERE programs over the FY2009 levels, such as a 222 percent increase for wind energy, a 156 percent increase for solar energy, and a 142 percent increase for geothermal energy. The proposed budget also included a $57.5 million line-item for facilities and infrastructure at DOE's National Renewable Energy Laboratory. In addition to the funding for EERE, the proposed DOE budget included $500 million to support an estimated $3 to $5 billion in loan guarantees for renewable energy and energy efficiency projects.[5]

The American Recovery and Reinvestment Act (Recovery Act) had $23 billion of additional funds dedicated to renewable energy research development, manufacturing, deployment and commercialization activities, which would leverage $43 billion in private investment. For example, DOE used Recovery Act funds to support its solar PV incubator program, which worked with two firms, FirstSolar and Solyndra. The DOE dollars supported competition between thin-film crystalline silicon materials like cadmium telluride (Cd-Te), and copper indium 21 gallium selenide (CIGS). It was anticipated that advances in these technologies could reduce the costs of solar panels considerably by 2015. In addition, the Recovery Act allowed DOE's pre-incubator and incubator programs to support breakthrough work in nanomaterials and organic materials, that could drive down costs even further.[4]

DOE believed that near-term improvements gained under Recovery Act funding would cut the cost of solar power in half, as second generation thin-film solar panels such as the rapidly emerging CIGS and Cd-Te technologies would compete with ever improving traditional silicon-based panels. The agency was working toward the goal of making the cost of solar power cheaper per kilowatt hour (kWh), than electricity from the grid, from roughly

$0.20/kWh to $0.10/kWh for solar electricity generated at people's homes. If these breakthroughs in technology could bring costs down to $0.06/kWh by 2030, then solar power would be cheaper than retail electricity from the grid, even without government incentives. At that cost, an average household with rooftop solar panels could save more than $400 each year in its electricity bills.[4]

Obama further showed his commitment to solar energy R&D and commercialization by announcing in October 2010, that solar technology would be installed on the White House. The system chosen by DOE Secretary Steven Chu was a photovoltaic array and solar watering heating panel, which was designed to provide hot water in the White House residence. Chu said, "This project reflects President Obama's strong commitment to U.S. leadership in solar energy and the jobs it will create here at home."[6] No sooner had the announcement been made, when political critics started comparing Obama' solar decision to one-term President Jimmy Carter. Carter was the first president to have solar panels installed in the White House, and conservatives applauded when his successor President Reagan had them dismantled. Obama's political opponents tried to paint this Obama's decision, as showing the same failed judgment as Carter. The solar industry, however, was pleased with Obama's support and Scott Sklar, president of the Stella Group said, "It's about time for the United States to reposition itself as a global leader in solar and the entire portfolio renewable energy and energy efficiency technologies critical to our economic and national security."[7]

The Recovery Act funded two large wind turbine R&D test centers. One of the centers was designed for turbines, and the other one for blades. These centers would allow development and testing of the next generation of large-scale, wind-turbine, drive-train systems and blades in the U.S. Wind turbine sizes have increased with each new generation of turbines, and they have outgrown the capacity of existing U.S. drive-train testing facilities. It was hoped that these domestic facilities would help enhance the performance, durability, and reliability of U.S.-manufactured wind turbines and blades.[4]

The Recovery Act funded two manufacturers of wind turbines with groundbreaking concepts that may out compete international competitors in renewable energy technologies sales and generation.[4]

- PAX Streamline Inc.'s Adaptive Turbine Blades received $3 million to develop a prototype "blown wing" wind turbine at the 100 kW scale. Unlike typical wind turbine blades, which have fixed airfoils, a "blown wing" turbine blade can be adjusted to maximize power under a wide range of wind conditions. While blown wing technology has been demonstrated on aircraft by the U.S. military, it had not yet been demonstrated for wind turbines.
- FloDesign Wind Turbine Corp.'s Shrouded Wind Turbines was granted $8.3 million to developed a novel, enclosed wind turbine, similar to jet turbine designs, which would deliver significantly more energy for its size than existing wind turbines.[4]

One of the challenges of trying to increase the number of clean energy developments on federal land using Recovery Act funds, or any other government funding, is reducing the obstacles for approval. In December 2009, Department of the Interior (DOI) Secretary Salazar convened nine federal agencies with authority over the siting processes on federal land, to sign an MOU. This agreement designated DOI as the lead agency to coordinate federal authorizations, and help streamline the process. The DOI provided fast-track approval for 30 renewable projects by late 2009, which were scheduled to be up and running by December 2010. For solar applications, DOI set aside over 1000 square miles of land. For wind resources, DOI established in conjunction with the Federal Energy Regulatory Commission, a process for granting leases, easements, and rights of way for projects on the Outer Continental Shelf.[8]

Some congressional Democratic members became upset, and called for suspension in DOE Recovery Act funding, when they learned in 2010, that some of the dollars were going to support firms and jobs overseas. Senators Schumer (D-NY), Casey (D-PA), Brown (D-OH) and Tester (D-MT) wanted to add a new "Buy America" provision to the Recovery Act which would apply to all programs under the jurisdiction of the act. This concern surfaced when a report done by the Investigative Reporting Workshop was released. The report documented that since September 2009, 79 percent of DOE's $2 billion in renewable energy grants had gone to foreign firms. Schumer said, "We are demanding that the Obama Administration suspend this program immediately....(and) indefinitely. We are sending a letter to (Treasury) Secretary (Timothy) Geithner asking him to halt all payouts on this program until we in Congress can go back an fix this law."[9] While the Recovery Act had very restrictive "Buy America" provision for construction projects, it did not apply to high technology or complex manufactured goods, such as those funded with the DOE monies.[10]

It was learned late in 2010 that the Obama Administration, in order to speed the implementation of Recovery Act projects, had provide more than 179,00 "categorical exemptions" from compliance with the National Environmental Policy Act (NEPA)that requires an environmental impact statement (EIS). To provide these exemptions, the Obama Administration relied on voluntary disclosures by companies on whether the Recovery Act project would pose any environmental harm. This included those firms who already had long records of environmental violations. In fact, DOE granted waivers to 99 percent of the Recovery Act projects it funded, including: (1) an electric power grid upgrade project in Kansas City performed by Westar Energy, which recently paid a half billion dollars in environmental fines and remediation costs; (2) a wind farm project in Texas that was performed by Duke Energy, which is involved in a decades long air pollution case; and (3) a clean burning biofuels project managed by DuPont who has faced two class-action lawsuits over water contamination by its toxic chemical C8.[11]

Even with DOE cutting corners on NEPA compliance, the agency's Inspectors General (IG) cited issues with DOE's pace in distributing Recovery Act dollars, and its recipients in using them. The IG reported in August 2010, that while DOE had awarded $2.7 of $3.2 billion in block grant Recovery Act funds, the recipients had only used 8.4 percent after more than a year. The IG found that spending delays were most prevalent with the larger grantees receiving $2 million or more. The IG noted that spending of funds at the federal, state and local levels "was hampered by numerous administrative and regulatory challenges associated with implementing a new program."[12]

Clean Technologies Deployment Venture Capital Fund: *Barack Obama and Joe Biden will create a Clean Technologies Venture Capital Fund to fill a critical gap in U.S. technology development. This fund will partner with existing investment funds and our National Laboratories to ensure that promising technologies move beyond the lab and are commercialized in the U.S.*

Obama did not create a Clean Technologies Venture Capital Fund, and it may not be lawful for the government to become an investor in the development of a private corporation. But Obama did received $6 billion in a loan guarantees under the Recovery Act for clean energy innovation to be administered by DOE.[13] The conditions for the DOE 1705 renewable loan guarantee program were that each project had to have the potential to create or save more than 5,000 construction and permanent jobs, lead to more than 3 GW of clean power generating capacity, and avoid more than 30 million tons of $CO2$ per year. It was estimated that the 1705 program loan guarantees would leverage more than $4 debt and equity for every $1 of loan guarantee subsidy.[4] Loan guarantees are not dollars given to the firms, but the government agrees to payback the loans, if the company defaults on a loan from a private lender to finance the project. Emily Mendel, vice president of the National Venture Capital Association, said "While a venture capital fund was not created, the loan guarantee program in the (Recover Act) was a good thing."[14] She further indicated that the DOE loan guarantees would be going to firms further along in the development process than a venture capital fund would, so the technology would get to market faster, provide more jobs sooner and be less risky for the government.[14]

The 1705 renewable loan guarantees were to be administered by the DOE "Energy Bank," which provides guarantees for a wide range of innovative energy technologies, including nuclear. The Energy Bank earned the wrath of Senator Jeff Bingaman (D-MN) in early 2009, when after receiving $42 billion in authorizations for loans from Congress since 2005, it had not issued even one loan guarantee. Bingaman had heard from unhappy nuclear energy lobbyists that the Energy Bank had a backlog of $122 billion in requests for 21 nuclear reactors. The negative performance of the Energy Bank halted a preliminary request from the Obama Administration for a clean energy loan guarantee program worth $50 billion. In fact, Bingaman was so unhappy with the Energy Bank, he asked DOE Secretary Chu to consider establishing a separate "Clean Energy Bank" and even drafted legislation to make the program a separate entity.[15]

Congress and Obama were facing a dire economic situation in summer 2010, with the prospect of 300,000 teachers, police and other civil servants across the nation being laid off, due to state budget cuts. Congress moved quickly to assemble a $26 billion spending bill which Obama signed in order to prevent furloughs and maintain services To find the dollars to fund the state bailout bill, $1.5 billion was taken from the Recovery Act 1705 renewable energy loan guarantee program, supporting solar wind and alternative energy companies. This was in addition to the $2 billion taken from the program earlier in the year for an extension of the car trade-in program, known as Cash for Clunkers. The renewable energy industry expressed "strong opposition" to Speaker Pelosi over the rescission[16] and had former Vice President Al Gore weigh in saying "although this is an important initiative, this $1.5 billion cut is on top of the $2 billion taken out of the renewables fund to pay for an extension to the Cash for Clunkers program. Taken together, this is more than one-half of the $6 billion allocated to the Energy Department for the Renewables/Transmission Loan Guarantee Program under the Recovery Act. These rescissions put into jeopardy the green jobs that the administration have touted as part of the clean energy future and put us further behind the rest of the world."[10] Pelosi's staff said that she would work to restore the 1705 funding at a later date, but that never happened.[13] Unfortunately, in this instance, Obama did not prevent a repeat of the roller coaster support that has plagued federal renewable energy funding in prior administrations.[10]

Then, in November 2010, a memo to Obama from assistant for energy and climate change, Carol Browner was leaked. It proposed several paths forward for 1705 renewable loan guarantee program. All the problems that Bingaman had outlined in 2009 regarding the Energy Bank were still plaguing the institution, especially the slow processing. In fairness to DOE, it should be noted that other agencies such as the Office of Management and Budget (OMB) and the Department of the Treasury (Treasury) had to sign off on each loan guarantee, and that added to slow pace and cumbersomeness of the process. Browner was concerned that Congress might use the rescission process to defund the 1705 loan guarantees and reprogram the funds non-clean energy purposes. The memo outlined four possible options: (1) limit OMB and Treasury oversight role: (2) make the process work better by establishing clear policy principles; (3) reprogram 1705 loan dollars to 1603 tax credit/grants which were about to expire; and (4) streamline and accelerate OMB and Treasury reviews with project prioritization.[17]

In early December 2010, Senate Majority Leader Reid announced that an extension of the 1603 tax credit/grant for the renewable energy industry was to be included in the lame duck tax package, that included the continuation of the Bush tax cuts, and an extension of unemployment benefits.[18] The Obama Administration declined to push for renewal of the 1705 loan program and allowed the transfer of remaining funds to the 1603 tax credit/grant program. The same renewable energy industry that Gore represented as being concerned about the 1705 de-funding for the Cash for Clunkers program and for state government, was ecstatic about this move. Denis Bode, chief executive of the American Wind Energy Association said, "Orders will be on the rise for new wind power, and investors will put more capital into the U.S. economy."[19] Rhone Resch, chief executive of the Solar Energy Industries Association stated, "It was kind of a roller coaster there. There were a lot of projects that were getting close to being canceled. Now this gives them some flexibility to get their financing together and start construction at a time when they need it most." Resch added, "It keeps the lights on, keeps us growing. There are a lot of happy people in the industry today, and 2011 is looking like it will be a true breakout year."[19]

Production Tax Credit: *Barack Obama and Joe Biden the federal Production Tax Credit (PTC) for 5 years to encou deployment of renewable technologies.*

When Obama signed the Recovery Act, it ha which extended the Production Tax Credits (PTC) o systems until December 2012, and for open-loop-sys December 2013. Closed loop systems are wind, solar, geothermal, and bioenergy (using dedicated energy crops). Under the Recovery Act language, they are eligible for a 2.1 cents per kilowatt-hour (kWh) PTC for the first ten years of the renewable energy facility's operation. Open-loop systems such as biomass using farm and forest wastes (rather than dedicated energy crops), incremental hydropower, small irrigation systems, landfill gas, and municipal solid waste (MSW), are eligible to receive a PTC of 1.0 cent per kWh. In addition, the Recovery Act also extended the PTC for electricity produced by wave and tidal energy through 2013.[20] Rob Gramlich of the American Wind Energy Association said, "It was a longer extension than we have ever had and the (Obama) Administration worked very hard to restructure the mechanism to work in the changed economic environment. So we give the administration very high marks on the tax credit."[21]

Offshore Drilling: *Barack Obama fought against offshore drilling in the U.S. Senate, and he supports maintaining current moratoriums on new offshore oil and natural gas drilling.*

Obama broke his commitment on keeping current moratoriums in place for offshore drilling in late March 2009. From behind the podium and in front of the news media, Obama announced his bipartisan plan to expand energy production, which was to open up areas along the southern coastline of the Atlantic Ocean and Gulf of Mexico to offshore drilling. He would also allow continued drilling on the North Slope of Alaska, but not off the coast or in Bristol Bay.[21] In making the announcement, Obama said, "we'll employ new technologies that reduce the impact of oil exploration. We'll protect areas that are vital to tourism, the environment, and our national security. And we'll be guided not by political ideology, but by scientific evidence."[22]

The action to open the southern portion of the Atlantic coast from the northern tip of Delaware to mid-Florida was spurred by Senators Warner (D-VA) and Webb (D-VA) who had sent a letter to Interior Secretary Salazar stating, "We would urge you to promptly commence these steps in order to ensure that the Virginia lease sale is conducted in a manner that is timely and consistent with the interests of environment and national security."[23] It was estimated that 130 million barrels of oil and 1.14 trillion cubic feet of natural gas could be tapped off the coast of Virginia. Upon hearing of Obama's decision, Warner said, "This is good news and a positive step forward as we work to expand our nation's domestic energy production."[23]

Some of Warner's Senate colleagues were not happy. Senator Frank Lautenberg (D-NJ) said, "Drilling off the coast of Virginia would endanger many of New Jersey's beaches and vibrant coastal economies. Giving Big Oil more access to our nation's waters is really Kill, Baby, Kill policy; it threatens to kill jobs, kill marine life and kill coastal communities that generate billions of dollars. Offshore drilling isn't the solution to our energy problems, and I will fight this policy and continue to push for 21st century clean energy solutions."[23]

Coincidentally, a few weeks after Obama's much heralded offshore drilling announcement, the Deepwater Horizon Gulf Oil Spill occurred. It created one of the worst environmental disasters the U.S. had ever seen, releasing 172 million gallons of oil into the fragile Gulf of Mexico ecosystem.[24]

Then eighteen months later in December 2010, the Obama Administration announced that it was not opening the Atlantic or Pacific coasts, or the eastern Gulf of Mexico, to offshore oil drilling. This announcement was very low key, with no president, no podium and no press conference. Instead Salazar sent out a press release and did a phone call with reporters. Salazar said, "The plan we announced in March was based on our best science at the time. There has been significant additional information that has been gained since April 20 until now"[24] Senators Mendez (D-NJ), and Bill Nelson (D-FL), said they regretted that it took the spill in the Gulf for the Obama Administration to realized that offshore oil drilling was not safe.[24]

Develop and Deploy Clean Coal Technology: *An Obama administration will provide incentives to accelerate private sector investment in commercial scale zero-carbon coal facilities. In order to maximize the speed with which we advance this critical technology, Barack Obama and Joe Biden will instruct DOE to enter into public private partnerships to develop 5 "first-of-a-kind" commercial scale coal-fired plants with carbon capture and sequestration.*

When an environmentalist tells Obama in February 2010, "It's got to be renewable energy. No more clean coal. …It's a unicorn. It doesn't exist."[25] Obama responded, "No, no, no ….I disagree with you. I disagree with you. I am going to defend. …We are not going to get all our energy from energy from wind and solar in the next 20 years. …Don't be stubborn."[25] Obama has stated repeatedly, that he believes in clean coal technologies, and wants to have them as part of his global warming and energy security initiatives.

Clean coal research is conducted by DOE within its Fossil Energy section. That section's budgets for Coal Technology have been declining with its FY2009 funding set at $681 billion,[26] FY2010 at $404 billion and the FY2011 request at $403 billion.[27] The major cause of the reductions has been the elimination of the Clean Coal Power Initiative (CCPI). The CCPI was started in 2003 during the Bush Administration, and had a FY2009 budget of $288 billion,[26] but the Obama Administration requested zero in FY2010[26] and FY2011.[27] The Obama Administration says that was due to the clean coal funding provided under the Recovery Act.[28] In the FY2010 Fossil Energy budget, the Obama Administration did ask for an increase in carbon sequestration R&D from the FY2009 $145 billion to $179 billion.[26] However, Congress only approved $154 billion in FY2010,[25] and the Obama Administration dropped its request for carbon sequestration R&D to $143 billion in FY2011.[27]

The Recovery Act contained $3.4 billion in funding for clean coal projects and carbon sequestration initiatives. This breaks down to $800 million for clean coal, $1.5 billion for industrial carbon capture and storage, $70 million for geologic sequestration site characterization, training and research, and $1 billion carbon capture and storage (undefined).[29] (For more information on the

Recovery Act's "$1 billion carbon capture and storage (undefined)," see the paragraphs below on FutureGen.)

During 2009 and 2010, Energy Secretary Chu announced the awards of numerous projects promoting clean coal and carbons sequestration technology. Using CCPI and Recovery Act funding, Chu's intention was to build the technological base that will yield five to ten commercialized systems fulfilling Obama's goal.

- Hydrogen Energy International LLC received $308 million to design, construct, and operate an integrated gasification combined cycle power plant that will take blends of coal and petroleum coke, combined with non-potable water, and convert them into hydrogen and CO2. The CO2 will be separated from the hydrogen using a methanol-based process. The hydrogen gas will be used to fuel a power station, and the CO2 will be transported by pipeline to nearby oil reservoirs where it will be injected for storage and used for enhanced oil recovery.[30]
- American Electric Power (AEP) was granted $334 million to design, construct and operate a chilled ammonia process that is expected to effectively capture at least 90 percent of the CO2 (1.5 million metric tons per year) in a 235 megawatt flue gas stream at the existing 1,300 megawatt power plant. The captured CO2 will be treated, compressed, and then transported by pipeline to injection sites located near the capture facility.[31]
- Leucadia Energy, LLC and Denbury Onshore LLC were awarded $260 million to capture and sequester 4.5 million tons of CO2 per year from a new methanol plant in Lake Charles, Louisiana. The CO2 will be delivered via a 12-mile connector pipeline, and used for enhanced oil recovery in a local oilfield, starting in April 2014.[32]
- Archer Daniels Midland Corporation was granted $99 million to capture and sequester one million tons of CO2 per year from an existing ethanol plant in Illinois,

starting in August 2012. The CO2 will be sequestered in a saline reservoir located about one mile from the plant.[30]

- NRG Energy, Inc. received $154 million to construct a 60-megawatt carbon capture demonstration facility integrating several important advanced technologies, including a carbon capture process, an advanced carbon dioxide compression system, and a highly efficient co-generation system to provide the necessary steam and electricity. The project was intended to show that post-combustion carbon capture can be economically applied to existing plants when the facility has the opportunity to sequester carbon dioxide in nearby oilfields.[33]

One of the more controversial energy decisions made by the Obama Administration was the restarting of a low-carbon project known as FutureGen. This project located in Mattoon, Illinois, Obama's home state, had been started by the Bush Administration in 2003. It was supposed to be the first commercial-scale, fully-integrated carbon capture and sequestration project in the nation. The facility would deploy both integrated-gasification, combined-cycle technology, and greenhouse gas emission control. However in early 2008, DOE de-funded FutureGen citing future cost overruns. The agency planned to restructure the dollars going to the project, so that DOE was only paying for the carbon capture and sequestration. Before leaving office, the Bush Administration and DOE had not made of final decision on the matter.[34]

The U.S. Government Accountability Office did an analysis of the FutureGen project releasing a report in March 2009 stating that DOE had mischaracterized the project's costs using calculations of constant dollars, and not factoring in inflation over the period ending in 2017.[35] The Washington Post noted that very same month, "Deep inside the economic stimulus package (Recovery Act) is a $1 billion prize that, in five short words, shows the benefits of being in power in Washington. The funding, for 'fossil energy research and development,' is likely to go to a power plant in a small Illinois town, a project whose longtime backers include a group of powerful lawmakers from the state, among them President Obama."[35] Then, in June 2009, the Obama

Administration, through DOE, announced that it was restarting FutureGen with a $1 billion commitment from the Recovery Act, and that the industry partners, comprised of 20 firms, would be contributing $400 to $600 million over a four to six year period. Obama's critics howled, with Senator Coburn (R-OK) stating, "This costly and gratuitous earmark calls into question the integrity of the Recovery Act. This decision appears to have more to do with politics and geography than science. FutureGen 1.0 was called 'YesterGen' because it had little scientific value."[36] Those criticizing Obama's decision, failed to notice that the Bush Administration in FY 2007, FY2008 and FY2009 had submitted earmarks for FutureGen funding totaling $318 million.[28, 37]

In February 2010, Obama named an Interagency Task Force on Carbon Capture and Storage composed of 14 cabinet and independent agencies with over 100 staff. The group was to develop, by August 2010, a plan to overcome barriers to carbon capture and storage (CCS) within the decade. The Task force would help to meet Obama's goal of having five to ten commercial demonstrations in place by 2016. The Task Force reported back with recommendations and findings that included:

- There are no insurmountable technical, legal, institutional, or other barriers to the deployment of CCS technology;
- Widespread utilization of CCS is best achieved with a price on carbon, but there are other market drivers which may support near-term adoption;
- Additional federal actions and coordination, such as the creation of a standing federal agency roundtable and expert committee would assist in commercialization;
- CCS deployment has significant industry liability issues that may need federal government involvement;
- DOE and EPA need to track regulatory implementation; and
- Federal agencies and other public and private partners need gather information and evaluate potential key concerns about CCS, including environmental justice issues.[38]

The bottom line for the report can be found in this one sentence, "While there are no insurmountable technological, legal, institutional, regulatory or other barriers that prevent CCS from playing a role in reducing GHG (greenhouse gas) emissions, early CCS projects face economic challenges related to climate policy uncertainty, first-of-a-kind technology risks and the current high costs of CCS relative to other technologies."[38]

Safe and Secure Nuclear Energy: *Nuclear power represents more than 70 percent of our non-carbon generated electricity. It is unlikely that we can meet our aggressive climate goals if we eliminate nuclear power as an option. However, before an expansion of nuclear power is considered, key issues must be addressed including: security of nuclear fuel and waste, waste storage, and proliferation.*

In his January 27, 2010 State of the Union Speech, Obama reiterated his support for "a new generation of safe, clean nuclear power plants."[39] A few weeks later, he followed that up in his FY2011 budget request to Congress, asking for $36 billion in loan guarantee authority for DOE in nuclear power plant construction. This would be in addition to $18.5 billion for nuclear plants that DOE already has.[39]

Obama's request did not, however, match the nuclear industry's wish list which included a $100 billion increase in loan guarantees, an extension of nuclear energy production credits through 2025, the removal of the 6,000 megawatt limitation on tax credits, a 30 percent investment tax credit or grant instead of the production credit, tax credits for new or expanded manufacturing and worker training, and decreasing or cutting entirely the tariffs on nuclear components.[40]

Chu told members of Congress that the $36 billion in loan guarantees would finance seven to ten new plants, and encourage an industry that has not seen expansion in decades. The Obama Administration proposal was praised by some in the Republican Party like Senator Judd Greg (R-NH) who said the move was "very constructive in moving the process forward."[40] Some saw Obama's move as way to build relationships with the opposition party, in preparation for the global climate change bill negotiations that would be happening later in the year. Senator Carper (D-DE) said,

"If the Republicans are interested in helping to ensure a renaissance for nuclear power in this country, I think the path is clear for how we might do that. They want to see as many as 100 plants built in the next 40 years. We will find out if they are really serious about getting started. If they are, they've got a great opportunity to work with us."[40]

The Achilles heel of the Obama plan was nuclear waste storage. Obama was in the process of de-funding the research into the long-term storage facility at Yucca Mountain in Nevada, and many Republicans did not know how he could be talking about nuclear power plant expansion. (See Chapter 8. Healthy Communities, section "Protecting the Public from Nuclear Material" for more information on Yucca Mountain.) Senator Richard Burr (R-NC) said the increase in nuclear loan guarantees meant nothing without long-storage being addressed, "Temporary storage does not meet the requirement for shareholders to aggressively invest in the build out of nuclear generation."[40] In agreement with that thinking was Senator McCain (R-AZ) who stated, "His secretary of energy says they won't recycle, and they won't restore. That's a nonstarter, so I do not pay attention."[38]

Joining the nuclear industry and Republicans, in their lack of enthusiasm for the Obama's proposal to expand nuclear loan guarantees, was the environmental community. Edwin Lyman a nuclear expert with the Union of Concerned Scientists said, "I am reluctant to say this, because I admire the Obama Administration, but this nuclear strategy no longer appears to be coherent. It does not have a plan for (storing) radioactive waste from a generation of nuclear power plants. That is irresponble."[39]

When the White House was drafting it budget plan to increase nuclear loan guarantees, the OMB dramatically cut funding for research on reprocessing and small reactor research. Chu sent a strongly worded letter to the White House arguing for full funding for both initiatives, and Chu won. However, DOE sees research on spent fuel reprocessing as a long-term science based R&D program. In addition, it views small-modular reactors as the future of the nuclear industry. Without the necessary research being funded adequately in the U.S., other counties may end up dominating the market, and their designs may pose nuclear proliferation risks.[39]

The DOE nuclear loan guarantee program from the Energy Bank approved its first two loans in 2010. This was the same troubled Energy Bank that Bingaman took to task in early 2009 for not issuing a single loan since 2005. This is the same Energy Bank that was so slow in issuing renewable energy loans, that Congress and the Obama Administration transferred its remaining renewable energy funds to a program outside its purview. (For more information on the Energy Bank see the section "Clean Energy Technologies Deployment Venture Capital Fund" in this chapter.)

The first nuclear loan guarantee was announced in February 2010 for Southern Nuclear. It totaled $8.3 billion for two 1,100 megawatt reactors along side two existing reactors nears Waynesboro, Georgia.[39] The second guarantee for $2 billion went to the French firm AREVA, that was planning to build the Eagle Rock Enrichment Facility near Idaho Falls, Idaho. This facility was to provide uranium enrichment services to U.S. nuclear plants coming on line as early as 2016.[42] Of course the reactions to these Obama loan guarantee decisions brought different reactions from the industry and environmental community. Marvin Fertel, president of the Nuclear Energy Institute said, "This loan guarantee, and others to follow, will act as a catalyst to accelerate construction of new nuclear plants and other low- and non-emitting sources of electricity."[41] On the other hand, Jim Riccio, nuclear policy analyst at Greenpeace thought the nuclear guarantee "is a dirty and dangerous distraction from the clean-energy future the president promised America."[41]

5.

ENERGY EFFICIENCY

Overhaul Federal Appliance Efficiency Standards. *The current Department of Energy has missed 34 deadlines for setting updated appliance efficiency standards, which has cost American consumers millions of dollars in unrealized energy savings. Barack Obama and Joe Biden will overhaul this process for appliances and provide more resources to his Department of Energy so it implements regular updates for efficiency standards. They will also work with Congress to ensure that it continues to play a key role in improving our national efficiency codes.*

The issue of appliance efficiency standards had been bouncing among the Congresses, administrations and courts for years. Three weeks into his administration, President Obama dedicated his administration to fulfilling the commitment of developing appliance efficiency standards, as proscribed under the Energy Policy and Conservation Act of 1975, and the Energy Policy Act of 2005. He signed an Executive Order in February 2009 covering 30 appliances in total, but focused on 15 of the 22 that had been the subject of a court decree in 2006.

The prior Bush Administration had been sued for not following the law in setting appliance standards, and agreed to move forward with the appliances covered in the final court agreement by August 2011.[1] According to the new Obama Administration Executive Order, rules for some appliances including ovens, microwaves, lamps, dishwashers and commercial boilers would be set by August 2009. With efficiency increases between five to forty percent, Americans utilizing all the different types of appliances covered by the Executive Order, were estimated save as much as $500 million over 30-year period.[2]

Department of Energy (DOE) Secretary Chu soon announced an aggressive schedule for appliance standards to be issued, including:

- March 2009 – dishwashers, incandescent lamps and residential clothes washers;
- April 2009 – microwaves, kitchen ranges and ovens;
- July 2009 – fluorescent lights and incandescent reflector lamps, commercial heating, air conditioning and water-heating equipment;
- August 2009 – beverage vending machines;
- December 2009 – commercial clothes washers;
- February 2010 – small electric motors; and
- March 2010 – residential water heaters, direct heating equipment and pool heaters.[3]

The DOE's lighting standard for fluorescent bulbs, which was released in the summer 2009, was projected to save more than three trillion kilowatt hours (kWh). It was the single largest energy savings appliance standard ever enacted by the U.S. government. It was estimated to reduce energy cost to energy customers by $70 billion, and cut mercury pollution by more than nine million tons over 30 years.[4] Chu announced new standards in 2010 for residential water heaters, pool heater and direct heating equipment, like gas fireplaces. Together these standards would save $10 billion in energy costs, prevent 164 tons of carbon dioxide emissions and reduce nitrogen oxides, mercury and other emissions, equivalent to taking 46 million cars off the road.[3]

The DOE's 2010 multi-year plan for appliance standards documents the agency's accelerated pace of proposing, and finalizing, appliance standards. It estimated that since Obama came to office, the agency has issued or codified new efficiency standards for 20 different products, saving energy customers between $250 and $300 billion. DOE, by late 2010, had met the deadlines as outlined in the 2006 consent decree. So it began development of a work plan to go beyond the minimum statutory requirements, with the resources and flexibility to address other appliances and performance guidelines.[5]

The Obama Administration was supportive of the National Consensus Appliance Agreements Act (NCAAA) introduced by Senator Bingaman (D-NM) in September 2010. The NCAAA was intended to enact low-cost, energy efficiency standards for several home appliances and lighting equipment. It would reduce energy use by 1.2 billion quadrillion BTUs through 2030 and save energy customers $50 billion. For approximately a year and a half, the manufacturers of the named products agreed to the energy efficiency provisions of NCAAA, along with energy and consumer groups. The bill had wide support including Senators Lugar(R-IN), Klobuchar (D-MN), Kerry (-MA), Bayh (D-IN), Cardin (D-MD), Johnson (D-SD), Warner (D-VA), Whitehouse (D-RI), Feingold (D-WI) and Merkley (D-OR). Similar bills to this were passed and signed into law in 1988, 1989, 1992, 2005 and 2007.[6] However, this one died at the end of the 111th Congress in December 2010.[7]

The Obama Administration demonstrated additional support for energy efficient appliances by announcing a rebate program for appliances funded with $300 million of American Recovery and Reinvestment Act (Recovery Act) dollars. The program was not only intended to jump start the economy, but to get more energy-efficient, Energy Star appliances in peoples homes, in order to reduce energy loads, and save consumers money.[8]

Make Federal Buildings More Efficient: *Barack Obama and Joe Biden will ensure that all new federal buildings are zero-emissions by 2025, and they will ensure that all new federal buildings are 40 percent more efficient within the next five years. They will also make retrofitting existing federal buildings a top priority and seek to improve their efficiency by 25 percent within five years.*

The Recovery Act included $4.5 billion to upgrade federal facilities into high-performance green buildings. These dollars were targeted to new heating and cooling systems, improved insulation and energy-efficient lighting. The Obama FY 2010 budget listed an unspecified additional amount funding for green buildings, which would be allocated to help federal buildings meet a "25 percent energy efficiency improvement goal by 2013."[9] With the federal government occupying more than 500,000 buildings nationwide, Obama signed two Executive Orders in 2009, which together, required federal agencies to increase energy efficiency, reduce greenhouses gases, conserve water, reduce waste and support sustainability principles. More specifically he ordered:

- Increased energy efficiency by agency of 30 percent, with 15 percent achieved by 2015;[10]
- Implementation of the 2030 net-zero-energy building requirement;
- Submission of greenhouse gas reduction targets for 2020;
- 50 percent recycling and waste diversion by 2015;
- 26 percent improvement in water efficiency; and
- Compliance with the 2007 Energy Independence and Security Act stormwater provisions.[11]

Helping to implement these building strategies was the federal government's General Services Administration (GSA). GSA is the nation's largest landlord owning or leasing more than 340 million square of office space in more than 8,500 buildings.[12] For FY2011, GSA had a capital investment funds of $1.4 billion to support green buildings, with $676 million for new construction and $703 million for renovations. [10]

Following up on his two 2009 Executive Orders focused on federal building, Obama signed a third one in early 2010. This order mandated energy used reductions targeted at achieving lower greenhouse gas emissions from federal facilities. The emissions goals for 35 different agencies use a 2008 baseline to target cuts of 646 trillion BTUs, reductions of 88 million tons of emissions, and energy savings of $8 to $11 billion. Upon signing the order, Obama announced, "As the largest energy consumer in the United States, we have a responsibility to American citizens to reduce energy our energy use and become more efficient. Our goal is to lower costs, reduce pollution and shift federal energy expenses away from oil and towards local, clean energy."[12]

Energy efficiency is not just about proper building design and technology selection, but also about having the personnel with the expertise to operate facilities to their maximum potential. In December 2010, Obama signed the Federal Buildings and Personnel Act. The legislation provided GSA with the resources to develop, or identify, certification courses for federal personnel managing buildings. This included understanding energy management, sustainability, water efficiency and electrical safety, as well as, performance metrics, such as energy saved and water conserved.[13]

Expand Federal Efficiency Grants: *Barack Obama and Joe Biden will work to provide incentives for energy conservation by ensuring utilities get increased profits for improving energy efficiency, rather than higher energy consumption. They will provide early adopter grants and other financial assistance from the federal government to states that implement this energy efficient policy. Barack Obama and Joe Biden will create a competitive grant program to award those states and localities that take the first steps in implementing new building codes that prioritize energy efficiency. They will also provide a federal match for those states with public benefits funds that support energy efficiency retrofits for existing buildings. Barack Obama and Joe Biden will expand federal grant programs to help states and localities build more efficient public buildings that adopt aggressive green building provisions like those provided by Green Globes and the Leadership in Energy and Environmental Design program of the U.S. Green Buildings Council.*

Obama dedicated $6.3 billion of Recovery Act funding to state and local government energy efficiency grants under two distinct programs. The Energy Efficiency and Conservation Block Grant, which distributed $3.2 billion, was a new initiative that had not been previously funded.[14] While $400 million was granted to states and local governments under a competitive grant program, the remaining was distributed under a formula with $1.9 billion going to cities with populations greater than 35,000, and $770 million were provided to state energy offices. Mass transit, energy efficient street lights and traffic signals were all eligible under the block grant program, but the main thrust was building energy efficiency.[15]

The second program was the State Energy Program, which has been a long-standing, state-federal partnership assisting the states to address their unique energy needs and opportunities. This program was funded at $44 million in FY2008, but sky rocketed to $3.1 billion in FY2009 with the addition of Recovery Act funding. This new funding waived the standing provision that the states provide a 20 percent match, or cost share, and that capital investment be limited to a maximum of 50 percent of federal funds. States had to submit applications under a competitive grant program, detailing the proposed uses of the funds, which could include energy efficiency, renewable energy and alternative transportation programs, projects and policies.[14]

The states accepting these dollars, however, had to agree to adopt the new buildings energy efficiency code, ASHRAE 90.1-2007. ASHRAE, which stands for the American Society of Heating, Refrigeration and Air Conditioning Engineers, is a private nonprofit organization that is the nation's first developer of energy efficiency standards for buildings. Various certification programs, like Leadership in Energy and Environmental Design (LEED) and Green Globes, refer to ASHRAE in defining their building performance criteria. Many were skeptical that the states would adopt the ASHRAE standard and cited the experience with previous federal efforts to incentivize tighter state energy standards.[15] However, as of mid-2010, only 14 states had not adopted ASHRAE 90.1-2007. Lynn G. Bellenger, president of ASHRAE said his organization "is committed to continually improving building energy performance, so we are pleased with this call from the Department of Energy encouraging states to meet the target codes. …To encourage energy conservation in buildings, we must strive toward higher efficiencies." [16]

The states submitted numerous proposals under these programs to make investments in energy efficiency. All of them focused on building a foundation for increased private efforts to grow the nation's economy. The program was intended to create local green jobs, while at the same time save consumers money, reduce energy consumption, and decrease reliance on foreign energy sources. Here are a few examples of how the states used a portion of the energy efficiency dollars that they received under these programs.

- Connecticut – The state used their funds to upgrade 12 state buildings and facilities with energy efficient technologies. One of the buildings retrofitted was the health campus at Uncas-on-Thames in Norwich, which received $2.58 million for the installation of low-wattage LED lighting and occupancy sensors throughout the campus.

- Louisiana – The Home Energy Rebate Option (HERO) has been a successful program in Louisiana for years providing $2,000 rebates for energy efficiency upgrades for homeowners of existing homes. The grant allowed the state to expand the program to include new homes and existing commercial properties and increasing the rebate to $3,000. The rebate was calculated on the measures installed on the property and their projected energy saving per kWh over a 15 year period.
- Minnesota – Project ReEnergize was a homeowner program started in Minnesota that provided rebates on EnergyStar windows of $250 to $300, air sealing of attics at $800 and wall insulation at $800. The maximum rebate allowed per home was $4,000. For every one dollar of rebate money spent, homeowners were found to be spending an addition five dollars.
- Utah – The University of Utah was adding a new facility in the vicinity of eleven other buildings that each had their own low-efficiency chillers. The state and the university decided to upgrade all those buildings, and serve the new facility by investing $19.5 million in a high efficiency centralized chiller. In addition the university did a lighting retrofits on the existing buildings, and added a solar energy system to the new facility.[17]

Fully Fund LIHEAP and Weatherize One Million Homes Annually. *To address the immediate challenge this winter, we must fully fund LIHEAP and ensure that everyone who needs it has access to heating assistance. Over the long-term, a significant part of the answer for low income families is home weatherization. Barack Obama and Joe Biden will make a national commitment to weatherize at least one million low-income homes each year for the next decade, which can reduce energy usage across the economy and help moderate energy prices for all.*

Vice President Biden, acting his role as the Obama Administration's manager of Recovery Act funds, chaired a multi-agency working group, known as the Middle Class Task force (MCTS). The MCTS developed and released in October 2009, a strategy called Recovery Through Retrofit. It was intended to increase the adoption of energy efficiency products and techniques in homes, in order to decrease energy use, reduce emission, save homeowners money and increase employment. The report outlined two major issues regarding home energy efficiency. The first was the lack of reliable information for the homeowner on total home energy performance and attainable financing to assist homeowner in borrowing money for energy efficiency retrofit projects.[18]

Biden's MCTS charged DOE and Environmental Protection Agency (EPA) with developing an energy performance label for existing homes, similar to the EnergyStar. While new homes could earn the EnergyStar label, there was no such federal label available for existing homes. The end result would be an easily recognizable benchmark that energy auditors, retrofitters, lenders, realtors, and consumers could use to compare home energy performance, and identify the most energy efficient houses. In addition, DOE and EPA were asked to establish a standardized home energy performance measure, applicable to every home in America. The measure was intended make it much easier for consumers to understand how much they can save by retrofitting their home. An added benefit was that it gave lenders the information needed to work with homeowners who were looking to invest in home energy efficiency improvements.[18]

The MCTS also recommended three initiatives to reduce high upfront costs, and make it easier for homeowners to borrow money for home energy retrofits, including:

- Encouraging local governments to adopt property tax or municipal energy financing to allow the costs of retrofits to be added to a homeowner's property tax bill, with monthly payments generally lower than utility bill savings;
- Expanding the use of energy efficient mortgages to simplify the process of obtaining and financing energy retrofits at a home's point of sale; and
- Increasing state revolving loan funds from 16 states to all 50 states to leverage private capital and achieve economies of scale necessary to produce consistent and affordable loan products.[18]

The HomeStar legislative initiative, also known as Cash for Caulkers, was unveiled in March 2010 as an outgrowth Biden's MCTF Recovery Through Retrofit Report. The program, to be funded at $6 billion, was to provide 3 million homeowners with rebates for energy efficiency improvements, and would also provide needed employment throughout the U.S.[19] The program had two levels of rebate. The Silver Star level would consist of rebates of 50 percent totaling $1,000 to $1,500 for simple upgrades such as new insulations, duct sealing or water heater. The Gold Star level would require the home to be evaluated by a certified energy auditor, who would recommend the necessary improvements to achieve a 20 percent reduction in utility bills. The homeowner opting for the Gold Star level would receive a rebate of $3,000. The legislation did not pass in the 111th Congress.[20]

Biden and Secretaries Chu, Donovan and Solis announced two software programs in November 2010 that addressed other needs expressed by the MCTF report. The Home Energy Score program would provide utilities and contractors performing energy audits, with a standardized system of assessing energy efficiency, and generating a score which could compared to other homes. In addition, it would produce a simple, understandable, homeowner friendly report, indicating the best energy efficiency improvements to be made. Biden and the secretaries also introduced the Power Saver loan program to give homeowners access to information on local and national, financing options, for low-interest loans from multiple mainstream lenders.[21]

Chu announced in April 2010, the recipients a new nationwide $450 million program called Retrofit Ramp-Up. The program was intended to encourage greater homeowner and small business investments in energy efficiency upgrades, and was estimated to save $100 million annually in utility bills. The Retrofit Ramp-Up program piloted innovative processes for accelerating energy efficiency investments in hundreds of thousands of homes, and businesses, in a variety of communities. It was hoped that these successful pilot projects would be taken nationally, saving consumers billions of dollars on their utility bills. The program was funded from the city and local government portion of the Energy

Efficiency and Conservation Block Grant.[22] Some examples of the energy efficiency projects funded under Retrofit Ramps-Up include:

- Indianapolis received $10 million to retrofit a 470 square block neighborhood into an energy efficient community by providing investments in energy efficiency education, and performing outreach to community support organizations;
- Boulder County was granted $25 million to coordinate large-scale retrofits through the "Two Techs and a Truck" program, to provide energy efficiency outreach, audit, and implementation services to businesses, tenants, and homeowners; and
- Los Angeles County got a $30 million grant for the Retrofit California project. This was an ambitious program to provide energy outreach and education, utility allowances for affordable housing, group purchasing options for retrofits, and data tracking on energy savings, and retrofit rates of return.[23]

The Obama Administration received $5 billion in Recovery Act funding to provide energy efficiency products and services to America's low-income families through the Weatherization Assistance Program. This was the largest single investment in home energy efficiency in U.S. history. It was intended to provide needy families with both funding, and technical assistance from local agencies, performing home energy audits and weatherization services.[24] Republican Minority Leader, and now Speaker of the House of Representatives, John Boehner was unimpressed said, "if you look at the $500 billion worth of spending, a lot of it's going to fix up federal buildings, and - $6 billion to community action programs to do weatherization programs. It is more of the same kind of wasteful spending that we have seen in the past. I was really – I was shocked."[25]

In December 2009, the Obama Administration reported that it was on track to weatherize the homes of half a million low-income homes by the end of 2010.[24] A report from the Inspector General of the DOE in early 2010 indicated that the federal government had spent $659 million of the $5 billion on 80,000 homes for an average of $8,237 per house. To meet the federal goal of 593,000 homes weatherized by March 2012, the program would have to average 25,650 houses per month.[26] In addition, the report documented that of the ten service-providers that received the largest grants, only two had completed more than 2 percent of their planned units. Those in New York had finished 280 out of 45,400 units, in Texas zero were completed out of 33,908 and in California 12 of 43,400.[27]

Those who support the DOE's weatherization program pointed out that this was a three-year program, and it would take time to ramp up. After all, the Congress provided the weatherization program with a 20-fold increase in funding, going from about $200 to $250 million annually to $5 billion. In addition, for the first time ever, Congress required that all the weatherization workers be paid based on the Davis-Bacon Act, which meant requirements had to be established, and legally negotiated in each region. Lastly, the Office of Management and Budget issued a new set of rules and monitoring requirements for the program. The DOE dedicated six months to plan the strategy to meet programmatic goals for the number of homes to be weatherized. It also had to work through the legal and procedurals step required in the new Davis-Bacon, and OMB regulations. An additional challenge was that the states were in a period of fiscal austerity. Many had hiring freezes in place, so even with federal dollars in the state coffers, new staff could not be hired to advance weatherization goals. To meet their on-the-ground personnel needs, DOE had to develop new channels of hiring.[28]

The Low Income Home Energy Assistance Program (LIHEAP) assists low income households to pay their utility bills. The FY2010 LIHEAP budget totaled $5.1 billion, the same as FY2009.[29]

Invest in a Digital Smart Grid: *Barack Obama and Joe Biden will pursue a major investment in our national utility grid to enable a tremendous increase in renewable generation and accommodate 21st century energy requirements, such as reliability, smart metering and distributed storage. Barack Obama and Joe Biden will direct federal resources to the most vulnerable and congested urban and rural areas where significant renewable energy sources are* *located. They will work toward national transformation of our energy grid in partnership with states and utilities.*

The Recovery Act included $4.7 billion for smart grid technology, to upgrade the nation's electric transmission.[30] Smart grid allows better information, measurement and control of energy use by the companies and people who produce, transmit and use electricity. Through automated sensors, computers and specialized software, smart grid assists utilities and customers to make more intelligent decision regarding energy efficiency. Also, with the intermittent nature of renewable energy, smart grid permits a better integration of their generating capacities into the system.

Obama announced in October 2010 that $3.4 billion in smart grid awards were made to 100 firms nationwide, leveraging $4.7 billion in private capital to the table.[31] These dollar were divided among major categories of technologies and systems to help make smart grid a reality, including.

- Empowering Consumers to Save Energy and Cut Utility Bills - $1 billion. These investments were to create the infrastructure and expand customer access to smart meters
- Making Electricity Distribution and Transmission More Efficient - $400 million. These were investment in several grid modernization projects across the country to significantly decrease transmission losses.
- Integrating and Crosscutting Across Different "Smart" Components of a Smart Grid - $2 billion. These dollars were for systems integration of smart meters, smart thermostats and appliances, automated substations, plug in hybrid electric vehicles and renewable energy sources.
- Building a Smart Grid Manufacturing Industry - $25 million. These fund were to expand the domestic manufacturing base for components like smart meters, smart appliances, smart transformers, and other systems technologies.[32]

Chu announced in the fall 2009, that DOE was funding a $100 million program to train workers in the installation techniques and technologies to upgrade transmission system to be smart grid compatible. He also announced a related $44 million grant program for state public utility commissions to foster greater adoption of smart grid systems.[33] Later that year, Chu granted an additional $620 million, matched by $1 billion in private investment, to demonstrate advanced smart grid technologies, and integrated systems, aimed at making the nation's electricity system more resilient and efficient. This included 32 demonstration projects, such as large scale energy storage, smart meters, distribution and transmission system monitoring devises and a range of other smart technologies.[34]

Biden and Chu released a report in August 2010 detailing the progress in the utilization of Recovery Act funds in the national development of smart grid. The report indicated that 875 transmission system sensors, known as "phasor measurement units," had been installed top detect irregularities, and prevent minor disturbances in electricity transmission from causing large blackouts. In addition, another 700 substation were equipped with a different type of transmission sensor, and 200,000 advance transformers were installed, both to increase power reliability.[35]

On the energy user side of the equation, Recovery Act fund purchased 18 million smart meters, which added to the eight million that were already in use. Projections indicated that 26 million smart meters would be use by 2013, which according to the report, is on target for the goal of having 40 million smart meters in operation by 2015.[35]

The report indicated that consumer based software to maximize energy efficiency in smart grid application was moving forward with venture capital firms backing smaller firms, and larger corporations investing their own funds. This included a wide range of devices such as smart thermostats, smart appliances, in-home energy displays, energy management and information service. There is also an effort of the National Institute of Standards and Technology to develop standards allowing for the integration of renewable technologies, providing consumers with new energy reduction tools, and increasing transmission reliability, as well as security.[35]

6.

CLEAN AIR

Clean Air Act: *Barack Obama and Joe Biden will restore the force of the Clean Air Act*

The regulation of greenhouse gases was certainly the crown jewel in President Obama's campaign promises on air quality. However, he also committed to greater enforcement of the Clean Air Act. The setting of stricter rules and regulations would be a major component of the strategy to meet that goal. Within hours of taking office, Obama through his chief of staff Rahm Emanuel, put a halt to all proposed Bush Administration federal regulations pending a 60-day review by the Obama Administration. This not only included the printing of new or proposed regulations in the Federal Register, but also the withdrawal of regulations that had not yet been printed. His action positively affected not only air quality regulation and EPA, but impacted all federal agencies and environmental issues, ranging from mining, logging, water quality and endangered species.[1]

Not long after arriving in office, Obama received a report from a coalition of environmental and health groups listing their priorities for clean air during his administration. While the groups recognized, and agreed, that climate change was the preeminent issue, their other top priority was cleaning up coal-fired power plants. These facilities are the leading sources of snoot, smog, and airborne toxics. The groups wanted greater emphasis on power plant sulfur dioxide, nitrogen oxides, air toxins and mercury, than they had seen during the Bush Administration. In addition, their report highlighted other issues, such as improving the 2008 ozone standards, cleaning up soot pollution from commercial ships, fixing air pollution monitors nationwide, and speeding up EPA's air pollution enforcement efforts.[2]

The Obama Administration quickly signaled that their environmental regulation and rule making would rely more on science advisors, and less on corporate intermediaries. In February 2009, when Environmental Protection Agency (EPA) Administrator, Lisa Jackson starting setting new air quality standards for nitrogen oxide, in accordance with a June 2009 court imposed deadline, she decided EPA would not be issuing an advanced notice of proposed rulemaking (ANPR). The ANPR, which is not legally required, was adopted during the Bush Administration. It only added layers of red tape to the process and gave corporate interests increased time to push back on new or modified rules and regulations.[3]

Another signal of the winds of change being heralded by the Obama Administration was the March 2009 EPA repeal of the Bush Administration's aggregation rule. This rule was enacted in the final weeks of the Bush Administration. It said that in order for activities to be aggregated at a facility, and trigger a New Source Review (NSR) under the Clean Air Act, they had to be technically or economically interconnected. This created a loophole so that regulated industries, making modifications to processes, did not have to install best available pollution control technologies.[4]

The innovative nature of the air quality regulation that Jackson brought to EPA became evident in October 2009. The agency announced that it was pursuing a multi-pollutant strategy to provide clearer guidelines for environmental investments by regulated industries. The policy was targeted at instituting a more business-friendly approach, that would allow industry sectors to invest in technologies that address multiple pollutants, rather than focusing on one pollutant at a time.[5]

The agency initiative seemed well-timed, because numerous new rules were in the works, including the Maximum Achievable Control Technology (MACT) for the utility sector, and a re-working of the Clean Air Interstate Rule (CAIR). In addition in 2011, EPA was scheduled to perform a review of the standards for all six of the criteria pollutants under it jurisdiction. The multi-pollutant approach has garnered praised from both the environmental and industry communities. One the challenges for the strategy is the underpinning statues, that provide EPA the authority for regulation of air pollutants, may not allow the flexibility that most believe is necessary to fulfill the multi-pollutant approach.[5]

The Clean Air Interstate Rule (CAIR), promulgated during the Bush Administration to reduce soot and smog from electric utility generating plants in 28 Eastern states, and the District of Columbia, was stuck down by a judge in July 2008. However, it was reinstated in December 2008, and sent back to EPA for redrafting. The court said the rule was "fundamentally flawed," and it failed to "connect states' emission reductions to any measure of their own significant contributions."[6]

In July 2009, EPA release a revised version of CAIR which would reduce electric utility generating emissions that crossed state lines in 31 states from as far West as Kansas, Oklahoma and Texas and as far East as Massachusetts, North Carolina and Florida. EPA stated that with implementation slated for 2012, it projected emissions reductions over 2005 levels in sulfur dioxide of 71 percent by 2014, and nitrogen oxide reductions of 52 percent.[6] The agency further stated that it believed the regulation would provide between $120 and $290 billion in health and welfare benefits by 2014, in preventing 14,000 to 36,000 deaths. The costs for implementation were projected to be $2.8 billion annually.[8]

The EPA, under the Obama Administration, proposed the first change in nitrogen dioxide emissions, since the standard was first established in 1971. EPA staff and scientists recommended the establishment of a new one-hour standard between 50 and 200 parts per billion (ppb), with a strong opinion supporting a level below 100 ppb. Based on these findings, in June 2009, the agency proposed a one-hour maximum standard between 80 and 100 ppb. While EPA decided to maintain the average annual standard of 53 ppb, it did outline new requirements for NO2 monitoring.[9]

A proposed rule that would reduce particulate, sulfur dioxide and nitrogen oxide emissions, and require cleaner burning fuel and engine modifications in cargo ships, was proposed by EPA in October 2009. It would affect the shipping industries operating in the Great Lakes, and within 200 miles of the coasts. The rule was targeted to reduce smog and acid rain, which are known to effect a number of illnesses from heart disease to asthma.[10] However, in the EPA FY2010 appropriations , House Appropriations Chairman Dave Obey (D-WI) was able to insert language providing an exemption for 13 Great Lakes cargo ships to the low-sulfur fuel requirement.[11]

Smog and Soot: *Barack Obama and Joe Biden will fight for continued reductions in smog and soot.*

New ozone regulations affecting the generation of smog pollution found in urban areas were released by EPA in January 2010. The agency made this move, because ozone-forming pollutants from cars, utilities, oil refineries and other sources were impacting human health, and the environment. These new standards overturned the Bush Administration's 2008 level of 0.075 parts per million (ppm), and proposed standards in the range of 0.060-0.070 ppm. The agency also proposed "a distinct cumulative season secondary standard, designed to protect sensitive vegetation and ecosystems, including forests, parks, wildlife refuges and wildness areas."[12]

However in December 2010, EPA indicated that it would be delaying completion of these rules until July 2011, in order to gather more information from its Clean Air Science Advisory Committee.[13] Some in the environmental community were concerned that this delay was less for scientific reasons, and more for political reasons. The proposed standards had received significant pushback from Republicans, who will be in the majority in the House of Representatives in January 2011.[14]

The last time the soot standard was revised was during the Bush Administration in 2006, and it was set at 35 to 65 micrograms per meter in a 24-hour period, and 15 micrograms per meter annually. That was counter to the advice of EPA staff and scientists at the time, who had recommended an annual standard of between 13 and 14 micrograms. EPA was sued and in 2009, a federal appeals court reviewed the scientific data and concluded the standards were flawed "in several respects, contrary to law and unsupported by adequately reasoned desion-making."[15]

A report released by EPA in March 2010 stated that the agency was considering setting the soot standards in such a manner that the annual standard would protect the public health, in both long- and short-term exposures, and the 24-hour standard would strictly address peak levels. There were two different proposals offered that would meet the criteria outlined in the court ruling. The first would maintain 24-hour level at 30 to 35 micrograms, and annual level of 12 to 13 micrograms. The second proposal would set peak standards at 25 to 30 micrograms, and the annual standard at 10 to 11 micrograms.[15]

Toxins: *Barack Obama and Joe Biden will combat toxins that contribute to air pollution.*

New rules covering toxic emissions from boilers and waste incinerators were proposed in April 2010 to meet court decreed deadlines. The first rule was targeted toward industrial, commercial and institutional boilers and process heaters. New sources would have to emit less than 10 tons per year of any one toxic air component, or 25 tons in combination. Coal-fired facilities would have to meet restricted mercury and carbon monoxide standards, but biomass and oil-fired plants would have only carbon monoxide requirements. The agency also adopted new standards for existing and new commercial and industrial incinerators, however, it exempted plants that burn their own waste.[16]

In December 2010, EPA filed a motion in federal district court to delay the deadline for new boiler emissions regulations, until April 2012. Some within the agency have suggested that the proposed standards may be too strict, and that new information has come to light. Many in the environmental community are concerned that the real reason for the delay is a new Republican majority in the House of Representatives taking office in January 2011.[14]

The toxics assessment rule for the utility sector, promulgated in the final weeks of the Bush Administration, was set aside by EPA in October 2009. It was one of the regulations that Obama Administration was able to freeze when taking office on January 2009. Upon further review, Jackson found that the rule might not accurately reflect the risk posed by petroleum refinery emissions. The original Bush rule would have kept 1995 air toxics standards in place for refineries, and not required any additional toxics reductions.[17]

Pursuant to a court order, in October 2010, EPA released a draft rule covering the first six of 28 total updates of the National

Emissions Standards for Hazardous Air Pollutants (NESHPA). This rule covered six industry sectors: (1) chromium electroplating and anodizing; (2) polymers and resins; (3) marine tank vessel loading; (4) pharmaceuticals; (5) printing and publishing; and (6) steel pickling and hydrochloric regeneration.[18]

However, the new rule received less than a stellar reception from the environmental community, with Jane Williams of the Sierra Club stating, "We haven't waited 20 years for the implementation of the Clean Air Act and sued the agency to have them promise these rules and just sit by and have nothing happen."[17] For example, the EPA determined that there is an "acceptable" increase in the risk of cancer from chrome plating facilities, so it did not propose any changes to the industry's Maximum Achievable Control Technology. The industry would be required to make only minor changes. Most of these changes would be required during periods of startup, shutdown and malfunction. This is inline with another court ruling against EPA, stating that industry exemptions in these three instances were violations of the Clean Air Act. The Supreme decided not to intervene in the case, so EPA must review and enact toxic standards for over 100 industry sectors.[18]

Mercury: *Barack Obama and Joe Biden will reduce health risks caused by mercury pollution.*

In February 2009, the Obama Administration withdrew a Bush Administration request to the Supreme Court to review EPA rules on mercury emissions from electric utilities. In making the motion, the Obama Administration stated that EPA was dropping the Bush Administration's cap and trade approach to mercury regulation, and intends to promulgate regulations for individual plants.[19] EPA was on track to release a new rule on coal and oil electric generating utilities by March 2011, and finalized it by November 2011. It has been estimated that the standards for mercury controls for new and existing plants may be in the range of 85 to 90 percent removal. If EPA advances MACT for hazardous air pollutants, then all coal-fired utilities will be installing advanced scrubbers and particulate controls by 2015.[20]

7.

CLEAN WATER

Clean Water State Revolving Fund: *Barack Obama and Joe Biden support full funding for the Clean Water State Revolving Fund, which funds water quality protection projects for wastewater treatment, nonpoint source pollution control, and watershed and estuary management.*

When President Obama unveiled his budget for FY2010 in February 2009, $3.9 billion was dedicated to the Environmental Protection Agency's (EPA) Clean Water and Drinking Water State Revolving Funds. In addition, there was $3.8 billion slated for the Department of Agriculture's rural water and waste water loans. This was in addition to the approximately $6 billion previously appropriated under the American Recovery and Reinvestment Act (Recovery Act). The Obama Administration estimated that these new dollars would help to fund more than 1,000 clean water and 700 drinking water projects nationwide.[1]

Once the House and Senate acted on Obama's budget recommendations, and came to agreement on the conference report, a total of $3.6 billion was allocated by Congress for water infrastructure projects. Included in the appropriations were $2.1 billion for the Clean Water Revolving Fund, $1.38 billion for the Drinking Water Revolving Fund and $157 million for direct grants to municipalities.[2] This was a sharp reversal from the Bush Administration years that saw significant declines in water infrastructure funding.[1]

In October 2010, EPA released a sustainability policy report to assist local communities in creating strategies, and locating funding, to upgrading older waste water facilities. The policy report endorsed the concept of adding green infrastructure in the clean water treatment process, in order to increase local employment, bolster neighborhoods, and reduce expenditures. The techniques outlined in the report included green roofs and pervious pavement. EPA encouraged communities to move forward with green construction by utilizing resources from the Clean Water State Revolving Fund. EPA Deputy Administrator, Bob Perciasepe stated, "Through cost-effective, resource-efficient techniques – like green water infrastructure alternatives – this policy aims to make our communities more environmentally and economically sustainable. These smart investments in our water infrastructure, along with increased awareness of the importance of these investments, can keep our water cleaner and save Americans money."[3]

A report tracking the expenditure of federal Recovery Act dollars was released in December 2010, stating that the entire $5.5 billion in environmental infrastructure funding had been spent, which included $4 billion allocated to the Clean Water Revolving Fund.[4]

Drinking Water Standards: *Barack Obama and Joe Biden will reinvigorate the drinking water standards that have been weakened under the Bush administration and update them to address new threats.*

EPA Administrator Lisa Jackson announced, at a conference of metropolitan water agencies, that the federal government would be taking a new approach to safe guard drinking water. The new approach would not require new laws or regulations, but would use existing authorities more effectively. The overall strategy would have four components: (1) dealing with contaminants in groups, not individually; (2) advancing research on novel treatments; (3) employing multiple laws on the books to protect safe water; and (4) improving collaborations with local and state partners. Jackson also announced that standards for four potentially cancer-causing chemicals were going to be strengthened. This included tetrachloroethylene, trichloroethylene, acrylamide and epichlorohydrin.[5]

This followed the announcement that EPA would investigating whether to take into account children's health when regulating perchlorate, which is a chemical often used in fireworks, flares and solid rocket propellant. Perchlorate has found it way into over four percent of the nation's drinking water systems, and health experts have raised concerns about its effects not only on children, but adults. This was a significant shift in policy from the Bush Administration, which had determined not to regulate perchlorate.[6]

A report, released in December 2010, detailed the levels of a known carcinogen, chromium-6, found in drinking water systems in cities across the United States. The chemical, which is also called hexavalent chromium, is commonly found in the mills making stainless steel and other metal alloys. The movie, *Erin Brockovich*, had brought the chemical to the public's attention. Currently, EPA does not have a standard in place for chromium-6. Instead, the agency limits all chromium content to 100 parts per billion (ppb) in drinking water systems. However, that limit includes the relatively less dangerous chromium-3.[7]

California has set a maximum safe standard of 0.06 ppb for chromium-6. Of the cities listed in the report, Bethesda, Maryland had a reading of 0.19 ppb, Chicago, Illinois a level of 0.18 and Honolulu, Hawaii a level of 2.0 ppb. All of these communities had concentrations of chromium-6 more than three times the level deemed safe in California. The release of the report prompted a hastily assembled meeting among Jackson and a bipartisan group of Senators in Senator Dick Durbin (D-IL) office on Capitol Hill. Jackson assured the Senators that her agency would review its chromium-6 standard, and try to assess the sources. In addition, she stated that EPA would oversee a peer-reviewed analyses of chromium-6 by later summer 2011.[7]

Major Water Bodies: *Barack Obama and Joe Biden support a comprehensive solution for restoring our national treasures – such as the Great Lakes, Everglades and Chesapeake Bay – including expanded scientific research and protections for species and habitats from threats such as industrial pollution, water diversion, and invasive species.*

Great Lakes

During the campaign, Obama was out in front on Great Lakes issues. Being from Illinois, a Great Lakes state, he was familiar with the issues, and knew how close they are to the hearts of the people in the eight-state region. All of the governors in the Great Lakes basin had recently signed the Great Lakes Compact, and it was passed by Congress in the fall 2008. The agreement put strict limitations on water diversions to outside the basin.[8] These actions followed up on earlier work in the region to limit to diversions and consumptive uses, as outlined in the Great Lakes Charter. This agreement was signed in 1984 by the eight U.S. governors and two Canadian premiers, and is recognized in federal law under the 1986 Water Resources Development Act.[9]

Obama often criticized his rival Senator John McCain for not supporting funding to protect the Great Lakes from the invasive Asian carp. However, Obama showed his strongest support for Great Lakes issues, when he called for the full implementation of the recently signed Great Lakes Compact. In addition, he announced that he would commit $5 billion of new federal funds for Great Lakes sewage treatment plant upgrades, toxic chemical cleanup, wetland restoration, reductions in mercury pollution and invasive species control.[8]

Obama started making good on his promises when he proposed, and passed through Congress, his FY2010 budget for the Great Lakes, that included $425 million for implementation of the Great Lakes Restoration Initiative. The Great Lakes Restoration Initiative operationalizes the Great Lakes Regional Collaborative Strategy, which took many years and multiple stakeholders to develop. The funding President provided for the Great Lakes were targeted to five major focus areas:

- Toxic substances and areas of concern, including pollution prevention and cleanup of the most polluted areas.
- Invasive species, including efforts to institute a "zero tolerance policy" toward new invasions and self-sustaining populations of invasive species, such as the Asian carp.
- Nearshore health and nonpoint source pollution, including a targeted geographic focus on high priority watersheds, and reducing runoff from urban suburban and agricultural sources.
- Habitat and wildlife protection and restoration, including bringing wetlands and other habitat back to life, and the first-ever comprehensive assessment of the 530,000 acres of Great Lakes coastal wetlands for restoration and protection.

- Accountability, education, monitoring, evaluation, communication and partnerships, including the implementation of accountability measures.[10]

Everglades

It was estimated that an investment of $10.7 billion would be needed to fully restore the Everglades. Obama, in his first year in office, was able to bring approximately $250 million to the effort, with about $100 million of those funds coming from the Recovery Act. Multiple federal agencies are also involved in the effort such as the Army Corp of Engineers, which provided an award of $53 million, paying for construction of a pump station, blockage of 13.5 miles of canals and removal of 95 miles of roadways in the preserve.[11]

However, Everglades restoration has been behind schedule. The effort missed a 2006 deadline that had been set in 1994 to decrease phosphorus levels to 10 ppb. Monitoring in the preserve indicated phosphorous levels, in six different testing areas, ranged from 13 to 93 ppb. Most the phosphorous is from runoff from fertilizer applications. In April 2010, a Florida judge ruled that EPA was not enforcing the Clean Water Act, and ordered the agency to develop a new enforcement plan by September 2010.[12]

EPA released its Everglades restoration plan on schedule in early September 2010, and it required the State of Florida to double the size of its man-made marshes, to over 100,000 acres. In addition, EPA called on the state to improve its pollution monitoring and reporting program. Environmentalists in the state were ecstatic. Government and business leaders were more reserved, and wanted time to review it; hoping to find some flexibility. After reviewing the EPA plan, Florida officials called it both unrealistic and unreasonable. Their major concerns were the deadlines, and the mandate for the state to contribute $1.5 billion to the effort without any federal match. However, EPA stated the plan was a "thoughtful, science-based blueprint for water quality improvement in the Everglades."[14]

Chesapeake Bay

The Obama Campaign planned to release a comprehensive Chesapeake Bay Initiative in the fall 2008, similar in scope to the Great Lakes Initiative detailed earlier in the year. It was intended to not only bolster environmental enthusiasm in the seven-state region, but also increase support by local government officials and agricultural communities, who were bearing the brunt of the cost of the watershed restoration. The financial collapse of the banking industry and Wall Street in September 2008, put those plans on hold, and the Chesapeake Bay Initiative was never released.[15]

The Obama Energy and Environment Work Group, however, did prepare a special commentary on Chesapeake Bay issues that was published in newspapers in the Mid-Atlantic region. It was assembled using existing campaign commitments, and outlined Obama's support for numerous initiatives to reduce nutrient and sediment pollution. The commentary focused on the three sectors that have the most effect on local water quality and the health of the Chesapeake region: (1) waste water treatment plant upgrades; (2) agricultural run-off; and (3) land use change and development.[16]

The campaign work on the Chesapeake Bay Initiative was useful after the election, when in May 2009, Obama released an Executive Order entitled, Chesapeake Bay Protection and Restoration. It named the Chesapeake Bay a national treasure, and set a 2025 deadline for cleanup. More importantly, the order increased federal participation in the restoration effort, and for the first time named a federal leadership committee, chaired by the EPA administrator and was comprised of cabinet level officers.[17]

A year later in May 2010, EPA released its Chesapeake Bay strategy that outlined each federal agency's role and responsibility. EPA committed to: (1) implementing a Total Maximum Daily Load (TMDL); (2) expanding regulation of urban and suburban stormwater runoff; (3) drafting new rules for concentrated animal feeding operations (CAFOs); (4) increasing enforcement activities; and (5) bolstering funding for state regulatory programs. USDA detailed its plans to provide farmers with the resources to prevent soil erosion, and reduce nitrogen and phosphorous pollution leaching into waterways. The Department of the Interior dedicated itself to launching a collaborative Chesapeake Treasured Landscape Initiative, expanding land conservation, providing community assistance, and increasing public access to waterways. NOAA and the Army Corps of Engineers committed to enhancing a bay-wide oyster restoration strategy, in partnership with Maryland and Virginia.[18]

    The states in the Chesapeake Bay watershed were required to submit to EPA draft Watershed Implementation Plans, indicating how they would reduce pollution from water treatment plants, farms, CAFOs, urban stormwater and other sources.[19] This regulatory strategy differed from earlier approaches, dating back in 1983, in that EPA said it was ready to rigorously enforce the state plans. The agency was threatening direct actions, such as challenging operating permits for specific municipal water treatment facilities or agricultural operations, and overreaching the state agency regulators to prosecute polluters under the Clean Water Act. By the year 2025, full implementation of the TMDL was projected to reduce nitrogen by 25 percent, phosphorous by 24 percent and sediment by 20 percent. In quantitative terms, that would be reductions of 185.9 million pounds of nitrogen, 12.5 million pounds of phosphorous and 6.45 million billions pounds of sediment.[20] The end result would be that 55 of the Chesapeake Bay's 92 would meet quality standards in 2025, while only three do today.[19]

Gulf Coast: *Barack Obama and Joe Biden will help the Gulf Coast restore the wetlands, marshes and barrier islands that are critical to tamping down the force of hurricanes and serve as critical fish and wildlife habitat. As president, he will immediately close the Mississippi River Gulf Outlet, which experts say funneled floodwater into New Orleans.*

    No environmental issue, except climate change, received as much attention in the first two years of the Obama Presidency as did the Gulf Oil Spill. It is ironic that within just weeks of Obama reversing his long-standing opposition to offshore oil drilling, the nation's largest oil spill would consume nearly three months of his time in office, and be spread daily across the newspapers and cable TV. The American public was mesmerized watching their television screens and computer monitors, as an underwater camera documented the volumes of oil being released into the Gulf waters second by second.

Obama followed up on his campaign pledge to address Gulf Coast environmental issues after Hurricane Katrina, by naming in October 2009, a Louisiana-Mississippi Gulf Coast Ecosystem Restoration Working Group. The group was to be co-chaired by the White House Council on Environmental Quality and the Office of Management and Budget. The group laid the foundation for the March 2010 unveiling of the *Roadmap for Gulf Coast Ecosystem Restoration Focused on Resiliency and Sustainability*. The Roadmap welcomed state participation and enacted a long-term governance structure. It had a series of goals including increasing federal agency coordination, setting clearer priorities, developing better science, and securing more federal and state funding. Regarding resources, the Roadmap hoped to build on its record of receiving funds during the Obama Administration: (1) $45.6 billion in the proposed FY2011 budget for the Louisiana Coastal Area (LCA) restoration program, restoration of key fish and wildlife habitat, and integration of ocean and coastal mapping; (2) $18 million to the LCA in 2010; and (3) $439 million to restore barrier islands along the Mississippi coast in the Recovery Act.[21]

On March 31, 2010, Obama abandoned his stance against offshore oil drilling, and announced he was willing to open up areas along the south coast of the Atlantic Ocean and the Gulf of Mexico.[22] In less than three weeks of that announcement, the Gulf Oil Spill began on April 20, 2010. Early estimates of the leak were reported to be 1,000 barrels of crude oil per day (bpd). By April 28, those estimates were increased to 5,000 bpd. Some scientists were skeptical of that number based on the size of the plumes they were seeing, and Steve Wereley a researcher at Purdue University pegged the spill at 70,000 bpd on May 13.[23] A month later on June 20, government scientists finally increased the official estimate to 40,000 bpd,[23] while internal documents from BP indicated that the spill may have been releasing 100,000 bpd.[24]

Obama's earliest responses to the oil spill were very measured. On April 28, he pledged "every single available resource", including the US military, and stated that BP was responsible for the cleanup.[23] He traveled to the Gulf Coast in early

May, and told the American people that we were facing "a massive and potentially unprecedented environmental disaster."[25] After seeing the oil company executives testify before Congress on May 14, Obama commented, "I did not appreciate what I considered to be a ridiculous spectacle during the congressional hearings into this matter. You had executives of BP and Transocean and Haliburton falling all over each other to point the finger of blame at somebody else…it is pretty clear that the system failed, and it failed badly."[23] Then on May 26, it was leaked that Obama ended a briefing on the Gulf Oil Spill with the exasperated comment, "Plug the damn hole."[23]

The situation surrounding the oil spill became so grave, that in June 2010, eighteen months into his presidency, Obama decided to give his first Oval Office address to the nation. He laid out a proposed compensation program for the businesses and workers, who lost money during the spill, and detailed a long-term environmental restoration program to bring back the marshes, regional seafood, fishing and tourism. Obama also used the opportunity to call for changes in the nation's energy policy. He said, "For decades, we have known the days of cheap and easily accessible oil were numbered. For decades, we have talked and talked about the need to end America's century-long addiction to fossil fuels. And for decades, we have failed to act with the sense of urgency that this challenge requires. Time and time again, the path forward has been blocked – not only by oil industry lobbyists, but also by a lack of political courage and candor."[26]

One of the most notable aspects about the speech was not what it said, but what it did not say. Obama did not repeat the line from his June 2 speech calling for "finally putting a price on carbon." It was noted by the environmental community that Obama did not use the environmental disaster in the Gulf to further the legislative fight on Capitol Hill on global climate change.[26]

On August 4, more than 100 days after it began, the Gulf Oil Spill was finally capped. It was a major challenge to the Obama Administration, and it called Obama's leadership into question many times. This should have been a time of celebration for the Obama team, but they made one of the worst communications mistakes of the Obama Presidency. Government officials went on television, and distributed press releases, stating that 74 percent of the oil leaked into the Gulf had dissipated. It had just disappeared.[27] The Obama Administration had pie charts showing that 25 percent had evaporated or dissolved, 17 percent was directly recovered from the well-head, 16 percent naturally dispersed, 8 percent was chemically dispersed, 5 percent was burned and 3 percent was skimmed.[28] However these number were just unbelievable. To the general public, who had watched for months, on their computers and televisions, the images of the oil plumes gushing from the well, they knew it was not true.

Restore the Wetlands: *Barack Obama and Joe Biden are a advocates for preserving our wetlands and support a broad range of traditional conservation programs, including: (1) the Wetland Reserve Program in the Farm Bill; (2) full funding for the North American Wetlands Conservation Act and fulfilling the goal of "no-net loss;" (3) extending the swamp buster provisions of the Farm Bill; and (4) amending the Clean Water Act to clarify that it protects isolated wetlands. They will work with local governments to develop the best strategies for protecting and expanding wetlands*

To increase funding for the North American Wetlands Conservation Act, Obama requested a $10 million increase for the program in his FY2010 budget. However, Congress only approved a $2.5 million increase, bringing total funding for the program to $45.6 million. Obama's campaign commitment to extend the swamp buster program, which offers incentives for farmers to preserve wetlands on their agricultural operations, has not yet been further authorized. But there is still time, because the program does not expire until 2012. Prior to the Obama Administration, the Supreme Court ruled that EPA did not have the authority to regulate some wetlands, because they were not connected to navigable waters, as defined in the Clean Water Act. A Senate committee approved a bill that would have restored EPA's broad federal authority over wetlands, however, the Senate adjourned in December 2010 without taking action on the bill.[29]

8.

HEALTHIER COMMUNITIES

Protect Children and Families from Toxic Health Hazards: *As president, Barack Obama will continue his fight, begun as a community organizer, to protect our children from health hazards and developmental disabilities caused by environmental toxins, such as lead, mercury, particulate matter, and industrial land waste.*

The General Accountability Office (GAO) released a report in January 2010, which was highly critical of the Environmental Protection Agency's (EPA) efforts over the past decade in protecting children from toxic chemicals. The report detailed EPA's reduced "emphasis on children" and "high-level failures to act" to benefit children's health.[1] Specifically, the GAO stated that the EPA was initially very responsive, when the 1997 Executive Order 13045 was issued, directing federal agencies to place a high priority on children's risks. EPA had included children's issues in its 1997 and 2000 strategic plans. It created an Office of Children's Health, and took advice from the Children' Health Advisory Committee. However, GAO said that children's health was missing as topic of concern in EPA's 2003, 2006 and draft 2009 strategic plans.[1]

The report documented that the Children' Health Advisory Committee had proactively made 607 recommendations to EPA, most of which had been ignored, and the agency had only sought the committee's advice three times in the past decade. Additionally, GAO found that the Office of Children's Health had four acting directors from 2002 to 2008, which resulted in "inconsistent leadership and direction," that hurt the office's ability "to fulfill its priorities and commitments."[2] At a hearing in March 2010, Senator Lautenberg (D-NJ) summed up the report by saying efforts to protect children from environmental hazards "ground to a halt during the Bush Administration," and the EPA Office for Children's Health "withered on the vine."[1]

GAO presented Congress and EPA with a list of nine recommendations to heighten the sensitivity of EPA leadership and staff to children's health issues when considering regulations. Some of the most pertinent recommendations were:
- Congress may want to consider re-establishing a government-wide task force on children's health issues, to identify the principle threats to children, and develop national strategies;
- EPA should strengthen the data system that identifies and tracks development of rule making, to ensure they comply with the policy to evaluate health risks to children;
- EPA should re-evaluate it policy to ensure consistency with new scientific research, demonstrating the risks childhood exposures can have on disease development later in life; and
- EPA should use the Children's Health Protection Advisory Committee more proactively, as a mechanism for receiving advice on regulations, programs, plans or other issues.[3]

EPA stated that it agreed with all the recommendations of GAO, and began the process of implemented them. In fact, in March 2010, EPA Administrator Jackson sent memo to EPA staff stating that "protecting children's environmental health is central to our work at EPA. Let me affirm that it is EPA's policy to consider the health of pregnant women, infants and children consistently and explicitly in all the activities we undertake related to human health protection, both domestically and internationally. We must be diligent in our efforts to ensure that dangerous exposures and health risks to children are prevented."[1]

Later that month, Peter Grevatt, Director of the EPA Office of Children's Health Protection and Environmental Education, testified before the Senate Committee on Environment and Public Works, and described the agencies multi-pronged strategy to address the concerns raised by GAO study. Grevatt indicated the EPA would be putting an increase emphasis on the best science to reduce the potential for the exposure of children to toxins. This would be accomplished through rulemaking, policy, enforcement and research focused on prenatal and childhood vulnerabilities. The agency would be revisiting it rules regarding ground level ozone and smog, which are closely linked to childhood asthma and other respiratory diseases. Additionally, EPA has been re-evaluating food pesticides to provide more safety for children.[4]

However, Grevatt testified one of the major impediments for better protection of children was inadequacy of the Toxic Substances Control Act (TSCA), and the fact that there are over 80,000 existing chemicals, of which few have been reviewed for their risk on children.[4] Jackson testified about TSCA in December 2009, and she stated that the act, when signed into law in 1976, "grandfathered in" all chemicals then being manufactured and in use for commercial purposed without any further evaluation. In addition, the statute did not give EPA the authority to re-evaluate existing chemicals, even if new concerns were recognized, or data emerged. TSCA also does not require manufacturers of new chemicals to conduct testing on their products. The only requirement is that they provide existing data to EPA, and in most cases, it is not sufficient to assess risks to human heath.[5]

Jackson outlined her recommendations to Congress on how the law should be revised, including:

- EPA should be granted the authority to establish human health and safety standards for chemicals based on the best available science;
- Industry should be responsible for providing adequate health and safety information for proper regulation;
- EPA should have authority to take risk management actions, when chemicals do not meet safety standards under a range considerations, such as children's health, economic costs, social costs and equity concerns;
- EPA should have clear authority to set priorities for conducting safety reviews;
- EPA must be given the flexibility to encourage innovation in green chemistry, and other strategies that will lead to safer, and more sustainable chemicals and processes; and

- EPA and the TSCA law needs to be adequately and consistently funded, with chemical manufacturers supporting agency implementation.[5]

In the interim, Jackson vowed to use the full extent of TSCA authority to label, restrict, or ban chemicals to protect the general public and environment. EPA has already selected an initial group of chemicals related to hazard, exposure and use, for potential action. Following an evaluation, the agency would complete and make public a series of "action plans." EPA said it intended to release a new list of chemicals and "action plans" every four months.[5]

There seemed to be wide spread agreement in government, and the nonprofit environmental community, that TSCA needed to be revised. The surprising fact was that many in the chemical industry agreed, and Cal Dooley, President and CEO American Chemical Council had outlined a series of revisions to TSCA that were consistent with many of the recommendations of Jackson.[6] One factor that may have pushed the industry's position, was that some states were not waiting for the federal government to act, and were creating a patchwork of local regulations across the country. However, as the 2010 congressional election approached, the tenor of industry negotiations changed. It appeared that many in chemical manufacturing industry would prefer to wait, and see if a more Republican Congress in 2011 would give them the additional flexibility that they would like in a revised TSCA statute.[7]

Formaldehyde is case in point about the short comings of TSCA, and some the political aspects that come into play in doing a chemical assessment. EPA has been trying since 1998 to change its assessment of formaldehyde, from a "probable" to a "known" carcinogen. After receiving a preliminary assessment from the National Cancer Institute, EPA began an internal agency assessment of the chemical in 2004. Senator Inhofe (R-OK) requested, and received from EPA, an agreement that a full outside review by the National Cancer Institute would be conducted. That study took five years, and was released in May 2009. It found that of the 25,000 workers exposed to higher levels of formaldehyde over a 30 year period, 37 percent had a greater risk of death from blood and lymphatic cancer, and a 78 percent had greater risk of leukemia, than those exposed to lower amounts. So in the summer 2009, EPA began another internal assessment, but Senator Vitter (R-LA) objected, requesting another outside review by the National Academy of Sciences. To make his request more pointed, he put holds on the confirmation of two Obama EPA appointees. Jackson eventually agreed to Vitter's request in December 2009, however, she said the study would be conducted under a compressed time frame.[8]

The EPA published its Toxics Release Inventory (TRI) in December 2010, which tracks information on waste management and pollution prevention, as well as, toxic disposals, and releases to the land, air and water. The TRI indicated that in 2009, 3.37 billion pounds of toxic chemicals were released to the environment. That was a 12 percent reduction from 2008. Data from 650 chemicals and 20,000 facilities were analyzed to determine that, toxic releases to the air in dropped 20 percent, releases to surface water decreased 18 percent and releases to land decreased four percent. In addition, releases of persistent, bioaccumulative and toxic chemicals, such as lead, dioxin and mercury were also down. Mercury disposal and release were down three percent from the previous year, and both dioxin and lead decreased by 18 percent. One statistic of concern, however, was the number of facilities reporting to EPA was down by seven percent.[9]

Other federal agencies, such as the Consumer Product Safety Commission (CPSC), also have roles in protecting children's health from toxic substances. In the summer 2010, the CPSC in partnership with McDonald's, executed a voluntary recall of promotional drinking glasses with images of Shrek. This occurred due to high levels of cadmium in the paint on the exterior of the glasses.[10]

As children eat and lick their fingers, any toxics from the paint on the outside of the glasses can easily enter their digestive systems. That is why the allowable levels of other toxics, like lead, on children's products are set lower than those for adults. Currently the CPSC limit on lead in children's products is 0.03 percent.[10]

Unfortunately, the Shrek glasses are not the only ones in the marketplace. Promotional drinking glasses with images of

Superman, Wonder Woman and the Tin Man from the Wizard of Oz, have recently been distributed by movie studios and fast food restaurants. The paint on these glasses have tested and found to contain between 16 and 30.2 percent lead. That is more than 1000 times the federal limit for children's products. Federal regulators at the CPSC must decide whether these products are marketed for children, because many of the companies distributing the glasses, say they are for adult collectors. An even more challenging issue for protecting children's health is that when lead content in paint goes down, manufacturers often substitute cadmium, a more dangerous chemical for children.[10]

The CPSC had set limits for the amount of cadmium in toys, but not until October 2010, had it set a protocol for other products, like children's drinking glasses. The agency determined that children's exposure to 0.1 micrograms/kilogram of body weight/day over an extended period, and 11 micrograms per day all at once, was below the threshold for which no health effects are expected. This determination was consistent with the findings of the U.S. Centers for Disease Control.[11] Using these parameters, the CPSC is negotiating with various industry representatives to set a voluntary standard for cadmium in a wide range of children's products, including those from jewelry, fashion and drinking glasses. [11]

The Chairman of the CPSC Ines Tenenbaum said, "The agency is required to give industry a chance to craft standards before the government acts."[11] The voluntary bar that the CPSC has set for industry, essentially triples the allowable limits for cadmium. It would let the cadmium tainted children's jewelry that CPSC recalled in January 2010, and the Shrek drinking glasses that were pulled in June 2010, to remain in the marketplace.[12]

Brownfields: *Barack Obama and Joe Biden will fight to clean brownfields and restore abandoned industrial riverfront sites.*

The U.S. Conference of Mayors released a national brownfields report in November 2010 entitled, *Recycling America's Land: A National Report on Brownfields Redevelopment (1993-2010)*. The study documents that 54 cities reported creating 161,880 jobs through the redevelopment of 2118 brownfield sites. These jobs can be defined as 64,730 jobs in pre-development/remediation and 97,150 permanent positions. Fifty cities estimated that starting in 1993, $309 million in local tax revenues resulted from the redevelopment of 654 brownfield sites. Looking to the future, 58 cities estimated that if they could move forward with brownfields redevelopment on known sites in their communities, tax revenue increases would range from $872 to $1.3 billion yearly. Eighty-four percent of the surveyed cities had successful brownfields redevelopment with 65 of those communities cleaning up 1,010 sites totaling 7210 acres. In addition, 70 cities noted that they are presently redeveloping 906 sites totaling 4,683 acres. The top four programs that the mayors found helpful to these efforts were: EPA Assessment Funding, Private Sector Investment, EPA Clean Up Funds, and State programs such as Voluntary Clean Up programs.[13]

The Obama Administration must have been listening to the mayors. In its FY2011 budget request, EPA proposed to eliminate the Brownfields Economic Development Initiative, and increase the budget for the much larger Clean Up program. This would give the program an annual budget of $138 million, which is a $38 million increase[14] and bring total Obama brownsfield funding in FY2011 to $215 million.[15] To give the program more focus and achieve greater success, EPA said it was hoping to target 20 poorer communities with brownfields funding by 2012. EPA proposed to help state and local governments in assisting the targeted communities to achieve the implementation of their goals.[14]

The EPA announced a total of $4 million in funding in 2010 for the redevelopment of brownfields targeted toward 23 cities. This effort unveiled a new strategy of not only performing environmental cleanup of the brownfields, but also assisting in the rebirth of the neighborhoods in the surrounding area. It was part a much larger Obama Administration effort known as the Partnership for Sustainable Communities (PSC), a multi-agency effort involving EPA, HUD and the Department of Transportation.[16]

The PSC is intended to coordinate federal investments in infrastructure, facilities and services, in order to better meet multiple economic, environmental and community objectives.

Guiding the PSC are six livability principles that cut across the three agencies involved:
- Provide more transportation choices;
- Promote equitable, affordable housing;
- Enhance economic competitiveness;
- Support existing communities;
- Coordinate and leverage federal policy and investment; and
- Value communities and neightborhoods.[17]

Control Superfund Sites and Data: *As president, Obama will restore the strength of the Superfund program by requiring polluters to pay for the cleanup of contaminated sites they created.*

When the Obama Administration released its FY2010 budget in February 2009, it included a plan to reinstate polluter fees that would raise funds to cleanup Superfund sites. This plan would bring back the Superfund excise taxes, which expired in 1995, but they would not be reinstated until 2011. It was anticipated that these excise taxes would yield more than $1 billion a year dedicated to Superfund cleanup, and would permit EPA to increase the number of sites remediated. [18]

One of the challenges of the Superfund program is that the less contaminated sites, or the low hanging fruit, have already been cleaned up. The sites left for remediation are more challenging, and because the Superfund excise tax expired in 1995, and went bankrupt in 2004, tax dollars have been the primary source of cleanup resources. Many were critical of the Bush Administration for the low numbers of Superfund sites receiving attention. Some in Congress were equally as critical of the Obama Administration, when it announced projected cleanup numbers similar to the Bush Administration. However, the key difference is that the Obama Administration was out in front, supporting the reinstatement of the excise tax, to bring in the funds to accelerate the number Superfund sites. The Bush Administration was not.[19]

Data on the Superfund program indicated that of the 527 sites still requiring Superfund remediation, 40 were almost completed, needing removal of contaminated dirt, construction of a treatment plant to process groundwater of contaminants, or capping the landfill. The other 1060 hazardous waste sites remaining on the list, have all the construction completed, and are in the final stages of restoration. The Obama Administration requested $1.31 billion in its FY2010 budget, and $600 million in the American Recovery and Reinvestment Act (Recovery Act), to address some of the Superfund needs.[19]

Congress moved forward on several bills to reinstate the Superfund excise tax. Representative Frank Pallone (D-NJ), representing a state with one of the largest numbers of Superfund sites, introduced the Superfund Polluter Pays Act (HR 832) in February 2009. Representative Earl Blumenauer (D-OR) introduced a similar bill (HR 564). Senator Lautenberg (D-NJ) also of New Jersey, committed to introducing companion Superfund legislation in the Senate. All of these bill were referred to committees respectively, in the House and Senate, where they all ultimately died.[20]

The Obama Administration, not satisfied with the pace or tenor of the House and Senate bills, developed it own draft Superfund bill, and sent it to Congress in June 2010. It would reinstate the Superfund excise tax through a set of four different fees on crude oil, imported petroleum, chemical products and corporate taxable income. As Jackson stated in the letter transmitting the draft legislation, this plan "would ensure that the parties who benefit from the manufacture or sale of substances commonly found in contaminated sites contribute to the costs of cleanup"[21.] The Obama Administration's draft legislation was projected to yield $18.9 billion over a 10 year period.[21]

The amount of activity on Capitol Hill combined with the weight of the Obama Administration for reinstating the Superfund excise taxes, caused some concern among the regulated industries. The American Chemistry Council (ACC) decided, in mid-summer 2010, that it was time to strengthen its lobbying arm against the proposed excise tax. The ACC hired two veteran lobbying firms to bolster its hand, Morgan, Lewis & Brockius and Williams & Jensen. Cal Dooley, president of ACC, said that the reinstatement of the Superfund excise tax would be "a lose-lose for the environment and economy."[22] He further asserted that the tax would hurt U.S.

businesses, and push jobs over seas. Ed Hopkins, the director of the Sierra Clubs' environmental quality program was pleased to see the Obama Administration weighing in saying "It is signaling to Congress that the administration is serious about having companies be responsible for clean up. It appears the administration is willing to invest some political capital in seeing this passed, and that could help a lot." [22]

Protect the Public from Nuclear Material: *As president, Obama will make safeguarding nuclear material both abroad and in the U.S. a top anti-terrorism priority. In addition, we will protect Nevada and its communities from the high-level nuclear waste dump at Yucca Mountain, which has not been proven to be safe by sound science. In terms of waste storage, Barack Obama and Joe Biden do not believe that Yucca Mountain is a suitable site. They will lead federal efforts to look for safe, long-term disposal solutions based on objective, scientific analysis. In the meantime, they will develop requirements to ensure that waste stored at current reactor sites is contained using the most advanced dry-cask storage technology available.*

Early in his term, Obama proposed eliminating funding for the nuclear materials repository being built and tested at Nevada's Yucca Mountain. This was the first, and possibly fatal step, in killing the plans for the site altogether. Over the 22-year time period that the project has been being pursued, it has consumed more than $7.7 billion in public funding. The original plan, which was determined by Congress, was the Yucca Mountain site would begin accepting spent nuclear materials from 104 reactors nationwide in1998. More than a decade later, spent nuclear fuel was being stored at 121 above ground sites in 39 states, in close proximity to 161 million people.[23]

Presently, 57,000 tons of spent nuclear materials are being stored next to their reactors. Nuclear plants in the U.S. produce about 2,000 tons of new waste every year. Not having a long-term solution for spent fuel storage is a major impediment to the nuclear industry, which is anticipating building more than 30 new reactors in the coming decades. However, recent tests have shown that Yucca Mountain is more porous to water infiltration than was previously believed. Water passing through spent nuclear material raised concerns that radioactive leaks into the groundwater could contaminate drinking water supplies in Nevada.[24]

In addition to the plans to zero-out the budget, the Obama Administration signaled its intention to withdraw the project's pending license application before the Nuclear Regulatory Commission. The license review request was submitted by the Bush Administration. It is a lengthy process where, if taken to its conclusion, a license might be granted in 2012. Some believe that even though the Yucca Mountain program was initiated by Congress, the Obama Administration could withdraw the application, halting the program. If that were to occur, opponents of the Yucca Mountain program would be examining the documents submitted to see if the application was withdrawn "with prejudice." That would mean the site is not suitable for nuclear materials, and could not be resurrected anytime in the future.[25]

The Obama Administration appointed a commission in January 2010, co-chaired by Lee Hamilton and Brent Scowcroft, to determine a "Plan B," or a set of alternatives to Yucca Mountain. In addition, the Obama Administration unveiled a new federal loan guarantee program, which had been requested by the nuclear industry, to accelerate the planning, design and construction of new nuclear power plants nationwide.[25]

In March 2010, the Department of Energy (DOE) formally filed a motion to withdraw the license review for Yucca Mountain from the Nuclear Regulatory Commission (NRC). When questioned by Congress about this action, DOE Secretary Steven Chu said that the Yucca Mountain site was not appropriate for nuclear material storage, due to the fissures in the mountain structure that could fill water with water. He postulated that, "we could maybe add a titanium shield, then you wonder if you are throwing good money after bad."[26] Chu further stated that salt domes may ultimately be a superior long-term storage solution for storing spent nuclear materials, saying that the domes, "have been stable for tens of millions, hundreds of millions of years."[26]

The Obama Administration received some bad new in June 2010, when a panel of administrative law judges from the NRC rejected Chu's request to withdraw the license review for Yucca Mountain. The full NRC, however, took up the case to determine whether the Obama Administration actually has the authority to withdraw a congressionally determined project, when numerous administrations have invested billions of tax payer dollars.[27]

Then, in October 2010, the NRC's Chairman Gregory Jaczko ordered his agency to stop reviewing the Yucca Mountain application. He said he was acting on the FY2011 budget guidance provided by the full NRC in February. He further stated that there was no timeframe under which the commission must rule on the Obama Administration's authority to withdraw the application, and that "the hearing takes its own path."[28] He did not have an estimate of the time it would take to restart the review process, if the commission ultimately decided that the Obama Administration was operating outside its authority. His final word was the review would remain shut down "absent some other guidance from Congress."[26] Jaczko's action prompted a letter from a former NRC member to the NCR's Inspector General requesting an immediate investigation, to determine if any "legal or other improprieties may have been committed."[28]

Strengthen Federal Environmental Justice Programs: *Barack Obama and Joe Biden will make environmental justice policies a priority within the Environmental Protection Agency (EPA). As president, he and Joe Biden will work to strengthen the EPA Office of Environmental Justice and expand the Environmental Justice Small Grants Program, which provides non-profit organizations across the nation with valuable resources to address local environmental problems. They will also work to ensure that environmental health issues in the wake of man-made or terrorist disasters are promptly addressed by federal, state and local officials. They will work to provide low-income communities the legal ability to challenge policies and processes that adversely affect the environmental health of low-income and minority communities.*

Jackson stated early in her tenure that, "Environmental justice is a priority for EPA and must be part of every action we take. By meeting people where they are and talking to them about the challenges they face, we can broadly expand the conversation on environmentalism."[29] Jackson's comments are the essence of environmental justice. Historically underrepresented communities need to be brought into the decision-making process, to make sure that disadvantaged populations are not unduly, and negatively affected, by government decisions on environmental matters.[29] To bring environmental justice considerations into every aspect of EPA regulation, and rule making, the agency used American Recovery and Reinvestment Act dollars to finalized a database, known as the Environmental Justice Strategic Enforcement Assessment Tool (EJSEAT). This tool would allow offices in EPA to assign an environmental justice score to their decisions by U.S. Census tract.[30]

After initiating an environmental justice tour, with the Congressional Black Caucus, to South Carolina, Maryland and Georgia in January 2010,[27] Jackson issued new guidance to her agency staff on environmental justice issues. This guidance stated, in part that, "relying on minimum notice and comment requirements is often not enough to achieve meaningful involvement for minority, low-income and indigenous populations. Promoting meaningful involvement often means special efforts to connect with populations that have been historically underrepresented in decision-making and that have a wide range of education levels, literacy or proficiency in English.[31]

The Interagency Working Group on Environmental Justice was re-convened at the White House in September 2010 with co-chairs Jackson and Council on Environmental Quality Chair, Nancy Sutley and members comprised of Attorney General, Eric Holder, Secretary of HUD, Shaun Donovan, energy and climate assistant Carol Browner, director of the science and technology policy, John Holdren, director of domestic policy, Melody Barnes and head of the General Services Administration, Martha Johnson. The working group was authorized under Executive Order 12898 by President Clinton, and was never convened during the Bush Administration.[32]

The meeting demonstrated the Obama Administration's commitment to environmental justice, and set the stage for more interagency collaborative work in the coming years. The group decided that its future agenda would include:
- Holding monthly meetings;
- Organize regional listening tours for 2011;
- Develop agency specific environmental justice strategies by September 2011;

- Host a White House forum on environmental justice;
- Identify opportunities for federal programs to improve environment, public health, sustainable economies and other issues of concern to environmental justice communities; and
- Identify opportunities to assist American Indian and Alaska tribes working to develop their renewable energy resources, to promote green jobs and economies, and reduce the impacts of climate change.[33]

9.

LAND AND WILDLIFE

Protect National Parks and Forests: *Barack Obama fought efforts to drill in the Arctic National Wildlife Refuge. Obama supports the Roadless Area Conservation Rule to keep over 58 million acres of national forests pristine. As president, he and Joe Biden will repair the damage done to our national parks by inadequate funding and emphasize the protection and restoration of our National Forests.*

President Obama's FY2010 budget for the National Park Service totaled $2.7 billion to both preserve and improve park lands. It was a $288 million, or 10 percent increase over the previous year's budget. Of these funds, $2.2 billion were designated for national park system operations, and approximately $15 million were targeted to a new grant program for park preservation. This was third straight year that federal funding for the National Park Service increased, and it was welcomed by Tom Kiernan president of the National Parks and Conservation Association who noted, "This bill demonstrates a concerted effort by Congress and the Administration to restore our national treasures in time for the 2016 centennial of the National Park Service."[1]

With numerous previous administrations short changing the National Park Service, many of the parks, including such popular tourist attractions as Grand Canyon and Yellowstone, have acquired a $580 million operating deficit, and have accumulated a backlog of $9 billion in deferred maintenance needs.[2] However, when Obama announced his 2011 budget priorities, the National Park Service saw a decline in funding to $2.4 billion,[3] and national park advocates were not pleased. This time Kiernan said, "Unfortunately this budget halts that progress – and additional years of such policies will diminish visitor services and the protection of America's special places. Through history, presidents have invested in national parks during difficult times. Our national parks received more money during the Great Depression than they had in all the years prior;

and Yosemite was set aside as a federal park during the Civil War. Now is not the time to pull back from investment in our national parks."[2]

During the 2008 presidential campaign, Obama pledged to enforce the Roadless Area Conservation Rule that was developed in the waning days of the Clinton Administration. The rule was intended to prevent logging in pristine areas of national forests, and protect approximately 60 million acres of national forest land in 39 states, from the destruction of old growth ecosystems, water pollution and the increased risk of fire. The Clinton Rule, however, was superceded by in 2005 by a Bush Administration rule to delegate the authority of determining roadless areas to state governors. Prior to leaving office, the Bush Administration approved exemptions of large portions of the national forest system, such as the Tongass National Forest in Alaska, and forests in Idaho. Those exemptions increased the likelihood of road construction and logging in those areas.[4]

Shortly after taking office, Obama provided Agriculture Secretary, Tom Vilsack with the sole authority to approve road construction, and logging, in any of the national forests covered by the rule. This halted much of the planned development in the short-term, and was hailed by the environmental community. Except at the same time, Vilsak approved a long-pending timber sale in the Tongass, which raised the hackles of the same environmental community. For example, Rolf Skar, senior forest campaigner for Greenpeace said, "…because of that one exemption, if there is wiggle room, we are going to keep seeing these proposals. Obama has signaled, 'If it's a tough sell, we'll cave in on this and let you go.'"[4]

The Obama Administration also addressed the Roadless Rule in the judicial system. August 2009 brought two important developments. The Ninth Circuit Court of Appeals upheld a lower court decision, and reinstated the Roadless Rule for most of the National Forest roadless areas. Its ruling found that the Bush Administration had violated the National Environmental Policy Act, and the Endangered Species Act, by substituting a state petition process for federal oversight. In addition, the Obama Administration decided to join the environmental community in appealing to the Tenth Circuit Court of Appeals, a 2008 Wyoming ruling which struck down the Clinton era Roadless Rule.[5]

The Obama Administration is crafting a new rule on how the entire national forest system is going to be managed. It is a planning rule, which implements the 1976 National Forest Management Act, and is a very valuable tool for forest service managers to use to carry out their duties. The rule defines the types of activities from logging, recreation and protecting wildlife habitat that will be conducted in 155 national forests and 20 national grasslands. All three of the previous rules developed in 2000, 2005 and 2008 have all been struck down by federal courts. This leaves the forest service using a 1982 rule which focuses primary on timber harvesting, and does not encompass the wide range of activities that the Forest Service generally employs today, such as the restoration of watersheds. The federal courts have recommended that any new rule developed, should have provisions assuring protections for species viability. Currently 68 of the 127 forest service plans are overdue for revision.[6]

Many in the environmental community are pleased that the Obama Administration is tackling head-on the issue of setting rules for management in the National Forest System. With the release of the new rule anticipated for January 2011, twelve environmental organizations banded together in December 2010 to make a strong push for a comprehensive rule. They purchased holiday ads in Washington DC political publications, and send out 10,000 holiday card to decision-makers, requesting a rule that would have strong standards for water quality, and wildlife protection, and a commitment to scientific review. As Jane Danowitz, U.S. public lands program director for the Pew Environmental Group stated, "President Obama has an opportunity to present the American people with a legacy that will stand the test of time: strong protections for our national forests. If well-protected, our national forests will be the gift that keeps on giving – providing clean water for millions of people, a safe home for fish and wildlife and a natural resource for generations."[7]

In 2010, the Obama Administration also introduced a climate change initiative to the National Forest system, requiring that all 155 national forests incorporate climate change and its consequences, into long-term management plans. The U.S. Forest Service has developed a 10-point scorecard that forest managers can use to develop their plans, and will be employed to evaluate their progress. The early stages of the score card are focused on employee education and training, while the later stages involve carbon sequestration measurement and sustainable development. The U.S. Forest Service hopes that each national forest management team is able to achieve seven out of the ten criteria by 2015.[8] The scorecard elements are:

- Employee education;
- Designated climate change coordinators;
- Guidance, training, plans of work;
- Integration of science and management;
- External relationships;
- Vulnerability assessment;
- Adaptation activities;
- Monitoring of species, watershed condition, forest and grassland health;
- Carbon assessment and management; and
- Sustainable operations such as reduced energy, water and other environmental footprints.[9]

Conserve New Lands: *Barack Obama is a strong supporter of increased funding for the Land and Water Conservation Fund, which supports land acquisition and maintenance of parks. As president, Barack Obama will lead efforts to acquire and conserve new parks and public lands, focusing on ecosystems such as the Great Plains and Eastern forests which do not yet have the protection they deserve.*

Obama's FY2010 budget, passed by Congress, included $420 million for the Land and Water Conservation Fund. This is the fund that provides the resources to the both the Departments of Agriculture and Interior, to acquire, preserve and protect environmentally sensitive land. Overall, Obama's budget for this program increased by 38 percent over the previous year, and placed it on a trajectory to reach the $900 million level by 2014.[10]

The Omnibus Lands Management Act of 2009, the most significant lands bill in decades, was signed by Obama in March of

2009. It was signed into law at the White House before a bipartisan group of Senators and Representatives that had shepherded the bill through both houses of Congress, including Senators Harry Reid (D-NV), Tom Coburn (R-OK), John Barrasso (R-WY), Mike Crapo (R-ID) and Speaker of the House, Nancy Pelosi (D-CA).[11] The bill: (1) designated more than 2 million acres across nine states as wilderness; (2) created thousands of miles of new trails, preserved battlefields and bolstered the National Park Service; and (3) safeguarded more than 1000 miles of rivers.[12]

Republicans in the House of Representatives were up in arms in the spring 2010, when they received word that Obama might be considering using his authorities under the Antiquities Act of 1906, to designate millions of acres of federally owned land as national monuments. This is the same authority that President Clinton used in 1996 for the 1.7 million acre site in Utah known as the Grand Staircase Escalante. A leaked memo to the Republican caucus indicated that Obama was considering 14 different areas, totaling 13 million acres for national monument status.[13]

When congressional Republicans asked the Department of the Interior to release any documents related to the designation of monuments, they received 383 pages of more than 2,000 documents related to the potential designations. Representative Jason Chaffetz (R-UT) said, "The federal government wants to steal millions of acres and put them into wilderness without much discussion or input."[13] Other Republicans were just as displeased. Representatives from six western states drafted a bill to exempt their states from the Antiquities Act, but Representative Virginia Fox (R-NC) upped the ante by introducing legislation to eliminate presidential authority to unilaterally designate monuments.[13]

The 21st Century Strategy for America's Great Outdoors, a Presidential Memorandum, was signed by Obama in April 2010. It was an effort to re-introduce the American public to the wonders of nature, and resurrect the spirit of President Theodore Roosevelt on how conservation can enhance each of our lives.[14] At the signing ceremony, Obama stated that the program was not a "big federal agenda being driven out of Washington," but rather focused on promoting community-level efforts to conserve outdoor spaces. The program was intended to encourage families to increase the number of hours spent outside, and would build on the First Lady's Let's Move initiative.[15]

Leading the program, Obama named four senior officials Vilsack, Interior Secretary Ken Salazar, Environmental Protection Agency Administrator, Lisa Jackson, and Chair of the White House Council on Environmental Quality, Nancy Sutley. They were charged with the steep challenge to revitalize the nation's conservation agenda during austere times, where there are few new federal dollars to be allocated. As Obama signed the memorandum, he listed some broad brush goals that he hoped the program would achieve, "forming coalitions with state and local governments and the private sector; encouraging outdoor recreation by Americans; connecting wildlife migration corridors; and encouraging the use of private land."[16]

Obama also directed the senior leaders, he appointed to head the Great Outdoors program, with developing an action plan to delivered by November 15, which would "reflect the constraints in resources available in, and be consistent with, the Federal budget."[17] Many in the environmental community believe that primary source of funding for the Great Outdoors activities and programs should be the Land Water Conservation Fund.[17]

The Obama Administration announced in December 2010 that it would reverse a Bush Administration policy, and permit millions of acres of undeveloped land to be eligible for federal wilderness protection. The 2003 edict, known by some as the "No More Wilderness Policy," signed by then-Secretary Gail Norton, stripped the U.S. Bureau of Land Management (BLM) of its authority to recommend areas for wilderness protection. Salazar intended to close millions of acres to commercial development, and was reviewing 220 million acres of BLM land to determine which should be given the new designation of "Wild Lands." While Congress must decide which lands receive permanent protection, "Wild Lands" can be named by the BLM after a public review process. "Wild Lands" can be managed under a plan with detailed protective measures. Some on the Republican side of the aisle in Congress were not happy, and Representative Doc Hastings (R-WA) said, "This backdoor approach is intended to circumvent both the people who will be directly affected and Congress."[18]

Partner with Landowners to Conserve Private Lands: *Barack Obama and Joe Biden will put an unprecedented level of emphasis on the conservation of private lands. They will advance legislation that works with landowners and follows in the tradition of the Wilderness Act, the Clean Water Act, and the Clean Air Act to focus federal attention and increased resources for this key environmental issue.*

Agriculture conservation funding for FY2010 under Obama totaled $887.6 million which was an increase of over $34 million from previous years. However, not all programs that would improve conservation and environmental protection in agriculture saw increases In fact, the Conservation Reserve Program was slated in the "Terminations, Reductions and Savings," document to lose $178 million over the period ending in 2019.[19] For more information on agricultural conservation programs, see Chapter 11. Agriculture.

The biggest disappointment in Obama's campaign pledges for land conservation is that no new overarching program has been developed, or proposed for private landowners.

Endangered Species: *Barack Obama and Joe Biden will fight to maintain the strong protections of the Endangered Species Act of 1973 and will undo the proposal from President Bush to eliminate the advice of independent government scientists in some endangered species reviews. We strongly support the goals of the Endangered Species Act, which has paved the way for a number of species - - such as the bald eagle - - to return from the brink of extinction. However, during the past 30 years the Endangered Species Act has not always worked perfectly. With all of its accomplishments, we have learned not only what works, but also what is ineffective. Consequently, the Endangered Species Act needs to be updated and improved. And that means moving past rigid ideological positions so that we can reach consensus on the right solutions.*

In March 2009, Obama blocked a key provision of the Bush Administration's interpretation of the Endangered Species Act, and environmentalists applauded the decision as strengthening the protections for endangered species and their habitats. The Bush Administration had finalized a regulation in December 2008, which allowed federal agencies to bypass consultation with government scientists at the U.S. Fish and Wildlife Service or the National Marine Fisheries Service, in determining the threat that a project, such as dam or a highway, may have on wildlife. The reason the Bush Administration gave for the change, was that these government scientists were too busy, and this would free them to perform more critical conservation work.[20]

The business community was opposed to Obama blocking the Bush Administration streamlining move, and said the consequences would be delays in energy, construction and other projects, which create employment. Obama countered when signing the memorandum, "Throughout our history, there's been a tension between those who sought to conserve our natural resources for the benefit of future generations, and those who have sought to profit from these resources. But I am here to tell you that this is a false choice. With smart, sustainable policies, we can grow our economy today and preserve the environment for ourselves, our children and our grandchildren."[20]

Obama also stated at that March 2009 ceremony, "Today, I have signed a memorandum that will help restore the scientific process to its rightful place at the heart of the Endangered Species Act, a process undermined by past administrations."[21] It was startling that just days later, Salazar removed endangered species protections from gray wolves in the Northern Rockies. From an environmental perspective, Salazar used a flawed analysis from the Bush Administration, which overturned more than 30 years of Endangered Species Act interpretation, to do so. Salazar defined the wolf populations using state line boundaries, rather than species populations, to exempt Wyoming from the areas where gray wolves were no longer considered endangered. This action allowed the hunting and killing of as many as 1050 of the 1350 wolves living in Idaho and Montana.[21]

Environmental organization reached out to Salazar on numerous occasions to draft a plan that would ensure the continued recovery of the gray wolf population, but they were rebuffed. At that point, thirteen environmental organizations jointly sued the Department of the Interior (DOI) in federal court.[21] The judge in the case ruled in November 2010 that the DOI could not divide endangered species designation along state boundaries, and reinstated the gray wolf's endangered species designation across the entire northern Rockies region.[22]

After the Gulf Oil Spill, the DOI and Council on Environmental Quality announced in May 2010 that they would be reviewing the Minerals Management Services' (MMS) protocol for licensing offshore oil and gas operation under the Endangered Species Act, and Marine Mammal Protection Act. Specifically, the agencies said they would beanalyzing MMS's performance under the two pieces of legislation to determine where processes can be improved, where they can be strengthened, and where they may have loopholes.[23]

Within two months of that announcement, the Center for Biological Diversity filled suit in federal court against the DOI and the MMS. The suit contended that the Endangered Species Act compels all federal agencies, including the MMS, to ensure that any action they carry out does not jeopardize a threatened or endangered species. And it charged that Salazar, "concluded that oil drilling in the Gulf would not jeopardize species: the Endangered Species Act requires agencies to revisit their conclusions about an action's impacts if new information calls those conclusions into question. The recent oil spill in the Gulf of Mexico triggers a legal obligation for the government to revisit its approvals of offshore and gas activities"[24] That litigation is ongoing.

The DOI declined to list the America Pika as an endangered species in February of 2010. This small rabbit-like mammal has a heavy coat, and its historical habitat range in the cool Sierra Nevada Mountains of California, and nine other Western states, has shrunken dramatically. Due to its coat, the pika can only survive for less than six hours in temperatures above 77 degrees. But government scientists say the animal can adapt to a wider range of temperatures, and rainfall, than had been previously believed.[25]

The pika was prime case for the DOI to consider the Endangered Species Act implications of climate change on a species, which may be threatened by logging on public land, or the permitting of electric generation stations. The Bush Administration had barred global climate change considerations in its reviews of endangered species protection for polar bears, and the Obama Administration said it concurred with that approach in May 2009. If the Obama DOI had picked up the mantel of including climate change in the deliberations over the pika's endangered species designation, it would have added the Endangered Species Act as an avenue for addressing global warming. Shaye Wolf a biologist with the Center for Biological Diversity, said, "That was a fight in the Bush Administration, and the Obama Administration isn't doing much better."[25]

The environmental community was stunned in November 2010 when it learned that the Obama Administration had denied protection to 251 plants and animals under the Endangered Species Act, and placed them on the list of candidate species. During its first years in office, the Obama Administration has provided protection to just 52 plants and animals, with only one of them having a habitat in the continental United States. The average yearly rate for the Obama Administration protection approval has been 26 species. By comparison, the Clinton Administration annual rate was 65 species approved, and the first Bush Administration was 58. Those who are being diplomatic may say that the Obama Administration does not have any urgency in endangered species designation, while Kieran Suckling of the Center Biological Diversity contends, "The Obama Administration has been abysmal when it comes to protecting our most vulnerable plants and animals."[26]

Six subspecies of Artic seals were proposed to be listed as threatened under the Endangered Species Act in December 2010,[27] but the Obama Administration announcement that everyone was wanting for, came later in the month, when it reaffirmed its decision to maintain polar bears as a threatened, not endangered.[28] Earlier in the year the Obama Administration set aside 187,000 square miles in Alaska as critical habitat to benefit polar bear populations.[29] In declining to name polar bears as endangered, the DOI stated that "its biologists had concluded in 2008 that the polar bear was not facing sudden and catastrophic threats (and) was still a widespread species that had not been restricted to a critically small range or critically low numbers."[28]

10.

TRANSPORTATION

Increase Fuel Economy Standards: *Barack Obama and Joe Biden will increase fuel economy standards 4 percent per each year. The plan, which will save nearly a half trillion gallons of gasoline and 6 billion metric tons of greenhouse gases, will establish concrete targets for annual fuel efficiency increases while giving industry the flexibility to meet those targets. Barack Obama and Joe Biden will double fuel economy standards within 18 years while protecting the financial future of domestic automakers. Their plan will provide retooling tax credits and loan guarantees for domestic auto plants and parts manufacturers, so that the new fuel-efficient cars can be built in the U.S. rather than overseas.*

    Within a week of taking office, President Obama signaled that his administration was open to states, like California, setting stricter auto emission than the federal government. This was seen as a repudiation of the policies of the Bush Administration, and was the first salvo in a negotiation with auto industry to raise Corporate Average Fuel Economy (CAFE) standards. In fact, he ordered the Department of Transportation (DOT) to begin talks with the auto industry to set higher fuel efficiency standards for cars by the 2011 model year. Obama knew that in allowing a number of different emissions standards to be developed by states, automakers would willingly come to the table and agree to increased emissions standards at the national level. It was estimated that 13 other states were in line to adopt stricter standards similar to California, if the Obama Administration sanctioned that approach.[1]

    This concerned the auto industry, because it would result in the adoption of a costly business model of building different cars for different states across the nation. The alternative would be to adopt the strictest standard for nationwide distribution. The shot across the bow of the auto industry made by Obama was, "The days of Washington dragging its heels are over. My administration will not deny facts; we will be guided by them. We can not afford to pass the buck or push the burden onto the states."[1]

The Obama Administration by early March 2009 had successfully negotiated with the auto industry, to not only secure their support for stricter mileage standards for cars, and trucks, but for a first-ever greenhouse gas (GHG) standard for vehicles. The agreement required an average mileage standard of 39 miles per gallon for cars and 30 miles per gallon for trucks by 2016. Linking the CAFE standard, and GHG standard, gave the industry the confidence that that the federal government would not be regulating these emission separately. The standard would phase in, starting in 2012, and be in full effect by 2016. The Obama Administration projected that these standards would save 1.8 billion barrels of oil, and reduce approximately 900 million tons of greenhouse gas emissions.[2]

When the final fuel efficiency rules were announced over a year later in April 2010, the average fuel efficiency for all vehicles manufactured for the 2016 model year would be 34.1 miles per gallon. This standard increased projected GHG savings to 960 million tons.[3] Some auto manufacturers like Porshe and Jaguar Land Rover hired lobbyists, and met with the Office of Management and Budget over the new standards. Because they produce fleets of high performance passenger vehicles, without an economy model, they stated that they would have difficulty meeting the 2016 standards.[4] Overall, the Obama Administration was pleased with amount of industry support, and David McCurdy, president and CEO of the Alliance of Automobile Manufacturers stated, "America needs a road map to reduced dependence on foreign oil and greenhouse gases and only the federal government can play that role."[3]

Less than a month after that major CAFE standard win, Obama signed an order that tasked the Environmental Protection Agency (EPA) and the DOT with creating a first-time national mileage, and GHG standard, for medium and heavy duty trucks. This would affect trucks manufactured in the 2014 to 2018 model years. In addition, Obama directed the setting of standards for cars and trucks beyond the year 2016, when the current national program ends. It is estimated that trucks use more than 2 million barrels of oil daily, and produce a fifth of nation's transportation-related GHGs. Transportation experts believe that efficiencies in tractor-trailer design could improve fuel economy by 25 percent.[5] EPA estimated that the new rules would cut greenhouse gas emissions by 250 metric tons, and reduce fuel consumption by 500 million barrels of oil.[6]

Obama heralded a new era of vehicle fuel economy, and GHG reduction, by stating that the previous stalemates had ended, and that in prior administrations, "progress was mired in a lot of old argument traded across entrenched political divides."[5] These sentiments were echoed by industry representative McCurdy, who stated, "The federal government is looking down the road and uniting all the diverse stakeholders to work toward the same national goal. This approach achieved success once before, so we are optimistic that we can do it again."[7]

The Obama Administration not only moved to improve the fuel efficiency of the vehicles produced in future years, but also targeted the pool of vehicles currently on the road through the Cash for Clunkers Program. Promoted as an economic recovery initiative to spur manufacturing, and job creation, through increased vehicle sales, a billion dollars was initially dedicated to the program. Owners of cars and trucks less than 25-years old, with a fuel economy of less than 18 miles per gallon, were eligible for vouchers toward more fuel-efficient vehicles. If they traded up to a vehicle with an improved fuel economy of four to ten miles, they received a $3,500 credit. If they traded up to a vehicle with a fuel economy of more than 10 miles, the credit was $4,500.[8]

The one billion dollar program which subsidized the purchase of 185,000 vehicles, quickly ran out of funds, and the Obama Administration asked Congress to authorize an addition $2 billion for the program, which passed Congress in August 2009.[8] To fund the second round of Cash for Clunkers, Congress took $2 billion of American Recovery and Restoration Act (Recovery Act) monies from the 1705 renewable energy loan program, administered by the Department of Energy (DOE) Energy Bank.

Mandate All New Vehicles are Flexible Fuel Vehicles.
Sustainably-produced biofuels can create jobs, protect the environment and help end oil addiction – but only if Americans drive cars that will take such fuels. Barack Obama and Joe Biden will work with Congress and auto companies to

ensure that all new vehicles have FFV capability – the capability by the end of his first term in office.

The Consumer Fuels and Vehicle Choice Act of 2009 was introduced by Senators Tom Harkin (D-IA) and Richard Lugar (R-IN), which if passed would have partially fulfilled Obama's commitment to mandate all vehicles be flexible-fuel vehicles (FFV) by 2013. A FFV is one that can operate using regular gasoline, and up to 85 percent ethanol (E85). The Harkin-Lugar Senate Bill would have required that 50 percent of all vehicles manufactured domestically would be FFV by 2011 and 90 percent by 2013.[9]

The Harkin-Lugar Bill ran into stiff opposition because some industry representatives believed that if a bipartisan proposal focused on E85 were to pass, it would discourage R&D on other fuel sources. In addition, it would force a technology into production, which might not be market ready. Auto manufacturers warned that current E85 fueling infrastructure was not sufficient to handle the current fleet of E85 vehicles, let alone the numbers that Congress and the Obama Administration would mandate. Industry figures showed that less that one percent of all fueling station in the U.S. were equipped with E85 pumps.[10]

While FFV mandates did not move in Congress, bolstering markets for E85, the EPA in October 2010, did approve that gasoline using up to 15 percent ethanol (E15) could be used in vehicles manufactured in model year 2007 and newer. It put on hold, however, the approval of E15 for vehicle model years 2001-2006 and rejected the request for vehicles manufactured prior to 2001.[11]

Partner with Domestic Automakers. *Barack Obama and Joe Biden will also provide $4 billion retooling tax credits and loan guarantees for domestic auto plants and parts manufacturers, so that the new fuel-efficient cars can be built in the U.S. by American workers rather than overseas. This measure will strengthen the U.S. manufacturing sector and help ensure that American workers will build the high-demand cars of the future.*

On Obama's path to assist the auto industry in retooling to make more energy efficient, low-emission vehicles, the American economy sunk into a great recession. Two of the three American auto makers teetered on financial collapse, and one actually went bankrupt. In his first year in office, Obama allocated $25 billion dollars in loan guarantees to the auto industry to speed up the transition to more fuel efficient vehicles.[12] For example, Ford moved forward with investments of $850 million in four of its Michigan plants scheduled for the 2011 to 2013 timeframe. Ford was beginning to make the changes necessary to develop, and build more fuel-efficient vehicles. It was estimated that this investment would create 1,200 new full-time positions in vehicle assembly and design. The investment built upon the $950 million that Ford dedicated to converting the Ford Michigan Assembly Plant from a large SUV factory, to a "state-of-the-art" car plant. That plant was scheduled to build the fuel efficient Focus, as well as the company's all-electric, and next generation hybrid, and plug-in hybrid vehicles by 2012.[13]

GM on the other hand announced that it would invest $190 million in its Lansing Grand River plant, adding 600 jobs to the plant's current 1,100 employees. A new small car would also be added to its Cadillac lineup. This was in addition to the redesigned Chevrolet Aveo, and the new Buick Verano. Chrysler announced it would invest $600 million in a manufacturing plant for small cars. Additionally, it would retool its Belvidere, Illinois plant to build new fleet of fuel efficient cars starting in 2012, including a small car to replace the Dodge Caliber. While Chryster said the investment would not create any new jobs, it would be able to retain the 2,349 jobs at plant, and a nearby parts stamping facility.[14]

However, before these companies could be reliable partners in the manufacture of more fuel-efficient, environmentally-friendly vehicles, the government had to assure that they would survive the economic collapse. Ford, the strongest of the three firms, refused government assistance. GM and Chrysler received over $35 billion under the Toxic Assets Relief Program (TARP), including $5 billion of assistance to GM and Chrysler parts suppliers. The Obama Administration told GM that it had until June 1, 2009 to restructure. At that time, the firm would receive an additional $12 billion, and its financing subsidiary would receive $7.5 billion.[15]

Obama did not believe that that the economic condition of the Big Three American automakers was totally a result of a faltering economy. As he had stated in a speech in 2007, "The auto industry's refusal to act for so long has left it mired in a predicament for which there is no easy way out. For years, while foreign competitors were investing in more fuel-efficient technology for their vehicles, American automakers were spending their time investing in bigger, faster cars."[16] In his book, *The Audacity of Hope*, Barack Obama said, "For years, U.S. automakers and the U.A..W. (United Autoworkers of America) have resisted higher fuel-efficiency standards because retooling costs money, and, Detroit is already struggling under huge retiree health-care costs and stiff competition."[16]

In early May 2009, a deal was brokered that secured the future of Chrysler. Obama announced that the U.S., and Canadian federal government, would provide more than $8 billion to Chrysler. The company could then go through a quick bankruptcy and reconfigure operations. Chrysler would be run by executives of the Italian car company Fiat, and a new board of directors would be recruited. In addition, with the wage, benefit and retiree cuts agreed to by the UAW, the union would become a 55 percent owner of the firm.[17]

GM filed for bankruptcy on June 1, 2009, and a week later, with the backing of the United States Treasury, a new firm called the New General Motors was formed to purchase the assets of the old firm. The new company was planning to issue an initial public offering (IPO) of stock in 2010 to begin paying back the government loans. The agreement was, that the Obama Administration would be holding 60 percent of the new company's stock, in exchange for relieving all but $9 billion of the loans it extended. At the same time, the government of Canada would loan GM $9.5 billion, forgive all but $1.7 billion and hold 12 percent of the new company's stock.[18]

The first IPO of New GM stock occurred in November 2010 On the first day of trading, the GM shares which were priced at $33, increased 3.6 percent. Financial experts said that was exactly the "sweet spot" of not too little, which would have been a vote of no confidence; or not too much, which would have meant the assets had been undervalued. While this was just a partial sale of the government's New GM stock holdings, it raised $20 billion of which $12 billion went to the US government.[19] Obama said,

"There were plenty of doubters and naysayers who said it couldn't be done, who were prepared to throw in the towel and read the American auto industry last rites."[20] He continued, "But we are finally beginning to see some of these tough decisions that we made in the midst of crisis pay off."[20]

Invest in Developing Advanced Vehicles and Put 1 Million Plugin Electric Vehicles on the Road by 2015. *Barack Obama and Joe Biden will invest in advanced vehicle technology that utilizes advanced lightweight materials and new engines. As president, Obama will continue this leadership by investing in advanced vehicle technology with a specific focus on R&D in advanced battery technology. The increased federal funding will leverage private sector funds and support our domestic automakers to bring plug-in hybrids and other advanced vehicles to American consumers. They will also expand consumer tax incentives by lifting the 60,000-per-manufacturer cap on buyer tax credits to allow more Americans to buy ultra-efficient vehicles. Barack Obama and Joe Biden will provide a $7,000 tax credit for the purchase of advanced technology vehicles as well as conversion tax credits. And to help create a market and show government leadership in purchasing highly efficient cars, Barack Obama and Joe Biden will commit to: (1) within one year of becoming President, the entire White House fleet will be converted to plug-ins as security permits; and (2) half of all cars purchased by the federal government will be plug-in hybrids or all-electric by 2012*

Obama has said "I don't want to have to import a hybrid car, I want to build a hybrid car here."[21] Putting America in the lead in production of hybrids, plug-in hybrids and electric cars has been a serious commitment for Obama. Administration officials say that is why he visited four different advanced battery plants in his first two years in office.[22] His administration also dedicated $2.4 billion in DOE electric technology grants to assist U.S. manufacturers to catch up to their Asian counterparts. These grants funded work in the design of advanced batteries, electric motors and other components for plug-in hybrids, and electric vehicles. [23] This included: (1) $1.5 billion for domestic battery manufacturers to expand battery recharging capabilities(2) $500 million for manufacturers to improve vehicle electric drive components, such as motors, electronics and drive trains components; and (3) $400 million for test demonstrations of plug-in hybrids and all-electric vehicles, installation of charging stations, and workforce training. In direct response the Gulf Oil Spill, Obama asked Congress for another $6 billion to advance these technologies.[24]

The massive infusion of taxpayer funds has helped the domestic industry become competitive worldwide in supplying advance batteries for vehicles. Federal investments assisted in financing 26 of the 30 electric-vehicle battery plants that were recently built. Of those plants, nine were lithium-ion battery manufacturing plants, with four of those expected to be operational by the end of 2010. The DOE projects that those 30 plants will have the capability of supplying 20 percent of the world's advanced battery market by 2012, and 40 percent by 2015.[22]

Market analysts are projecting healthy increases in plug-in hybrid sales in the coming years. Pike Research believes that plug-in hybrid sales in the U.S. by 2015 will be approximately 285,000 and worldwide it may reach 1,081,000. Frost and Sullivan are a little less bullish pegging global demand to increase by 127 percent, yielding worldwide sales of 756,000, with U.S. sales comprising half that number.[22] A report by Deutsche Bank from March 2010, indicates that automakers are receiving bids from battery manufacturers with delivery contracts in 2011 to 2012 timeframe in the range of $450 per kilowatt hour (kWh). Longer term, it is anticipated that battery performance will double in the next seven years, while prices will be lowered 25 percent in five years, and 50 percent in10 years.[21]

The Obama Administration was not able to extend the consumer tax credits on advanced vehicles, because it would have required an act of Congress. These tax credit were authorized under the Energy Policy Act of 2005, covering the period January 1, 2006 through December 31, 2010. Consumers could qualify for credits ranging from $250 to $3,400, when purchasing an advanced vehicle technologies, like a hybrid cars. The full tax credits were available to consumers, until a manufacturer's sales reaches the limit of 60,000 vehicles. Once a manufacturer has sold 60,000 vehicles, a one-year "phase out" would begin after the next calendar quarter, with only 50 percent of the credit available for that manufacturer's hybrids in the first two quarters of the phase out period, and 25 percent in the final two quarters.[25]

In early 2009, consumers were provide a $7,500 credit for the purchase of advanced technology vehicles, funded by legislation passed while Obama was still a Senator. Congress approved TARP in the fall 2008, which included a tax credit of up to $7,500 to consumers who bought one of the first 250,000 plug-in hybrid, or all-electric vehicles. These were models that were not on the market yet, but would soon be introduced. The plan was expected to cost the government about $1 billion.[26]

The Recovery Act signed by Obama in February 2009, included special tax credits for plug-in electric vehicles, like the Chevrolet Volt.[23] Building upon the TARP program, the Recovery Act increased the number of cars eligible for tax credits from 250,000 vehicles total, to 200,000 per manufacturer, either foreign or domestic. The consumer tax credit had a base level of $2,500 for a four kilowatt storage system, and added $417 for every additional kilowatt stored in a propulsion battery, up to a maximum of sixteen. For a Toyota Prius plug-in hybrid, with a 5 kilowatt battery pack, it would receive a tax credit of about $3,000. For the Chevy Volt plug-in hybrid, with a 16 kilowatt system, it would receive the full $7,500 tax credit. Obama officials anticipated that the Recovery Act would subsidize the purchase of some 1.8 million cars. The Recovery Act also included tax credits for small electric vehicles, including two-wheel and three-wheel plug-ins, plus conversions for existing hybrids to become plug-ins.[26]

Obama's has not been able to fulfill his commitment to convert the White House fleet to plug-in hybrids within one year. It does not look promising that he will be able to fulfill his other mandate that the federal government purchase plug-in hybrids, or all electric vehicles, to fill 50 percent of its fleet by 2012. To be fair, the deadline for the second commitment has not passed. However, in both cases the enthusiasm may have been ahead of the technology. The first plug-in hybrid, the Chevy Volt was not introduced to the market until late November 2010[27]. The all-electric Nissan Leaf entered the U.S. market in December 2010,[28] and there are no other mass-produced, all-electric vehicles, either domestic or international. The December 2010 sales for the Chevy Volt totaled 326[28] and the Nissan Leaf totaled 19.[28] While not meeting the goals by the dates stated, the White House has responded, "We are currently in the process of updating the fleet and we're making ever effort to make as much of the fleet as green as possible."[29]

Reform Federal Transportation Funding: *Barack Obama and Joe Biden will re-evaluate the transportation funding process to ensure that smart growth considerations are taken into account and he will also re-commit federal resources to public mass transportation projects across the country.*

Obama understood that federal programs and funding discourage smart growth development. Historically there have not been incentives for federal agencies to coordinate housing, transportation, water infrastructure, and economic development initiatives. So Obama took three steps early in his administration to promote smart growth concepts in federal policy and planning. The first was to establish the White House Office of Urban Policy, to assist in the coordination of more than a dozen agencies that affect urban life.[30] The second was to create the Partnership for Sustainable Communities (PSC), operated jointly by EPA, DOT and Department of Housing and Urban Development (HUD). The PSC has under its jurisdiction a $100 million Sustainable Communities Planning Grant Program, that provides resources for the development of sustainable policies at the state, regional and local government level.[31] The third was the development of the Livability Principles to guide government at all levels in creating communities that meet the needs of all their citizens.[31]

The Livability Principles are:
- Provide more transportation choices;
- Promote equitable, affordable housing;
- Enhance economic competitiveness;
- Support existing communities;
- Coordinate and leverage federal policies and investment; and
- Value communities and neighborhoods.[32]

The vision for the Livability Principles was to provide an avenue for federal agencies to work together. Obama hoped that this increased coordination would alter both the incentives and the funding, that federal agencies provide to communities. Over the years, numerous federal initiatives have barred smart growth considerations. That has made the sprawling suburbs and a dependence on cars, a fact of life for too many Americans. Some have criticized the Livability Principles for being too vague, given the myriad of rules and regulations that discourage, and in some cases make illegal, transportation plans for walking, transit and dense neighborhoods.[33] Others, however, hailed the principles as a step forward, by "improving building-level energy efficiency, cutting greenhouse gas emission through transit-oriented development, and taking advantage of locational efficiencies."[31]

    Smart growth is a concept whose time has come in the United States. For decades the urban cores of the nation's cities have decayed due to population declines, and increases in development in the suburbs and the exurbs. Many developers are now seeing greater opportunities in metropolitan areas, and are looking toward the inner-cities for building contracts. A survey of 26 of the nation's largest urban areas, has shown a doubling of residential construction during the past decade. Residential construction dropped to 600,000 units in 2008 from just 1.7 million earlier in the decade. However, hi-density residential construction in urban centers has remained level at 200,000 units. Mainstream America has joined the environmental community in seeing the benefits of urban redevelopment. People living in dense, transit friendly homes, help to conserve land, reduce pollution and decrease greenhouse gases.[31]

    More controversial is the Obama Administration's embrace of Congesting Pricing, which charges tolls to drivers who travel on the nation's road most frequently gridlocked highways. The dollars from these tolls can then be dedicated to improving urban highways, or other roads, that will help relieve traffic congestion. The Obama Administration believes that local and state government leaders, as well as the public, have not made the connection between highway tolls and reduced commuting times. Congesting Pricing has been promoted by the Obama Administration as a strategy to create new infrastructure. However the policy has not gained wide support and our urban traffic gridlock continues to be a problem.[33]

Many environmentalists remember with dismay the statement by Mary Peters, the DOT Secretary in the Bush Administration, when she "dismissed biking paths and trails as projects 'that are not really transportation' saying they had no place in federal transportation policy."[34] Then a "sea change" occurred in March 2009 when Obama DOT Secretary Ray LaHood said that in his agency, biking and walking projects would be given equal status to automobiles in transportation planning, and receiving federal funding. In FY2010, the Obama Administration allocated $1.2 billion on cycling and walking initiatives. This was a significant increase from the $600 million of the Bush Administration, and the $6 million that was dedicated to these types of projects 20 years ago. That follows a national trend which indicates that walking trips in the U.S. have increased from 18 billion in 1990, to 42.5 billion in 2009. Bike trips have also experienced an increase from 1.7 billion to 4 billion in the same timeframe.[34]

The primary legislative vehicle for federal transportation funding and policy is the Surface Transportation Authorization Act which is scheduled to passed Congress, and be signed by the president, every five years. A new bill was supposed to be passed in 2009, but due to a $140 billion shortfall in the Highway Trust Fund, Congress delayed the legislation until 2011. The Obama Administration was agreeable to this 18-month delay, and viewed it as an opportunity to negotiate a transformative, and environmentally friendly plan, that would incorporate mass transit issues.[35]

In January 2010, Obama and LaHood announced $8 billion of grants to large, high-speed rail projects. California received $2.25 billion to perform initial construction on new a system of 220 mph trains along four corridors: San Francisco and San Hose; Los Angeles and Anaheim: Fresno and Bakersfield; and Merced and Fresno. Florida was granted 1.25 billion to have a high speed line between Tampa and Orlando opened by 2014. Illinois was granted $1.33 billion to upgrade its Chicago to St. Louis line to speeds to 110 mph, cutting travel time from five and a half hours, to four hours. Wisconsin received $833 million to create a new high speed line between Madison and Chicago.[36]

Require States to Plan for Energy Conservation: *Barack Obama and Joe Biden will require governors and local leaders in our metropolitan areas to make "energy conservation" a required part of their planning for the expenditure of federal transportation funds.*

The Obama Administration introduced the concept of energy conservation into federal transportation funding, through the Transportation Investment Generating Economic Recovery (TIGER) grants. These grants were created under the Recovery Act.

These TIGER grants funded, through September 2011, made $1.5 billion available to state and local governments for highway, bridge, railway and port projects. They were awarded on a competitive basis, targeting projects that were deemed to have "a significant impact on the nation, a metropolitan area or a region." Several criteria played a role in determining which projects were funded. These included the economic impact, the contribution to longer-term U.S. economic competitiveness, improvements to safety, "livability," and "sustainability." DOT defines sustainability as "improving energy efficiency, reducing dependence on oil, reducing greenhouse gas emissions and benefiting the environment."[37]

There have been two rounds of TIGER grants. The first round totaling $1.5 billion focused on the development of new, or improved transit and rail services in the nation's largest metropolitan areas. This included funding for the: (1) renovation of Moynihan Station in New York City; (2) improvement of the freight rail system in suburban Chicago; and (3) creation of new streetcar or bus rapid transit lines in Boston, Dallas, Denver, Detroit, Las Vegas, New Orleans, Tucson, and Washington.[38]

The second round, with only $600 million available, meant that many of cities with more ambitious projects could not be funded. The biggest single grant, $47 million, went to Atlanta for the creation of a street carline between the Centennial Olympic Park downtown, and the Martin Luther King, Jr. historic district. Twenty million dollars was allocated to Los Angeles to leverage $546 million in federal funds for the Crenshaw light rail line. This may have been most significant grant, because it provided a new model for financing large infrastructure projects. A $16 million grant to New Haven, Connecticut was unique because it funded the first phase of its Downtown Crossing project. The work involved the removal of a portion of part of the city's central city highway, in order to reconnect the community that lives downtown, to the street grid. The overall plan in New Haven was to integrated the development of a streetcar line between downtown, and Union Station's intercity rail services.[38]

11.

AGRICULTURE

Combat Water Pollution in Rural America: *Barack Obama and Joe Biden will work to improve incentives that help farmers prevent runoff pollution from soil erosion, pesticides and fertilizer. Barack Obama and Joe Biden will also increase funding for the Conservation Security Program (CSP) and the Conservation Reserve Program (CRP) and will create additional incentives for private landowners to protect and restore wetlands, grasslands, forests, and other wildlife habitat.*

The environmental and agricultural communities, with the assistance of then Senator Barack Obama, fought hard for significant increases in conservation programs that are authorized in the 2008 Farm Bill. The programs, run by the U.S. Department of Agriculture (USDA), are the backbone of the efforts to improve rural water quality, and help farmers prevent soil erosion and runoff pollution. The Farm Bill sets mandatory spending levels for a variety of conservation programs for a five-year period. The 2008 Farm Bill directed an increase of $4 billion over the next five years for conservation programs.[1]

There are numerous programs that fall under conservation in the Farm Bill, but the four larger ones that are most closely linked to water quality are:

- Conservation Reserve Program (CRP) – This program offers farmers annual rental payments to plant trees or grasses along streams. These buffer strips reduce soil, nutrients and pesticides that would wash into rivers and streams.
- Conservation Stewardship Program (CSP – previously called the Conservation Security Program) – This program funds a wide range of conservation practices that improve soil, water, air, energy, plant and wildlife.
- Environmental Quality Incentives Program (EQIP) This program provides as much as 90 percent of the

cost of installation of new structures, or equipment, to reduce erosion or polluted runoff.
- Wetland Reserve Program (WRP) – This program offers farmers rental payments for creating or conserving wetlands.

Shortly after President Obama took office, he released his budget FY2010 budget. Many environmentalists were not happy, because his budget short changed conservation programs by $700 million dollars, from the levels agreed to in the 2008 Farm Bill. While the CSP numbers were on target, EQIP and WRP sustained major reductions. EQIP funding experienced a proposed cut of $250 million from the 2008 agreement. However, more concerning was the fact that WRP was targeted with a permanent reduction of 138,000 acres of wetland restoration, which translates into a cut of $350 million.[2] Craig Cox, Midwest vice president of the Environmental Working Group said, "These cuts to conservation undermine the Administration's goals of reducing global warming, cleaning up waterways and restoring balance and integrity to environmental programs. We still have a long way to go to reduce soil erosion, water pollution and declining wildlife habitat on agricultural land, and global warming will make these long-standing problems much harder to solve. EQIP and WRP should be front and center in President Obama's environmental program, not on the cutting room floor."[2]

The view of the Obama Administration operations of CSP was a bit more positive. Congress, who had retooled the Conservation Security Program into the Conservation Stewardship Program (CSP), held a hearing in October 2009 to learn the progress of the revamped initiative. The hearing demonstrated that the Obama Administration had been very aggressively moving forward to launch CSP, and the farm community was responding positively. The USDA unveiled the program in August 2009, with a deadline for farmers to apply by the end of September. USDA officials said even with the short sign-up time, they received more than twice number of applicants than could be supported by the $1.1 billion appropriation. That would allow USDA to enroll 12.8 million acres in CSP.[1]

The Obama Administration's FY2011 budget for farm conservation programs was not any more generous than the previous year's. In fact, it proposed cutting $1 billion from the 2008 Farm Bill baseline, with steep reductions anticipated in EQIP and WRP.[3] EQIP was slated for a cut of $380 million, giving it one third less than the 2008 Farm Bill allocation. This was viewed as unfortunate by those in the environmental and agricultural communities, who knew that there was already a large gap between the numbers of farmers who wished to participate in the program, and the amount of resources available.[4]

Limit EQIP Funding for CAFOs: *The 2002 Farm Bill lifted the cap on the size of livestock operations that can receive Environmental Quality Incentives Program (EQIP) funding, enabling large livestock operations to receive EQIP payments and subsidizing big CAFOs by as much as $450,000. Barack Obama and Joe Biden supports reinstating a strict cap on the size of the livestock operations that can receive EQIP funding so that the largest polluters have to pay for their own environmental clean up.*

The Obama Administration has not been able to limit Environmental Quality Incentives Program (EQIP) funding to Concentrated Animal Feeding Operations (CAFOs), because it would require new legislation from Congress. The parameters of EQIP funding had recently been decided on Capitol Hill, during the negotiation for the 2008 Farm Bill, and few in Congress had any interest in re-opening Farm Bill negotiations. A CAFO is a farming operation that raises livestock, and maximizes production by housing hundreds or thousands of animals indoors. With large numbers of animals in a confined space, the potential for large quantities of animal waste, dead animals, environmental issues and public health problems increase.[5]

CAFOs have massive waste issues that need to be addressed, but some operations are using limited federal EQIP funds to expand operations. There are numerous small- and medium- sized CAFO facilities currently in existence that do not meet water quality runoff regulations. As a presidential candidate, Obama agreed with those in the environmental community who believed that existing operations should get preference in EQIP funding over expanding operations. It was not until the 2002 that

EQIP began funding waste storage and handling equipment for those CAFOs with over 1,000 animal units. The firms owning CAFO operations saw an opportunity to secure federal EQIP subsidies to pay for expansion of individual facilities, and lobbied to have large CAFOs included in the 2002 Farm Bill. In addition, the industry successfully pushed for an almost ten-fold increase in the EQIP payment limit, taking it from $50,000 to $450,000 per individual contract.[6] It appears this is an issue that will have to wait until the 2012 Farm Bill negotiations.

Regulate CAFOs: *In the Obama Administration, the Environmental Protection Agency will strictly monitor and regulate pollution from large Concentrated Animal Feeding Operations (CAFOs) with fines for those who violate tough air and water quality standards. Barack Obama also strongly supports efforts to ensure meaningful local control.*

Prior to Obama taking office, the U.S. Environmental Protection Agency (EPA) finalized a rule in October 2008 to protect the nation's water quality, by requiring CAFOs to safely manage manure. Under this rule, EPA for the first time, required a nutrient management plan (NMP) for manure to be submitted as part of a CAFO's Clean Water Act permit application. The plan was to be reviewed by the permitting authority, and incorporated as an enforceable part of the permit The regulation also required that an owner or operator of a CAFO that discharges to streams, lakes, and other waters, must apply for a permit under the Clean Water Act (CWA). EPA estimated that nationwide, these CAFO regulations would prevent 56 million pounds of phosphorus, 110 million pounds of nitrogen, and 2 billion pounds of sediment from entering streams, lakes, and other waters annually.[7]

However in drafting that CAFO rule, EPA also called for CAFO operators who do not discharge, or propose to discharge, into waters, to show their commitment to pollution prevention, by obtaining a certification of zero-discharge.[7] The rule included the eligibility criteria that a CAFO must meet in order to become zero-discharge facility, including: (1) documenting the physical and operational conditions at the plant to ensure there will not be a waste discharge, and having a plan to accommodate changes at the facility; (2) developing, implementing, maintaining, and revising a no discharges nutrient management plan (NMP) for the plant; and (3) continuing to maintain internal documentation of the certification. The submission of this information entitles the facility to a zero-discharge certification, with no EPA review or approval of the documentation, or the NMP required.[8] Based on that provision, a group of environmental organizations filed suit against the EPA in February 2009 stating, "the targeted rule 'effectively exempted thousands of factory farms' from keeping animal waste out of waterways protected by the Clean Water Act."[9]

While that lawsuit was pending, EPA developed and released its Clean Water Act Enforcement Action Plan, and its emphasis on CAFOs was striking. It stated, "EPA will pursue new strategies to enforce existing rules limiting pollution from concentrated animal feeding operations (CAFOs), especially where they occur in areas close to imperiled waters. CAFOs have become larger and more densely located, placing more stress on waters in proximity to these locations. CAFOs result in a large pollution load to the environment and have been cited as an environmental justice concern in some areas. Where facilities with large numbers of animals are discharging without a permit or in violation of their permits, they can cause significant pollution problems of concern to communities. Many of the comments EPA received during its outreach for this Action Plan emphasized the need for EPA to move now to reduce pollution and address violations by these operations. EPA will review its existing enforcement tools to find ways to make progress in reducing violations and water pollution from these facilities, while additional solutions for reducing this pollution are being developed." [10]

Not everyone was impressed with EPA's new found commitment to CAFO discharge enforcement. Environmental attorney Nicolette Hahn-Niman said, "Obama has announced stepped up enforcement of the Clean Water Act, with specific reference to CAFOs, and it's making the meat industry nervous, of course. What I'd like to know is this: Will they finally be forcing all CAFOs to get CWA permits? If not, they are not going nearly far enough."[11]

That question was answered in May 2010, when EPA Administrator Lisa Jackson entered into a settlement agreement with the environmental groups that had filed suit over EPA's non-review, zero-discharge CAFO certification. The settlement stated that EPA would immediately issue new guidance "designed to assist permitting authorities in implementing the (CAFO regulations) by specifying the kinds of operations and factual circumstances that EPA anticipates may trigger the duty to apply for permits as discharging or proposing to discharge."[8] The Natural Resources Defense Council stated, "Under today's settlement, EPA will initiate a new national effort to track down factory farms operating without permits and determine for itself if they must be regulated. The specific information that EPA will ultimately require from individual facilities will be determined after a period of public comment. But the results of that investigation will enable the agency and the public to create stronger polluting controls in the future and make facilities are complying with current rules," [9]

Within days, to partially meet the obligations of the settlement, EPA issued a guidance document entitled, "Implementing Guidance on CAFO Regulations – CAFOs That Discharge or Are Proposing to Discharge." This document outlined the criteria for an objective assessment of whether a facility discharges or proposes to discharge. The criteria included proximity to rivers and streams, annual precipitation levels, discharge history, manure storage and animal mortality management practices.[12]

By May 2011, EPA anticipates it be issuing a new rule. It is expected to require 20,000 or more CAFOs to report information to EPA on how they dispose of manure and other waste. EPA will use that information to determine whether a CAFO needs a permit. The information required is likely to be data on the "animals housed at the facility, the generation of manure, management of manure, litter and wastewater, implementation of NMPs, recording keeping and history of applying for and/or complying with NPDES permits."[8]

The meat production industry expressed "deep frustration and anger"[9] over the EPA and environmental group settlement. Michael Formica, chief environmental counsel for the National Pork Producers Council, said, "With this one-sided settlement, EPA yanked the rug out from under America's livestock farmers. (The

National Pork Producers Council) is looking at all appropriate legal responses to EPA's disappointing course of action."[8]

Encourage Farmers at the Cutting Edge of Renewable Energy and Energy Efficiency: *Barack Obama and Joe Biden will encourage the use of methane digesters that are being used to produce power from animal waste. Barack Obama and Joe Biden will expand USDA projects that focus on energy efficiency and conservation.*

One of Obama's initiatives to encourage increased farm use of energy efficiency, and renewable energy technologies, was unveiled in the spring 2009. Secretary of Agriculture Vilsack announced the Rural Energy for America Program, Energy Audit and Renewable Energy Development Assist (REAP/EA/REDA) Grants The REAP/EA/REDA Grant Program was intended to provide grants for energy audits and renewable energy development assistance. The grants were awarded on a competitive basis, maximum grants totaled $100,000, and the eligible grantees included, state, tribal, or local governments, institutions of higher education, rural electric cooperatives, or a public power entities. The program was design to assist farmers, ranchers, and rural small businesses to become more energy efficient, and use renewable technologies. Recipients of the grants were required to pay at least 25 percent of the cost of an energy audit.[13]

In December 2009, USDA and the Innovation Center for U.S. Dairy signed a sustainability-focused Memorandum of Understanding (MOU), to work to reduce greenhouse gas emissions from dairy farms by 25 percent by 2020. Since the signing, USDA and the Center have partnered to increase the number of operating anaerobic digesters on farms, and encouraged research and development of new technologies, to help dairies reduce greenhouse gas emissions.[14]

On the one year anniversary of the signing Vilsack said, "The partnership between USDA and U.S. dairy producers to increase sustainability has achieved remarkable results over the past year. USDA has awarded funding to establish 30 anaerobic digesters, and we are assisting farmers with digester feasibility studies and energy audits to help producers reduce greenhouse gas emissions, while increasing on-farm income. The partnership is a demonstration of the Obama Administration's commitment to producing renewable energy, providing new economic opportunities to farmers, and preserving natural resources."[14]

Build Biofuel Distribution Infrastructure: *Barack Obama has been one of the strongest proponents in Congress for increasing the national supply of home-grown American ethanol and biodiesel. Barack Obama and Joe Biden will build on those efforts to improve the production, supply and distribution of advanced biofuels like cellulosic ethanol and biodiesel.*

The Obama Administration accepted the challenge of assisting industry to build a production, supply and distribution system for renewable transportation fuels. This included ethanol, and vegetable oil enhanced fuels, like E85 and B20. These are liquid renewable fuels that most Americans do not know anything about, nor do they have the vehicles that can use them.

The standard mix for ethanol and gasoline today is same as it was in the 1970s, when in the Midwest, it was called "gasohol;" 10 percent ethanol to 90 percent gasoline. That 10 percent ethanol mix is often referred to as E10. There are other levels of ethanol and gasoline mixtures that are trying to enter the transportation fuel market. These include a 15 percent ethanol to 85 percent gasoline mix, known as E15, and 85 percent ethanol to 15 percent gasoline, termed E85.

Ethanol can not only be derived from corn, barley and other grain through fermentation of the kernel, but it can also be produced from corn stalks, wood and other organic matter. These materials are first transformed through gasification, or hydrolysis, and then they are fermented. This is known as cellulosic ethanol. Since as an end product, it identical to kernel ethanol, it can be mix in the same proportions, and used as fuel in the same manner. Many experts see cellulosic as the future of the ethanol industry, because they believe the volumes available to be produced are much greater than from grain fermentation.

Ethanol is not the only renewable transportation fuel. There is also biodiesel, which is a mixture of vegetable oil and standard diesel fuel. Like ethanol, modern biodiesel had in origins in the Midwest, where there is an abundance of soybeans, and producing a local transportation fuel can have multiple economic benefits. A B10 biodiesel blend is 10 percent vegetable oil to 90 percent diesel fuel; B20 is 20 percent vegetable oil to 80 percent diesel; and B100 is pure vegetable oil.

The Energy Independence and Security Act of 2007 (EISA) supports the continued development and use of biofuels. It set a Renewable Fuels Standard (RFS) mandating a target of 36 billion gallons per year of renewable biofuels be in use by the year 2022. This standard covers cellulosic biofuels, biomass-based diesel, advanced biofuels and conventional biofuels. It charged the EPA with setting annual targets for oil companies to meet, in order to achieve greater use of renewable transportation fuels in the U.S.[15]

One of the major challenges for industry, government and the public, is that there is not a system in place to move E85 and B20 fuels from production and into the tank of consumers, like there is for gasoline, diesel fuel and E10. Blend technologies to ensure product consistency, proper UL listed storage tanks, separate pumps at the service station, easy to read pump labeling and vehicles with warranties to use the fuels, are all missing. This is all part of what is called the "supply chain."[16]

To address these issues, Obama signed a presidential directive in May 2009 naming Vilsack, Jackson, and Energy Secretary Stephen Chu to a new Biofuels Interagency Working Group (BIWG). BIWG was to increase collaboration among federal agencies by coordinating policies to positively impact the supply, transport, and distribution of biofuels, as well as, identify new policy options that would improve the environmental sustainability of biofuels feedstock production. [17]

The BIWG was also tasked to work on developing the policies to increase flexible fuel vehicle production, and assist in retail marketing efforts. The proposed policies were supposed to take into consideration land use, habitat conservation, crop management practices, water efficiency and water quality, and lifecycle assessments of greenhouse gas emissions.[17]

Obama specifically directed Vilsack to expedite and increase production of and investment in biofuels development efforts by: (1) refinancing existing investments in renewable fuels to preserve jobs in ethanol and biodiesel plants, renewable electricity generation plants, and other supporting industries; and (2) making renewable energy financing opportunities available within 30 days from the Food, Conservation and Energy Act of 2008. [17]

Obama also announced that $786 million from the American Recovery and Reinvestment Act (Recovery Act) would be provided to accelerate advanced biofuels research and development, and expand commercialization, by providing additional funding for commercial biorefineries. These efforts were to be overseen by DOE. The DOE Biomass Program was tasked with leveraging its national laboratories, universities, and the private sector partners, to help improve biofuels reliability, and overcome key technical challenges. This included the goal of developing more economic pathways to advanced biofuels like green gasoline, diesel, and jet fuels. The $786 million in Recovery Act funding was allocated across four main areas:

- $480 million solicitation for integrated pilot- and demonstration-scale biorefineries;
- $177 million for commercial-scale biorefinery projects;
- $110 million for fundamental research in key program areas; and
- $20 million for ethanol research.[18]

The BIWG reported back to the President in February 2010 and outlined the lead agency responsibilities for each supply chain segment of the comprehensive biofuels market development program. The responsibilities for each supply chain segment were are based on the core competencies and resources of the agencies:

- Biofuels Process Research – DOE.
- Feedstock Development and Production Systems – USDA (Research, Economics and Education (REE) and Forest Service (FS).
- Pilot-scale and Full-Scale and Biorefinery Demonstration – DOE Energy Efficiency and Renewable Energy (EERE), USDA Rural Development (RD) and FS).
- Regulatory compliance – EPA and USDA.
- Dissemination of Best Practices and Workforce Development – USDA (REE, FS, and RD) and USDA/State/Local Extension. [19]

Also, in February 2010, EPA determined that corn-based ethanol would meet the EISA RFS greenhouse gas standards. The agency found that the manufacture of the corn-based ethanol fuel, emits less than 20 percent of the "lifecycle" greenhouse gases of gasoline, which was required under the 2007 legislation. While corn-based ethanol met the standard, which pleased ethanol advocates, the industry continued to object with the methodology that EPA used measure the carbon footprint. Specifically, EPA continued to use factor of "international indirect land use changes" in its calculations. The parameter is a measure of the emissions that result from clearing grasslands and forests in foreign nations for cropland, because American corn and soybean are being diverted to manufacturing fuels.[20]

The RFS for 2011 for all four fuels, as required under EISA, was released by EPA in November 2010. In setting cellulosic ethanol at 6.6 million gallons, the Obama Administration was conceding that it would not reach the 250,000 million gallon target for 2011 set by Congress under EISA in 2007. Bob Dinneen, president of the Renewable Fuels Association said, "By reducing the standard for cellulosic biofuels, EPA is accurately reflecting the difficulties cellulosic biofuel technologies have encountered in obtaining the capital needed to fully commercialize. However, being aware of this fact, EPA should have been and must be careful to keep cellulosic biofuels targets ambitious so as to stimulate the kind of investment these technologies need to finish commericialization."[21] While that advice was provided to EPA, others were concerned that the Department of Energy had been slow in approving the loan for one of the biggest cellulosic plants planned which is backed by the oil company BP.[21]

Overall, EPA RFS standards indicated that in 2011, renewable fuels will comprise 8 percent of the fuel volume in comparison to non-renewable gasoline and diesel volume. On a volume basis, the gallons for each of the four fuels were:
- Cellulosic biofuels – 6.6 million gallons;
- Biomass-based diesel – 0.80 billion gallons;
- Advanced biofuel – 1.35 billion gallons; and
- Renewable fuel -13.95 billion gallons.[22]

EPA approved in October 2010, gasoline using up to 15 percent ethanol (E15) to be used in vehicles manufactured in model year 2007 and newer. It put on hold the approval of E15 for vehicle model years 2001-2006, and rejected the request for vehicles manufactured prior to 2001.[23] This approval, however, did not sit well with the National Petrochemical and Refiners Association (NPRA), who filed suit against EPA over this matter in early 2011. NPRA contended that "EPA does not have the authority under the Clean Air Act to approve a partial waiver that allows the use of E15 in some vehicles, but not in others."[24] Additionally, NPRA stated that E15 has not been adequately tested in vehicles made after 2007, causing engine damage, and drivers of cars built prior to 2007, may inadvertently pump E15 into their cars causing "misfueling."[24]

The ethanol industry has its own concerns about EPA's E15 ruling, and that was the label on the pump. The ethanol industry does not like the EPA orange label with the word "caution" on it, and has submitted a redesign in blue with the word "attention" instead. And while the EPA label tells consumers with cars manufactured earlier than 2007 that the E15 fuel may damage their engines, the industry label tells them that E15 is approved for vehicles made in 2007 and later.[25]

The Obama Administration brought good news to the B20 industry by including biodiesel in the Corporate Average Fuel Economy (CAFE) standards for auto manufacturers. For years, automakers have been able to include models deemed to be duel-fuel and flexible fuels vehicles (FFV), and dedicated alternative fuel vehicles (AFV), in their calculation to increase the average fuel mileage equivalents for their entire fleets. However, the federal government had previously said that B20 vehicles did not fall into either of those two categories. EPA issued a rule proposing that B20 vehicles could be counted as FFV and AFV credits, and could be calculated as part of the manufacturer's overall fleet fuel economy. This would provide an increased incentive for auto makers to manufacture B20 compatible vehicles that are warrantied for the higher level of biodiesel fuel.[16]

The tax cut bill passed by the 111th Congress during the lame duck session and signed by Obama in December 2010, was very friendly to ethanol and biodiesel. The legislation includes provisions that extend through 2011, the 45 cent per gallon ethanol tax credit, the 54 cent tariff on imported ethanol, and the 10 cent credit for small-scale U.S. manufacturers of corn based fuel. In addition to ethanol subsidies, the bill includes an extension of the $1 per gallon biodiesel tax credit through 2011.[26]

Develop the Next Generation of Biofuels: *Advances in biofuels, including cellulosic ethanol, biobutenol and other new technologies that produce synthetic petroleum from sustainable feedstocks offer tremendous potential to break our addiction to oil. Barack Obama and Joe Biden will work to ensure that these clean alternative fuels are developed and incorporated into our national supply as soon as possible. They will require at least 60 billion gallons of advanced biofuels by 2030. Barack Obama and Joe Biden will invest federal resources, including tax incentives, cash prizes and government contracts into developing the most promising technologies with the goal of getting the first two billion gallons of cellulosic ethanol into the system by 2013. Barack Obama and Joe Biden will also work to improve the national supply of advanced biodiesel.*

The Obama's BIWG designated the DOE Biomass Program as the lead research agency for facilitating the development, and transformation of new domestic biofuels. Through targeted research, development, and deployment, the Biomass Program was to assist industry in developing the next generation of cost-competitive biofuels, bioproducts, and biopower.[19]

The Biomass Program addresses technical barriers to producing advanced biofuels across the supply chain. Advanced biofuels are derived from renewable biomass other than corn kernel starch, and may include organic materials grown for the purposes of being converted to energy, such as agricultural wastes, forest resources, energy crops, and algae. The end product may be ethanol, methanol, biodiesel, or even renewable gasoline, diesel, kerosene and jet fuels. To develop a domestic biofuels industry capable of sustainably producing large enough quantities of advanced biofuels, the Biomass Program, in conjunction with USDA, developed an approach centered on the integrated biorefinery concept. A biorefinery is a facility similar in function to a petroleum refinery, which uses biomass, instead of crude oil, to produce fuels and a variety of useful co-products.[27]

The two primary conversion technologies that the Biomass Program focuses on are thermochemical and biochemical. The thermochemical R&D, funded at $28 million in FY2010, conducts research, testing, integration, and feasibility studies to convert biomass to fuels, chemicals and power. The DOE program focuses on conversion process such as gasification, pyrolysis, and catalytic hydrotreating and hydrocracking processing technologies. Some of the major technical challenges the Biomass Program addresses is increasing the understanding the feedstock requirements, and improving conversion technologies to produce fuel intermediates, such as clean synthesis gas and stable pyrolysis oils. In particular, efforts to develop and improve processes for converting syngas to advanced liquid biofuels, such as renewable gasoline and diesel, have been a primary focus. The Biomass Program leadership believes this would help to create the next generation of biofuels, and support future biorefinery validation projects.[27]

The biochemical conversion R&D, funded at $31.7 million in FY2010, was aimed at reducing the cost of converting lignocellulosic biomass to mixed, dilute sugars, and then to liquid transportation fuels such as ethanol. The Biomass Program has said that the further development of these technologies would advance multiple objectives. These include the conversion of a wider range of feedstocks, support for integrated biorefinery development, and ultimately, the launch of new commercial avenues for the production of cellulosic biofuels.[27]

Expand Locally-Owned Biofuel Refineries: *Barack Obama and Joe Biden believe we must ensure that local investment continues to play a significant role as the biofuels industry continues to expand and evolve. They will create a number of incentives for local communities to invest in their biofuels refineries, including expanding federal tax credit programs and providing technical advice to rural communities that are in a strong position to open their own refineries. They will also provide an additional subsidy per gallon of ethanol produced from new facilities that have a minimum of 25 percent local capital, and they will provide additional loan guarantees for advanced ethanol facilities with local investment.*

In February 2010, Obama expressed his support for the recommendations of BIWG, and its plan to accelerate the establishment and commercialization of the advanced biofuels sector. He also endorsed the BIWG's recommendation that named the USDA and DOE as the lead agencies in the biofuels supply sector, to advance the full-scale and widespread deployment of biofuels commercial facilities. This included:
- Provide financing for innovative first time commercial technologies;
- Development of first-of-a-kind, scaled-up commercial and multiple-commercial deployed 2nd and 3rd generation conversion facilities; and
- Continuation of 1st generation facilities.[28]

The leading program to fulfill these goals is the USDA Biorefinery Assistance Program which provides grants for demonstration-scale biorefineries, and loan guarantees for commercial-scale biorefineries that produce advanced biofuels. Loans under this program were limited to $250 million, and grants may be provided up to 50 percent of project cost. A total of $245 million was available for biorefineries in FY2010 funding. Two of the innovative advanced biofuels projects funded under the Biorefinery Assistance Program are Range Fuel of Soperton, Georgia and Sapphire Energy of Columbus, New Mexico.[28]

Range Fuel is a 20 million gallon per year (MGY) facility that has been producing cellulosic methanol from the initial phase of its first commercial plant. Private investors, such as Khosla Ventures, and an $80 million Department of Agriculture loan guarantee, are providing the financial backing for the firm. Range Fuel was initially using woody biomass from nearby timber operations, but plans to experiment with other types of renewable biomass as feedstock for the conversion process, including herbaceous feedstocks like miscanthus and switchgrass.[28]

The plant employs Range Fuels' two-step thermo-chemical process, which uses heat, pressure, and steam to convert non-food biomass, such as woody biomass and grasses into a synthesis gas, composed of hydrogen and carbon monoxide. The syngas is then passed over a proprietary catalyst to produce mixed alcohols, which are separated, and processed, to yield a variety of low-carbon biofuels.[28]

The cellulosic methanol produced from Phase 1 will be used to produce biodiesel. It may also be used to displace diesel in heating applications, used as a fuel additive in gasoline-powered motor vehicles, or used to power fuel cells. Range Fuels has plans to begin production of cellulosic ethanol from the plant in the late 2010. Range Fuels, which is permitted to produce 100 million gallons of cellulosic ethanol, plans to expand the capacity of the plant to 60 million gallons of cellulosic biofuels annually, with additional construction to begin in the summer of 2011. The plant had peak employment during construction of 250 and 70 plant employees at peak capacity.[28]

"We are ecstatic to be producing cellulosic methanol from our Soperton Plant, and are on track to begin production of cellulosic ethanol in the third quarter of this year," said David Aldous, Range Fuels' President and CEO. "This milestone is a giant step in overcoming the technological and financing challenges facing the commercialization of cellulosic biofuels."[29]

Sapphire Energy is the first 3rd generation biorefinery, and it is demonstrating that oil from algae can be refined into gasoline, diesel and jet fuel. The plant will produce 1 million gallons per year and can fix approximately 56 metric tons of CO_2 per day. Along with Boeing, Sappire completed the first two-engine 737-800 two hour test flight using synthetic algal based jet fuel.[28] Sapphire has financial support totaling $100 million from private sources like Bill Gates, and over $100,000 in Recovery Act grants and funding from the USDA. Sapphire has inserted genes into its algae that alter the hydrocarbons algae normally produce, making it more like petroleum, from which jet fuel and bio-diesel can be manufactured. The company has also inserted a Roundup-ready gene, which will allow their algae to survive spraying of ponds with the pesticide Roundup, to control any invasion of the crop by wild algae.[30] Sapphire has built a demonstration project containing 300 acres of open ponds in the New Mexico desert,[25] and is projected to have 750 direct and indirect jobs by 2011 and 30 positions directly operating the facility.[28]

Mike Mendez, a co-founder and vice president for technology at Sapphire Energy, the owner of the laboratory has said, "You don't want to take what algae gives you. You want to make the best product." He added, "My whole goal here at Sapphire is to domesticate algae, to make it a crop."[31]

Encourage Organic and Sustainable Agriculture: *Barack Obama and Joe Biden will increase funding for the National Organic Certification Cost-Share Program to help farmers afford the costs of compliance with national organic certification standards. They will also reform the U.S. Department of Agriculture (USDA) Risk Management Agency's crop insurance rates so that they do not penalize organic farmers.*

New legislation may be needed by Obama, if he wants to increase the payments for the National Organic Certification Cost Share Program (NOCCSP), beyond the increase that was provided in the 2008 Farm Bill. Depending in the state, NOCCSP or the Agricultural Management Assistance Program, makes financial assistance available to help defray the costs of organic certification for producers and handlers of organic products through their state departments of agriculture.[32]

Recipients must be certified locally by a USDA accredited agent under the National Organic Program. The 2008 Farm Bill reauthorized the NOCCSP, and provided an almost five-fold increase in mandatory funding for the program, from $5 million to $22 million. Producers and handlers can receive up to 75 percent of their annual certification costs. The maximum annual payment per operation was increased from $500 to $750,[32] which is the amount that USDA was offering in late November 2010.[33]

Obama followed through partially on his promise regarding reforming crop insurance rates to be more equitable to organic farmers. In August 2010, the USDA Risk Management Agency (RMA) said it would offer an organic price election for four crops during the 2011 production year, namely: cotton, corn, soybeans and processing tomatoes. RMA said it was eliminating the current five percent surcharge for organic crops insured under ten crop insurance programs. Affected programs are figs; Florida citrus fruit; Florida fruit tree; macadamia tree; nursery; pears; peppers; prunes; Texas citrus tree; and Texas citrus fruit. The agency further stated that it would continue to accumulate data that will allow for more precise rating of other organic crops.[34]

Secretary of Vilsack said, "USDA is working to provide producers of organic crops with improved opportunities and resources. We are taking aggressive action to improve delivery of our programs, with impressive results for our customers. The release of these reports and RMA's announcement of the price election mark another step in that continuing effort."[34]

Support Local Family Farmers with Local Foods and Promote Regional Food System Policies: *Barack Obama and Joe Biden recognize that local and regional food systems are better for our environment and support family-scale producers. They will emphasize the need for Americans to Buy Fresh and Buy Local, and they will implement USDA policies that promote local and regional food systems.*

Many in the local, regional and organic agriculture community felt that when Obama nominated Vilsack to be Secretary of Agriculture, that Vilsack would always side with large agribusiness and the biotechnology sectors. After all, Vilsack had been governor of one of nation's leading agricultural states, Iowa, and he had once been named "Governor of the year" by Biotechnology Industry. It surprised many when Vilsack named Kathleen Merrigan as his deputy. Merrigan was a staunch supporter of agricultural policies benefiting conservation, and sustainable land use, and in the early 1990s, had drafted the federal organic standards. Vilsack also burnished his local agricultural roots when he established a vegetable garden, right in front of the USDA headquarters building on the National Mall. Local food advocates began to see that Vilsack viewed local, regional and organic farmers on par with his other constituency, the large agribusiness and biotechnology firms like Monsanto. In fact, Carol Tucker Forman, a former USDA official and director of the Food Policy Institute of the Federation of America said about the changing climate of the department, "I have never seen conversations before about family farms and really small operations and local agriculture."[35]

However, not all was "small is beautiful" at USDA. Secretary Vilsack also appointed Roger Beachy to the director of the National Institute for Food. Beachy upset many in the local farming community when he said, "Scientific standards for food safety regulations should be the same across all farming systems. They should apply to big farms and small farms, including organic farms."[35] In addition, Islam Siddiqui was nominated as USDA's chief negotiator for global markets, and he was quoted in 1999 as saying, "We do not believe that obligatory GMO (genetic modified organism) labeling is necessary, because it would suggest a health risk where there is none. Mandatory labeling could mislead consumers about the safety of these products."[35]

After one year in office, the dual nature of the Obama agricultural policy was very evident to those in the local, organic and sustainable agriculture. On one side was the development of local, regional, and sustainable and organic food systems, and on the other was support for a agribusiness, biotech, and megafarm agriculture. The schizophrenic nature of the Obama agricultural policy came to a head in early January 2010 when USDA published final regulations concerning the limits on farm subsidy payments, and the "actively engaged in farming" rules that determine eligibility for subsidies. Those in the sustainable agriculture community felt betrayed. Obama had not fulfilled a campaign pledge, to close the loophole that allows megafarms to get around subsidy limits by dividing their operations on paper. The existence of these subsidizes allows millions of dollars to flow to corporate farms, and decreased the viability of small family farms and rural communities. The National Sustainable Agriculture Coalition felt so strongly they released this statement, "As Obama's USDA settles in and is forced to choose between taking concrete steps to advance a more sustainable agricultural system or the destructive status quo — between loving one son and the other— it's becoming clearer that it loves the destructive son best."[36]

In December 2010, Obama signed the Healthy, Hunger-Free Kids Act with the champion of the bill, First Lady Michelle Obama, standing by his side. There were a number of provisions in the bill that would benefit local and regional agriculture, but none more so, than one that helps communities to establish local farm to school networks, create school gardens, and ensure that more local foods are used in the school setting. One community-based agriculture advocate said, "These programs encourage schools to source ingredients from local farms, and create opportunities for children to learn about where their food comes from and how it grows. It's important for parents, teachers and administrators to understand that supporting children's health is a total package: we need to make healthy options available to them, we need to be good examples ourselves, and we need to help them make the connections between the health of the land, the health of their food and the health of their body, mind and spirit."[37]

Obama signed the Food Safety Modernization Act into law in January 2011, which is the first major overhaul of food safety regulations in nearly a century. The legislation, which is estimated to cost $1.4 billion over five years, provides the Food and Drug Administration (FDA) with the authority to increase risk-based inspections, require mandatory recalls of tainted food, and more effectively trace food borne illness outbreaks to their source. Two of the provisions of that legislation that appeals to local, regional and organic farmers include: (1) provides small farms, food processing facilities and community agriculture sellers, with the option of complying with state regulation or with modified, scale-appropriate federal regulation: and (2) gives FDA authority to either exempt low risk, or no-risk farms from the new regulatory requirements, or to modify particular regulatory requirements.[38]

When Michelle Obama planted an organic garden on the South Lawn of the White House, to highlight the importance of healthy diet for children, many in America applauded her efforts. No one knew what a controversy it would stir. Shortly after the announcement of the garden became public, the White House received a letter from Mid America CropLife Association that represents the companies selling chemical pesticides and fertilizers. The letter congratulated the Obamas on their new garden, but expressed a concern about its organic nature, by saying, in part, "we respectfully encourage you to recognize the role conventional agriculture plays in the U.S. in feeding the ever-increasing population, contributing to the U.S. economy, and providing a safe and economical food supply. America's farmers understand crop protection technologies are supported by sound scientific research and innovation."[39] Jeff Stier, associate director of the American Council on Science and Health said, "I think the Obama garden should come with a warning label. It is irresponsible to tell people that you should have to eat organic and locally grown food. Not everyone can afford that. That's a serious public health concern. People are going to eat fewer fruits and vegetables. Cancer rates will go up. Obesity rates will go up. I think if we decide to eat only locally grown food, we are going to have a lot of starvation."[40]

12.

CONCLUSIONS

"I think Ronald Reagan changed the trajectory of America in a way that Richard Nixon did not and in a way that Bill Clinton did not. He put us on a fundamentally different path because the country was ready for it. ....I think Kennedy, 20 years earlier moved the country in a fundamentally different direction. ...I think we are in one of those fundamentally different times right now where people think that things, the way they are going, just aren't working." [1]

President Obama, when he uttered those words, set a pretty high bar for himself, in aspiring to be a transformational president in the manner that Reagan, and Kennedy, are viewed in that context. Leadership styles and dimension were defined by noted scholar James MacGregor Burns, over 30 years ago. He famously defined transformational leadership, as inspiring followers to engage in the risky, and exhilarating work of changing the world. Transactional leadership was described as using reward, punishment and horse-trading, to gain followers in order to achieve goals.[1] A third leadership style, laissez-faire, was defined as exerting minimal effort, performing maintenance activities, and just keeping your head above water. Laissez-faire leaders do not really develop meaningful relationships with followers, or achieve significant new goals.[2]

In the previous chapters, we have examined in some detail, the environmental initiatives of the Obama Administration. Let's summarize those achievements, and challenges, along with how Obama has used the tools of the presidency in relation to: (1) cabinet secretaries; (2) executive office personnel; (3) executive orders, memorandums and agreements; (4) rules and regulations; (5) programs; (6) Congress; (7) courts; and (8) the American public. Then, we will assess whether Obama has demonstrated laissez-faire, transactional or transformational environmental leadership, during his first two years in office.

Cabinet Secretaries

Obama appears to have made wise choices in his cabinet secretaries with Steven Chu at the Department of Energy (DOE), Lisa Jackson at the Environmental Protection Agency (EPA), Ken Salazar at the Department of Interior (DOI) and Tom Vilsack at the Department of Agriculture (USDA). Each of them had considerable executive experience in running agencies with large staffs, such as being a governor, attorney general, head of a state agency, or a research laboratory manager. Over the past two years, all four of these Obama cabinet officials have moved forward rules, regulations, and funding programs that, as a whole, have had a positive impact on wide range of clean air, clean water, forest protection and smart growth development issues.

Chu has managed DOE's solar, wind, biofuels and clean coal research programs very well. He also rapidly rolled out a schedule to break the log jam on appliance efficiency standards. With his technical background, Chu was one of the primary members of the brain trust that developed the successful plan for capping the oil spill in the Gulf. Or as Obama referred to it, "Plug the damn hole."[3]

Jackson brought an innovative spirit, and a push-the-envelope approach, to EPA's regulatory agenda. This can be seen in the EPA proposals for multi-pollutant regulation of both air and water, as well as, the introduction of green infrastructure expenditures under the Clean Water State Revolving Fund. In history, Jackson's tenure at EPA will noted for her designation of greenhouses gases (GHG) as a threat to public health and welfare, and her issuance of rules to control GHG emissions from vehicles, utilities and oil refineries. Jackson also took a lead role in reviving the Inter-Agency Work Group on Environmental Justice, to bring underrepresented populations into the decision-making process regarding projects with environmental consequences in their communities.

Salazar is the only one of the group who has had a major agency scandal during the first two years of the Obama

Administration. Salazar addressed the basic corruption in Minerals Management Agency left over from the Bush Administration, but failed to follow up, and investigate, the actual procedure the agency was using in approving offshore leases.[3] Salazar has been a good environmental steward in the identification of Western lands as "Wild Lands," and in leading the multi-agency task group to break down barriers to deploying renewable energy technologies on federal property. However, Salazar's oversight of endangered species designations has not lived up to the expectations of the environmental community.

Vilsack has been walking the line between his large agribusiness constituents, and his small farm organic constituents. During his tenure at USDA, his agency has been a strong partner with DOE in the development of the biofuels supply chain and in the demonstration of the biorefinery concept. Vilsack surprised many of his environmental critics by following through with strong support for several organic farm initiatives, including reforms to crop insurance. He and Obama, however, have not seriously tackled some of the bigger issues, related to funding for agricultural conservation programs, and the criteria for participation in farm subsidy programs.

One criticism of the Obama environmental cabinet has been they were no where to be seen on cable, or network television. Obama, at times, seemed like the only administration spokesperson. One cable television political host said, about the Obama Administration, "It's hasn't leveraged its cabinet. It hasn't leveraged surrogates. It has not been a nationally power institution, like it could be."[4] That fact was not lost on the environmental community, who never saw Obama officials on television promoting climate change legislation.[5]

Executive Office of the President Personnel

Some in environmental community believe that Obama's chief of staff, Rahm Emanuel, and senior advisor, David Axelrod, were not fully on board regarding environmental issues taking a leadership role in the Obama Presidency. One commentator said, "Fundamentally, Rahm Emanuel and David Axelrod simply don't get global warming. They bought the nonsensical argument based on bad polling analysis that there was not good way to talk about it. They bought the even more nonsensical argument that comprehensive energy and climate legislation was not a politically winning issue."[6] Emanuel's phone calls to Senate Majority Leader Reid, suggesting that the Senate drop cap-and-trade legislation, certainly lend credence to that position.

Other staff members of the Executive Office of the President have been very productive in engaging Congress, and the American public in environmental issues. Carol Browner, White House assistant for energy and climate change, has been the crown jewel in that effort. Having been the longest serving administrator in EPA history, she brought a knowledge of EPA rule making, and a political sensibility that was unequaled. In addition, her political history and her established relationships on Capitol Hill, were key assets in the fast passage of climate change legislation in the House during 2009. Having a senior environmental official from the campaign in that position would have initially provided more policy continuity to the new administration, as well as, established relationships with senior Obama staff. However, in the long run, Browner was an excellent choice.

Larry Summers' role in advocating for climate change legislation was a surprise to many in the environmental community. The Harvard educated economist, who had been Treasury Secretary during the Clinton years, brought the financial the bona fides, and the gravitas, to make climate change a winner; especially when someone would try to pit environmental protection against economic development. His analogy that the Recovery Act and climate change legislation were two blades of the scissors, was pure genius.

Nancy Sutley's background in Los Angeles environmental politics helped her to advance the importance of environmental impact statements across the agencies, as well as help revive the long-neglected Inter-Agency Environmental Justice Work Group. Van Jones' commitment to green jobs was an asset that the Obama Administration could not pass up. While the concept of green jobs and the economic development aspect of renewable energy deployment was not a new one, Jones brought a passion and poetry that was unique. However, his past history with known communists, which he divulged readily during vetting, was too much for any administration official to survive.

There was much talk in the mainstream press, and in rightwing media, about the propriety of Obama having staff "czars" to lead particular issues, like green jobs and climate change. The discussion got to such a fevered pitch that a group of Republican Senators sent a letter to Obama, asking about the authority, qualifications and transparency of his staff. Further, they requested the he refrain appointing any more "czars."[7]

The bottom line is, presidents do not hire "czars." The press is the one that anoints a presidential staff member as a "czar." It was determined by an independent source, that while Obama had 32 czars, Bush had 35.[8] These are simply staff members working on a topical area for the president, who interact across agencies, within agencies at times and with members of Congress and their staff. The climate czar, green jobs czar and urban affairs czar, were located close to the White House, and performed important functions that cabinet members, managing huge bureaucracies, do not have the time or portfolios to do. Obama made a wise choice in continuing the tradition of having senior leadership staff at the White House level to shepherd priority environmental issues.

Another one of the challenges the Obama Administration faced was filling positions below the cabinet level. While 71 nominations out of 850 had been made prior to January 31, 2009, only six were made in month of February.[9] The vetting process became even more cumbersome after some high-level candidates were found to have tax issues in their backgrounds. At that point, candidates being considered, had to complete a 60-page questionnaire, and agree to an FBI investigation going back 20 years. This had a definite impact on pace at which the clean energy and green jobs aspects of the Recovery Act were able to be implemented.[10] More continuity from the campaign to the administration would have been useful in the identification of promising candidates. That may have avoided the situation where those who were close to the Obama campaign, described the administration's environmental hiring as a "mess" and "there is no process."[11]

Executive Orders, Memorandums and Agreements

Presidential signings are one way that presidents can send signals, and set directions, using only the power of their office to direct the executive branch. Because they are instructing their cabinet, and using existing budgetary resources, there is no need for congressional approval. Using his presidential powers, Obama was able to designate million of acres of land in the West as "Wild Lands," and protect them from commercial development. He also signed the presidential memorandum creating the 21st Century Strategy for America's Great Outdoors. This was a bold program to re-introduce America to the wonders of nature and increase the time that families spend outside. While there was no additional funding for the effort, Obama perceived this as a local or grassroots efforts that could be fostered by numerous federal agencies.

Signing a memorandum shortly after taking office, Obama reversed a Bush Administration policy of bypassing government scientists when considering endangered species in approving projects. Obama revived the scientific underpinnings of the Endangered Species Act by requiring the consultation with scientists at the U.S. Fish and Wildlife Service, or the National Marine Fisheries Service, before agencies fund projects, such as new dams or highways. However, the Obama Administration did not increase the pace of endangered species designation, and it used unscientific criteria in removing protections from the gray wolf in three Western States. The courts eventually struck down the Obama gray wolf ruling. Environmentalist were disappointed when Obama would not use the Endangered Species Act in the climate change fight with the American Pika, and were unhappy when the polar bear was not given endangered species protections

Obama signed three Executive Orders adopting government-wide a goals of reducing energy use in federal buildings by 15 percent by 2015, and dedicated $4.5 billion in Recovery Act dollars to achieve it. In addition, these orders implemented a net-zero-energy requirement by 2030, 50 percent recycling of waste by 2015, and reductions in GHGs of 88 million tons.

Obama created the Partnership for Sustainable Communities to provide a vehicle for EPA, HUD and DOT to collaborate in decisions regarding water infrastructure, housing and transportation. Through increase federal agency cooperation, Obama has been able to introduce smart growth into the federal funding formulas for multiple agencies. In addition, he as put more emphasis on the funding of high-speed rail, mass transit, biking and hiking infrastructure.

The Inter-Agency Work Group on Environmental Justice, which was created by Executive Order under President Clinton, was revived by Obama. Too often underrepresented and poor communities are required to bear the burden of governmental decision-making, which brings a larger percentage of environmental pollutants into their communities. Not only were multiple federal agencies reconvened to bring this subject into the foreground of decision-making, but EPA created a computer software program that imbedded environmental justice considerations into EPA's decision-making and project funding.

Obama and the First Lady Michelle Obama installed solar panels on the roof of the White House, and planted an organic garden on the South Lawn. These gestures by the Obamas indicated to Americans across the nation that the First Family had a personal commitment to a greener, healthier lifestyle. Critics, however, were quick to pounce, saying that Obama, in installing solar, was demonstrating the same failures in judgment as one-term President Jimmy Carter did. The First Lady was not immune to being the target negative rhetoric either. Opponents said her organic garden sent an unrealistic message to poor Americans, and if they followed her example of eating organic food, they would both starve, and become obese at the same time.

On the international front, Obama had a weak negotiating position as he entered into the United Nations Framework Convention on Climate Change (UNFCCC) 2009 Copenhagen, and 2010 Cancun meetings, because he did not have climate change legislation in hand. Unfortunately, the Copenhagen and Cancun agreements did not provide for greater GHGs reductions, or a path forward to an agreement once the Kyoto Protocol ends in 2012. During the Copenhagen meeting, Obama displayed boldness by barging into a meeting between China and India and threatening to leave the meeting unless they came to the negotiating table. The Copenhagen meeting ended with the countries agreeing to implement their own domestic programs, but not agreeing to new reductions. The Cancun meeting, which had a very small U.S. delegation and much lower meeting expectations, did provide developing countries with a commitment for $30 billion of 'fast start" assistance by 2012, additional clean energy technology assistance, and the adoption of UN's deforestation program, REDD. While both agreements were much less than most environmentalists would have hoped, if it were not for Obama's leadership, the talks would have totally collapsed.

Rules and Regulations

Within hours of taking office, Obama through his chief of staff Rahm Emanuel, put a halt to all Bush Administration proposed federal regulations, pending a 60-day review by the Obama Administration. This not only included the printing of new or proposed regulations, in the Federal Register, but also the withdrawal of regulations that had not yet been printed. The Obama Administration took proactive action that positively impacted a wide variety of environmental issues, such as, mining, air pollution, logging, appliance efficiency standards and endangered species. It has become a standard procedure for incoming presidents to freeze the regulatory actions of their predecessor, since President Reagan's order in 1981. Gaining control of the federal bureaucracy is one of the challenges of any new president, and Obama took effective action.

One of Obama's most historic achievements was putting the regulatory frame work in place to begin controlling GHGs. The Obama Administration issued a finding that GHGs threaten the public health and welfare. The finding was issued after a thorough examination of the scientific evidence, which determined that GHGs are a primary contributor to global climate change. The findings established the legal basis for EPA to regulate GHG emissions. The Obama Administration followed up and issued a schedule for rules, which in 2011 would begin to regulate GHGs from vehicles, electric utilities and oil refineries.

The Obama Administration demonstrated the innovative nature of its air quality regulatory agenda, when announced that it would pursue a multi-pollutant, regulatory strategy for various industry sectors. He also replaced the Bush Administration's proposed cap-and trade approach to mercury pollution, and set a timetable for a new mercury rule for electric utilities in 2011. In addition, the Obama Administration: (1) reconfigured the Clean Air Interstate Rule; (2) proposed the first new NO2 standard since 1971; and (3) rolled out tighter standards for ozone, soot and toxics from boilers.

However, the implementation of the ozone and the boiler toxic rules were postponed in December 2010. The Obama Administration said the ozone and boiler toxic rules needed further technical review. Some in the environmental community sensed the incoming House Republican majority, after the November 2010 election, may have had an impact these decisions. In addition, the courts had order updates to the National Emission Standards for Hazardous Air Pollutants, but the Obama Administration's draft rules for the first six industries were too weak for many in the environmental community.

The Gulf Oil Spill dramatically showed the environmental consequences of offshore drilling, coming only weeks after Obama announced the opening the south Atlantic, and Gulf coast, to more offshore drilling. The quiet withdrawal of the offshore drilling option in December 2010, in comparison to pomp and circumstance of the original announcement, said it all.

Obama moved rapidly in the examination of new drinking water standards for tetrachloroethylene, trichloroethylene, acrylamide, epichlorohydrin and perchlorate, but was caught flat footed by an independent report on chromium-6. In addition, the Obama Administration's use of voluntary industry standards by the Consumer Product Safety Commission to prevent cadmium poison in children is a pretty low bar. Especially, since the early 2010 voluntary recalls by industry, were for products with lower levels of cadmium than the current voluntary standard.

Other major regulatory and rules actions by Obama include:
- acted swiftly and decisively in moving the federal bureaucracy to advance 15 of 22 appliance efficiency standards that had been lagging for years;
- increased CAFE standards to 34.1 miles per gallon by 2016, has gotten the industry to agree to a new GHG

standard, as well as, a new medium and heavy duty truck standard;
- greatly increased concentrated animal feeding operations (CAFOs) water enforcement and closed the loophole for CAFO self-certification as zero-discharge facilities; and
- adopted the Clinton National Forest Roadless Rule, crafted a new forest management rule, and introduced climate change into forest management plans.

Programs

The creation of green jobs was a major thrust of not only of Obama's environmental agenda, but his economy recovery plan. Obama put several programs in place to bolster green employment training and opportunities. Obama started the Clean Energy Corps (CEC) which provided youth with the experience and vocational path to pursue a career in energy efficiency. CEC was funded out of the $1.1 million budget of the Corporation for National and Community Service. Obama was able modify and increase the funding for the Department of Labor's Veteran's Workforce Investment Program, creating his "Clean Vet Initiative. So that the unemployed could enter the green energy and smart grid workforce, $500 million in workforce training of was funded with American Recovery and Reinvestment Act (Recovery Act) dollars. A total of $2.3 billion from the Recovery Act were allocated by Obama in Advanced Energy Manufacturing Tax Credits to bolster green jobs in solar and wind manufacturing plants

To bolster domestic supplies of energy and increase energy security, Obama more than doubled R&D funding for solar, wind, biomass and geothermal energy resources and technologies. The Obama administration saw the potential to cut the costs of solar power in half, by creating competition between thin film and tradition silicon photovoltaic technologies. Supporting advanced wind turbines design was another Obama strategy to create green jobs, and maintain a strong domestic manufacturing base. Obama increased research on advanced biofuels with an emphasis on bolstering the supply-chain through biorefinery demonstration projects. E15 fuels were approved for use vehicles manufactured in

2007 and later, and B20 vehicles were given flexible/alternative fuel status to provide an incentive for manufacturers to build more. However, the Obama 2011 cellulosic ethanol Renewable Fuel Standard (RFS) was only three percent of the projected level, indicating the challenges cellulosic ethanol was facing in market commercialization.

His Cash for Clunkers Program (CCP), funded by $1 billion in the Recovery Act, was so successful in getting Americans to trade in older cars for more fuel effient new ones, that Congress provide $2 billion for an extension of the effort.. Many in the environmental community believed the efficiency requirements the new vehicles purchased under CCP could have been stricter. Obama has not been able to mandate that all vehicles be flexible fuel vehicles by 2013, or has he been able to convert the White House fleet to plug-in hybrids or have 50 percent of the federal government fleet be plug-in hybrids or all-electric vehicles. The commercialization of lithium-ion battery technology has been an Obama success, with the U.S. projected to supply 40 percent of the world's electric vehicle batteries by 2015.

The Obama believes that at least for the next decade or two, coal is going to remain a major fuel for electricity generation, and for providing Americans with jobs. Obama has decreased annual DOE appropriations for carbon capture and storage (CCS), and clean coal power technology (CCPI), but he has bolstered that research agenda with $3.4 billion of Recovery Act dollars. His administration has funded several CCS and CCPI projects in the hopes of finding a number of economically viable processes for commercialization. The Bush Administration's decision to de-funding FutureGen without proper analysis was inept, at best, or politically motivated, at worst. However, Obama's inclusion of a $1 billion presidential earmark in the Recovery Act for FutureGen, did not enhance the public perception of him as the "Change We Have Been Waiting For" in Washington.

In the energy efficiency arena, Obama established new state and local programs to foster innovation in addressing residential and commercial efficiency issues, many of which involved incentivizing utilities to promote greater energy efficiency. His agencies created new programs to rate home energy efficiency, and developed tools to increase information regarding financing options. The $5 billion low-income Weatherization Assistance Program has been slow to move into implementation, but with new congressional, federal agency and state agency restrictions, it had to develop alternative implementation strategies.

Obama took a leadership position in clean water programs. Funding for the Clean Water and Drinking Water State Revolving were significantly increased under Obama. Innovation was brought to both funds in allowing green infrastructure in the Clean Water Fund, and bringing multi-containment regulation forward in the Drinking Water Fund. Great Lakes, Everglades, Chesapeake Bay and Gulf of Mexico restoration efforts have benefited greatly from Obama's push for more federal involvement. However, Obama under funded conservation programs from the 2008 Farm Bill targeted levels, which makes increasing water quality in rural America more difficult.

Other programmatic actions by Obama included: (1) provided vital support to the nation's mayors in cleaning up brownsfields; (2) taken significant steps to reinstate protections for children's health through the EPA; (3) proposed increased then decreased funding levels for the National Parks; (4) provided level funding of organic certification programs; and (5) initiated reform of organic crop insurance programs.

Congress

Obama quickly found out his administration was not going to get Republican congressional cooperation. Obama said, "The strategy the Republicans were going to pursue was one of sitting on the sidelines, trying to gum up the works. …The unprecedented obstruction that has taken place in the Senate took its toll. Even if you eventually got something done, it would take so long and it would be so contentious, that it send a message to the public that 'Gosh Obama said he was going to come in and change Washington, and its exactly the same, it's more contentious that ever."[12] Senate Minority Leader Mitch McConnell even admitted that his number one priority was not creating jobs for the American people or bolstering the economy, but it was to keep Obama from being a two-term president.[13]

Add to that the fact, that congressional Republicans have never been enamored with renewable energy. Former Republican Senate Majority Leader, Trent Lott had said before the Independent Petroleum Association, "I'm sure all you petroleum folks understand that solar power will solve all our problems. How much money have we blown on that? This is the hippies' program from the seventies and they are still pushing this stuff."[14] Without congressional Republicans even understanding that photovoltaic solar is a high-technology, silicon-wafer product, manufactured by companies such as BP and Siemens, Obama's green agenda was going to have quite an up hill battle.

Early in the Obama Administration many were concerned about whether Obama and Speaker of the House Nancy Pelosi could work together. After a while, those close to the Obama-Pelosi relationship said, "I think (Pelosi) is the one who has kept the steel in the president's back – I think she represents that to Harry Reid, too."[15] Obama and Senate Majority Leader Harry Reid have had a longer, more complicated relationship, than the Obama-Pelosi one, because Obama served with Reid in the Senate.

Obama was able to pass the Recovery Act, on a mostly partisan vote, with great amount of assistance from both Pelosi and Reid. The legislation provided $100 billion in assistance to green jobs, renewable energy, energy efficiency and smart grid. This was the largest public infusion of funds into sustainable technology, and green job creation, in U.S. history. The funds were slow to be granted, however, due to problems with filling positions within agencies.

Obama did not achieve his goal of implementing cap-and-trade climate change legislation. Some commentators have suggested that he not only did not pass climate change legislation, but he also "poisoned the well for the next president."[16] While that remains to be seen, the Waxman-Markey bill did pass the House, once Obama became engaged. The determination of Pelosi, and the House Democrats, was the main reason that the Waxman-Markey bill passed within the first six months of 2009. Some have even suggested that members of the White House staff "seemed inconvenienced when House Speaker Pelosi made climate change a top priotity."[6] If not for the personal relationship between former

Vice President Al Gore and White House chief of staff Emanuel, and Gore convincing him to sit down to go over voting list, Obama may not have called House member to ensure their votes.[17]

When it came to the Senate, Obama never put his reputation on the line for any of the Senate climate change bills. In addition, Obama showed a lack of leadership by not objecting to Reid's multiple delays in taking up climate change legislation, especially because this was supposedly Obama's number one priority. Because Reid had helped Obama through the laborious Senate process to get the 60 votes to pass the Recovery Act, Obama took a hands-off approach, and let Reid take the lead when it came to climate change legislation in the Senate.

Obama had another lapse in leadership when Senator Boxer scheduled a committee vote for the Kerry-Boxer bill, without waiting the five weeks that Republicans requested for an EPA economic analysis. While Boxer was trying to meet the deadline for the UNFCCC Copenhagen meeting to demonstrate U.S. progress, pushing forward without the Republicans on the committee, permanently poisoned the waters for passage of the Kerry-Boxer bill. If Reid would not do it, Obama should have persuaded Boxer to delay the vote for the necessary five weeks to receive the EPA analysis.

Obama successfully extended the renewable energy Production Tax Credits (PTC) for three years under the Recovery Act. Also, he negotiated with Congress for a one-year extension of 1603 tax credit/grant, using the remaining funds from the 1705 renewable loan guarantees that the Energy Bank was not able to process. Earlier, Obama acquiesced to Congress raiding the 1705 renewable energy loan guarantee program to fund the Cash for Clunkers programs and the state government bailout.

With the passage of the the Edward M. Kennedy Serve America Act, Obama was able to create his Clean Energy Corps, giving disadvantaged youth the skills, experience and opportunity to pursue a career path in energy efficiency. In addition, Obama signed two pieces of legislation with significant organic farm provisions, the Healthy, Hungry-Free Kids Act and the Food Safety Modernization Act.

There were numerous pieces of legislation or amendments that remain vital to the Obama environment agenda that did not pass Congress. These include modifications to the Farm Bill, Clean Water Act, and Toxic Substances Control Act, as well as, reinstatement of the Superfund Excise Tax.

In his dealing with Congress, Obama was typically out in front offering concessions. This included his decisions to break his commitment to not allow offshore drilling, his request to increased nuclear loan guarantees, and his postponement of regulating GHGs until 2011.

Courts

The Obama Administration's green agenda has been impacted by the courts. Chu's early work on appliance efficiency standards was in response to court orders, as was Jackson's regulatory agenda on NO2, Clean Air Interstate Rule, soot, and air borne toxics. Taking a more proactive stance, Obama withdrew the Bush Administration appeal for the Supreme Court to review a cap-and-trade approach to mercury pollution from electric utility power plants. The Obama Administration instead, proposed to issue rules limiting mercury emissions by individual facilities. In addition, the Obama Administration joined the environmental community in appealing to the Tenth Circuit Court of Appeals, a ruling that struck down the Clinton Roadless Rules. On the gray wolf lawsuit brought by the environmental community, the court reinstated endangered species protections for the wolves. The court found that the Obama Administration had removed protections from the wolves based on political criteria delineated by state lines, not by a scientific methodology. Currently the courts are reviewing 150 lawsuits brought plaintiffs against EPA's GHG regulations. All the suits have been consolidated into three major cases the challenging the endangerment finding, the tailoring rule, and the light duty vehicle rule.

American Public

Obama, who was elected to office with the highest percentage of popular vote of any first-term president since Lyndon Johnson in 1964, saw his popularity drop in public opinion polls by

10.5 percent in this second year in office.[18] This is fairly typical of presidents facing harsh economic conditions on the domestic front. However, there was another factor in at play. Obama was known for his soaring rhetoric and positive messages during the campaign, talking about the larger issues of "hope," and "change," and "yes, we can." That seemed to end once Obama entered office.

One analyst said, "Republicans routinely speak in broad themes and tend to blur the details, while Democrats typically ignore broad themes and focus on details. The pre-presidential Obama powerfully made this kind of broad, patriotic appeal, both at his 2004 convention keynote address and in his stirring Jefferson-Jackson Day speak in Iowa in November 2007."[19]

Messaging became a real strategic challenge for Obama in his second year, as he seemed to be talking about nuts and bolts, and not visions of what America could be. He dropped his emphasis on green jobs as the year wore on, when the numbers of jobs did not increase as rapidly as everyone would have like. His references to a clean environment, and a healthy economy being linked, seemed to fade. There were three major mistakes that the Obama Administration made in messaging in the summer of 2010. The first was in the aftermath of the Gulf Oil Spill when the administration issued a press release, and officials went on television, to announce that 75 percent of the oil from the spill had disappeared. Remarkably, the Gulf had cleaned itself up in matter of days. The idea that millions of gallons of oil were gone was just not credible. One did not have to be an environmental specialist to know that did not happen. Those public statements and press release damaged the scientific credibility of the Obama Administration.

Second, the Obama Administration allowed the Republicans to brand climate change legislation as "cap-and-tax." This type of language tended to frighten the public and allowed the opposition to dominate in the discussion. The Obama Administration did not hit back hard, demonstrating that climate change legislation was part of the economic recovery, and long-term transition of the nation to cleaner economy. The Republicans were able to take the high ground of protecting the American people from higher costs, or "taxes," rather than Obama's being seen as a bold leader, taking the nation into a better future. Additionally, the cap-and-trade component of global climate change legislation provides market signals, to the real costs of the environmental resources that consumers are utilizing. Cap-and trade was originally a Republican idea, which provided a more flexible alternative to command-and-control environmental regulation. So not only did Obama have a vision of building the energy, and economic future of the nation, he was proposing to do it using Republican free-market principles. Those messages were never sent by the White House.

The third communications issue was also a real policy concern, and a leadership question. President Obama gave his first Oval Office address of his presidency in June 2010, to talk to the American people about the Gulf Oil Spill. This could have been a turning point in moving climate change legislation forward, by linking the oil spill to our nation's addiction to fossil fuels. Instead, he told the nation that we needed to reduce our fossil fuel consumption dramatically, but "we do not know precisely how we are going to get there."[17]

Not only did Obama have a policy and messaging problem, but he had an outreach issue as well. The candidate who had stunned the world with his campaign's mastery of the internet, and was heralded as the first internet president, had dismantled that machine at the end of his campaign. Email addresses and contact information for those dedicated to the Obama Presidency were transferred to the Organizing for America site. While email alerts were sent out from Organizing for America to those who had been interested and involved in the campaign, they came either from unknown individuals, or were copies of Obama Administration messages found on government websites. None of these messages ever inspired or mobilized the recipients, they way the ones during the campaign did.

In addition, many of those on the campaign who worked on policy groups, found there was no role for them once the transition and administration started. For example, the 500 members of Obama's Energy and Environment Work Group, who were the brain trust in during the campaign on energy and environmental issues, were told to join the eepolicy@groups.google.com.[20] No one from the transition or administration ever posted anything there, and in a couple of months, the board was filled with pornographic spam. The Obama Administration lost the services of 500 talented people, just in the energy and environmental field, who could have been useful later. It was unfortunate that Obama's internet campaign never developed a plan to become the Obama internet presidency.

Final Analysis

In moving his green agenda forward, Obama has not stolen the freedom or wealth of American citizens, as his rightwing critics had warned. The Obama Administration has not established neighborhood block captains, to ensure that Americans car pool to work, or to recycle their cans and bottles. No in-home surveillance systems have been mandated, to monitor whether families use energy-efficient lights, organic foods or smart metered electricity. Americans can still buy gas-guzzling SUVs, and purchase energy-hog homes with tens of thousands of square feet. Obama did add to the deficit. He invested $100 billion of the $787 billion Recovery Act in clean technology and green jobs, which is the largest commitment in U.S. history to sustainable infrastructure. However, this $100 billion added to the deficit, pales in comparison to the $2.1 trillion in Bush Administration tax cuts provided during the years 2001-2010.[21] Those tax cuts not only added to the deficit, but under funded U.S. infrastructure, and were paid with money borrowed from China.

The environmental beliefs of Obama are genuine. He has not betrayed the environmental community by using their support as a stepping stone, just to gain the political power of the presidency. As opposed to what some on the left may say, Obama has certainly not had a failed environmental presidency. He has advanced U.S. environment policy across the board, including everything from regulation of GHGs, support for green energy deployment, promotion of energy efficiency though stringent appliance standards, increased enforcement of clean water from CAFOs, protection of vast acres of wilderness in the West from commercial development, adoption of the Clinton Roadless Rule in National Forests and a myriad of other environmental initiatives.

Obama put environmental protection, climate change, green jobs and renewable energy, front and center in his administration. Green technologies have come along way since 1952, when the President Truman ignored his own Materials Policy Commission's recommendation to establish a federal agency to develop the potential of solar energy.[22] Thirty years before Obama's election, President Carter's DOE was reluctant to even participate in the very first Sun Day promoting renewable energy development.[22]

Obama was the first president to bring the concept of economic development and job creation through investment in green technologies to the federal level. However, the idea was not new. Since the 1980s, there have been numerous state and multi-state initiatives that have promoted the green jobs and economic development potential of clean energy technologies to benefit urban and rural areas.[23]

Obama led the first presidential administration that recognized the economic development potential of green jobs, and brought it to the federal level as a major policy initiative. He and his advisors married the short-term Recovery Act investments in green jobs, to the long-term market development impacts that climate change legislation would create in green industries.

Obama said it best, "The choice we face is not between saving our environment and saving our economy. The choice we face is between prosperity and decline. We can remain the world's leading importer of oil, or we can become the world's leading exporter of clean energy. We can allow climate change to wreak unnatural havoc across the landscape, or we can create jobs working to prevent its worst effects. We can hand over the jobs of the 21st Century to our competitors, or we can confront what countries in Europe and Asia have already recognized as both a challenge and an opportunity: The nation that leads the world in creating new energy sources will be the nation that leads the 21st Century global economy.[24]

Unfortunately, Obama's vision for the long-term market potential of climate change legislation has not been realized. Again, the nation has provided roller coaster funding to the renewable and energy efficiency industries, which has helped in the short-term, but ultimately did not truly build their capacities to succeed. More importantly, America did not experience the transformation of the economy, or the expansion of green jobs that the Recovery Act, and climate change legislation were targeted to achieve.

One commentator concluded, "In this context, it's clear that Obama stumbled in his quest to become a Reaganlike transformational leader. By pursing health care reform and climate legislation before satisfying a more basic concern of the American people – economic security – the president alienated some of his key supporters."[25] That assessment is incorrect, because it has the situation backwards. Climate change legislation would have provided that economic security. While it was true that health care reform would not create thousands of jobs and bolster economic vitality, climate change legislation would have. Climate change legislation was the central core of the Obama economic recovery package, and the long-term transformation of the American economy. It is precisely because Obama did not use all the tools in the presidential tool box, to pass climate change legislation, that he has not yet achieved the status of being a transformational president.

Let's look at the reasons. Obama made very good nominations and appointments to advance a strong environmental agenda. Using the tools of the executive branch at the disposal of Obama and his cabinet, they have achieved many of the goals of greater environmental protection. This includes signing executive orders, issuing new rules and regulations, and rolling out new programs. Most of Obama's environmental cabinet, and White House personnel choices, were solid individuals, with good backgrounds in their fields. They were not the most the most dynamic choices, and did not bring the media recognition or the inspiration of an environmentalist, like a Robert F. Kennedy Jr. But they have pushed the envelope on what can be achieved through government programs, rules and regulations. Obama's leadership in nominations and appointments has been between transactional and transformative.

President Obama's abilities, and at times his desires, to move an obstinate Congress on environmental issues, were not always in evidence. Some aspects of Obama's congressional relations could have been enhanced by engaging in more dialogue with the Republican leadership, and in not being so reluctant to get on the phone to push Democratic members. The Recovery Act passed Congress, the Waxman-Markey bill passed the House and Kerry-Boxer passed committee, all with deep party-lines votes. On the other hand, when the White House negotiated directly with Congress over the December 2010 tax bill, which passed with overwhelming majorities, the renewable energy industry saw the successful extensions of the 1603 renewable energy tax credit, ethanol tax credits, ethanol tariffs and biodiesel tax credits.

However, rather than engage with Capitol Hill during his first two years, Obama chose to try to lead Congress with an attitude of compromise, rather than with advocacy. Before he asked Republicans to offer anything, he committed himself to increases in nuclear power loan authority, opening up the Atlantic Coast to offshore drilling and postponing the enforcement of GHG regulations until 2011. Obama seemed to be negotiating with himself. He offered congressional Republicans exactly what they wanted, before they engaged in any discussions, so there was no reason for them to come to the table.

His compromise stance included his decision not to outline the details of the climate change bill that he wanted, and to allow the multiple delays of Majority Leader Reid in pushing climate change legislation off the agenda for other matters. Obama had said that climate change was his number one priority. Unfortunately, he never insisted to members of his own party that climate change was number one, and that it was critical to the economic recovery and job creation.

There were several pieces of legislation that were vital to the Obama environmental agenda in which he did not take on the entrenched interests, or develop a strategy to successfully engage with Congress. The eligibility rules for farm subsides in the Farm Bill need to be changed, especially the criteria for "actively engaged in farming." In addition, the Farm Bill provision for EQIP dollars going to large and/or expanding CAFOs should be removed. EPA's regulatory authority over wetlands should be fully restored in light of the Supreme Court's "navigable waters" ruling. Updating of Toxic Substances Control Act to the 21st century by stripping out the clauses that grandfather 80,000 chemical from regulation and providing a funding stream for regulatory review, would help ensure the long-term health of Americans. Additionally, the Superfund Excise Tax with its "polluter pays" provisions needs to be reinstated, so site clean up can be accelerated, and not be paid from taxpayer dollars.

Presidential leadership with Congress on environmental issues may have been lost in the fog of governance, given the fact that the White House staff was burnt out dealing with Obama's second priority, health care. By 2010, senior advisor, David Axelrod, was so fed up over the horse trading with Capitol Hill to move legislation, the advice he was giving to Obama was, "Fuck whatever Congress wants, we're not for them."[26] Overall, Obama has demonstrated a strategy between laissez-faire and transactional in his dealings with Congress.

Obama really needed to use the bully pulpit more often to influence the public that his environmental agenda was good for the future of both the health and economy of our nation. This could partially be accomplished by participating in a greater number of media interviews, press conference and addresses to the nation; where he puts his reputation on the line for environmental goals.

Obama displayed a lacked courage and leadership, when he let down the nation and the American people, during his Gulf Oil Spill address from the Oval Office. Obama did not seize the singular chance that history provided to him, to take America's biggest environmental disaster, and address it with dramatic environmental change - change that would have benefited the nation, the economy, and the generations to come. He did not use the Gulf Oil Spill to pursue a historic transformation of the American economy and energy use, by rallying the public, and endorsing climate change legislation. He gave up a once in a lifetime opportunity to pursue the larger moral argument, at the perfect moment in time for public education. When America had been watching daily, the environmentally disastrous consequences of its addiction to fossil fuels, it was a time that called for transformational presidential leadership. Overall, Obama's leadership in use of the bully pulpit to advance environmental issues has only been laissez-faire.

The high-tech internet tools that helped to elect Obama, were abandoned at the end of the presidential race. They were not available to be utilized to communicate with Obama supporters, in order to effectively pressure Congress to vote for environmental legislation of importance to the president and the nation. Of course, there are federal election laws that regulate what a President can do in public communications. However, it would be worth the investment of time to reconsider the situation, and develop a groundbreaking internet mobilization plan for future governance. While Obama may have been the nation's first successful internet presidential candidate, he has not yet become the nation's first internet president.

Obama, during his first two years in office, has been a good environmental president, maybe even a great environmental president, just by using the tools of the executive branch. He has not yet demonstrated that he is a transformational environmental president. The next two years, and possibly six years, will provide the answer to whether Obama adopts the strategies to become a truly transformational environmental president.

NOTES

Chapter 1. Introduction
1. "Joe Biden Biography," http://www.biography.com/articles/Joe-Biden-39995
2. "Rahm Emanuel Biography," http://www.biography.com/articles/Rahm-Emanuel-381074
3. Hendrix, Steve, and Michael D. Stone, *The Washington Post*, "Chief of Staff Pick's Flair for the Well-Timed Verbal Hand Grenade is Legendary," November 7, 2008.
4. *U.S. News*, "The Obama Team: Latest White House Staffers," November 19, 2008.
5. *The New York Times*, "David Pfouffe," January 25, 2010.
6. "Steven Chu Biography," http://www.biography.com/articles/Steven-Chu-9247820
7. Beinecke, Frances, *The Huffington Post*, "The Environmental Appointments: Obama Means What He Says," December 12, 2008.
8. Weisman, Jonathan, *The Wall Street Journal*, "Obama Picks Team to Guide Energy, Environmental Agendas," December 11, 2008.
9. *The New York Times*, "Ken Salazar," http://projects.nytimes.com/44th_president/new_team/show/ken-salazar
10. Brady, Jeff, *NPR News*, "Sen. Salazar Appointment Draws Mixed Reaction," December 16, 2008.
11. *The New York Times*, "Tom Vilsack," http://projects.nytimes.com/44th_president/new_team/show/tom-vilsack
12. Burros, Marian, *Politico*, "Obama Ag Policies Sow Confusion," February 11, 2010.
13. Romero, Frances, *Time*, "Energy Czar: Carol Browner," December 15, 2008.
14. Climate Solutions, "Van Jones Biography," http://climatesolutions.org/solutions/van-jones-biography
15. "Larry Summers Biography,' http://www.browsebiography.com/bio-larry_summers.html
16. Skomarovsky, Matthew, *Greanville Post*, "Evidence of an American Plutocracy: The Larry Summers Story,' January 10, 2011.
17. "The Council on Environmental Quality – Chair Nancy Sutley," http://www.whitehouse.gov/administration/eop/ceq/chair
18. "111th United States Congress," http://www.sourcewatch.org/index.php?title=111th_United_States_Congress
19. "About Harry Reid," http://reid.senate.gov/about/

20. "Mitch McConnell," http://www.sourcewatch.org/index.php?title=Mitch_McConnell
21. League of Conservation Voters, "LCV Members Elect Senate Minority Leader Mitch McConnell the New Don of the 'Dirty Dozen,'" April 8, 2008.
22. "Nancy Pelosi Biography," http://www.biography.com/articles/Nancy-Pelosi-38487
23. "Biography U.S. Representative John Boehner (OH-8)," http://johnboehner.house.gov/Biography/
24. Galbraith, Kate, *The New York Times*, "Boehner: Calling Carbon Dioxide Dangerous Is 'Almost Comical,'" April 21, 2009.
25. "Barbara Boxer Biography," http://www.biography.com/articles/Barbara-Boxer-597336
26. "Barbara Boxer," http://en.wikipedia.org/wiki/Barbara_Boxer
27. "Biography Representative Henry A Waxman 30th District of California," http://www.henrywaxman.house.gov/Biography/
28. *The Sun's Financial Diary*, "November 2008 Monthly Unemployment Rate at 15-Year High – Chart of the Day," December 5, 2008.
29. Allen, Mike, *Politico*, "Candidate Split on Strength of Economy," September 15, 2008.
30. "United States Presidential Election 2008," http://en.wikipedia.org/wiki/United_States_presidential_election_2008
31. Wagner, Mitch, *Information Week*, "Obama Election Ushering in First Internet Presidency," November 5, 2008.
32. Stone, Daniel, and Daniel Lyons, *Newsweek*, "Obama Harnessed the Grassroots Power of the Web to Get Elected. How Will He Use That Power Now?," November 22, 2008.
33. Horner, Christopher, *Power Grab: How Obama's Green Policies Will Steal Your Freedom and Bankrupt America*, Regnery Publishing Inc., Washington, DC, 2010, pg. 306.
34. Spencer, Roy, W., *The Bad Science and Bad Policy of Obama's Global Warming Agenda*, Encounter Books, New York, NY, 2010, pp. 37-38.
35. Pooley, Eric, *The Climate Wars, True Believers, Power Brokers, and the Fight to Save the Earth*, Hyperion, New York, NY, 2010, pg. 360.
36. Knickerbocker, Brad, *The Christian Science Monitor*, "Activists Frustrated at Obama's Environmental Record," July 25, 2010.
37. The Obama campaign promises listed in italics in Chapters 2-11 are taken from a number of documents. Most of the promises appear as they do in the campaign literature. Some promises where listed differently in different campaign documents. At times, those were differences in wording, and in others, they were differences in substance. In the later cases, the author has combined promises and eliminated duplicate content. In addition, the author has separated some promises into different categories, and, in other cases, has reformatted some promises for either brevity or appearance. The author has tried to stay true to campaign's intent, but apologizes in

advance he has inadvertently skewed any of the substance any of the promises. The documents used to compile the promises are:
Barack Obama and Joe Biden: Promoting a Healthy Environment.
http://www.barackobama.com/pdf/issues/EnvironmentFactSheet.pdf
Barack Obama and Joe Biden: New Energy for America.
http://www.barackobama.com/pdf/factsheet_energy_speech_080308.pdf
Barack Obama and Joe Biden: Strengthening America's Transportation Infrastructure.
http://www.barackobama.com/pdf/issues/FactSheetTransportation.pdf
Rural Leadership for Rural America.
http://www.barackobama.com/pdf/issues/RuralPlanFactSheet.pdf
Barack Obama: Supporting the Rights and Traditions of Sportmen..
http://www.barackobama.com/pdf/issues/additional/Obama_FactSheet_Western_Sportsmen.pdf
The Great Lakes, Chesapeake Bay and Everglades promises came from the 2008 Democratic Platforms.
http://www.democrats.org/party_platform
The Endangered Species Act promise came from
http://glassbooth.org/explore/index/barack-obama/11/environment-and-energy/7/

Chapter 2. Climate Change
1. *The New York Times*, "Transcript Barack Obama's Inaugural Address," January 20, 2009.
2. Pooley, Eric, *The Climate Wars, True Believers, Power Brokers, and the Fight to Save the Earth*, Hyperion, New York, NY, 2010, pg. 311.
3. Goldenberg, Suzanne, *The Guardian*, "Obama's Energy Secretary Outlines Dire Climate Change Scenario, February 4, 2009.
4. Lerer, Lisa, *Politico*, Climate Change to Bring Drought, Bugs, June 16, 2009.
5. Krugman, Paul, *The New York Times*, "Climate Change," Febuary 27, 2009.
6. *The New York Times*, Transcript President Obama's Address to Congress, February 24, 2009.
7. Pooley, Eric, *The Climate Wars, True Believers, Power Brokers, and the Fight to Save the Earth*, Hyperion, New York, NY, 2010, pg. 326.
8. Murray, James, *Business Green*, "Team Obama Hints at Delay to Climate Change Bill," February 24, 2009.
9. Lerer, Lisa, *Politico*, "Obama Officials Push Carbon Caps," April 22, 2009.
10. Javers, Eamon, *Politico*, "Obama Hears Concerns on Climate Plan,' May 20, 2009.
11. Lerer, Lisa, *Politico*, "Lawmakers Release Strict Carbon Plan," April 1, 2009.

12. O'Connor, Patrick, Politico, "Pelosi Vows Global Warming Bill by 2010.. April 2, 2009.
13. Lerer, Lisa, *Politico*, "Emission Bill Fuels Fight in Congress," April 7, 2009.
14. Climate Progress, "EPA Analysis of Waxman-Markey," http://climateprogress.org/2009/04/21/waxman-markey-epa-analysis/
15. Kucinich, Jackie, *Roll Call*, "Republicans Accuse EPA of Fuzzy Math," April 24, 2009.
16. Smith, Art, *The Conservative Reader*, "Tax and Trade Alert," June 30, 2009. http://theconservativereader.com/2009/06/30/tax-and-trade-alert/
17. Tapper Jake, ABC News, "President Talks Climate Change, 'Cash for Clunkers,' with House Democrats," May 5. http://blogs.abcnews.com/politicalpunch/2009/05/president-talks.html 2009.
18. Sheppard, Kate, *Grist*, "'Cause He's the Waxman," May 21, 2009.
19. Allen, Jared, *The Hill*, "Dem Mutiny on Climae Bill Grows, Says Peterson," June 10, 2009.
20. Lerer, Lisa, and Patrick O'Connor, *Politico*, "Dems May Make Trouble for Climate Bill," May 22, 2009.
21. Lerer, Lisa, *Politico*, "Ethanol Proposal May Derail Climate Bill," May 26, 2009.
22. Latta, Bob, *The Hill*, "GOP's Better Alternative to Waxman-Markey Bill," June 15, 2009.
23. Lerer, Lisa, *Politico*, "Four Keys to Solving Energy Stalemate," June 23, 2009.
24. Dickenson, Tim, *Rolling Stone*, "Climate Bill, R.I.P.," July 21, 2010.
25. Lerer, Lisa, and Patrick O'Connor, *Politico*, "House Democrats Strike Deal on Climate Bill," June 24, 2009.
26. Youngman, Sam, *The Hill*, Obama Presses House on Energy Bill, June 25, 2009.
27. Mulfason, Steven, and David A. Fahrenthold and Paul Kane. *The Washington Post,* "In Close Vote House Passes Climate Bill," June 27, 2009.
28. O'Connor, Patrick, and Glenn Thrush, *Politico*, "2010 Complete Election Coverage: Chaos and Arm-Twisting Gives Pelosi a Major Win," June 30, 2009.
29. Pew Center on Global Climate Change, "Pew Center Summary of H.R. 2454: American Clean Energy and Security Act of 2009 (Waxman-Markey)," http://www.pewclimate.org/docUploads/waxman-markey-detailed-summary-july2009.pdf
30. Snyder, Jim, *The Hill*, "EIA Says Cost of Climate Bill Modest at First," August 3, 2009.
31. Snyder, Jim, *The Hill*, "Climate Bill Could Cost 2 Million Jobs," August 12, 2009.

32. U.S. Senate, "Senate Action on Cloture Motions," http://www.senate.gov/pagelayout/reference/cloture_motions/clotureCounts.htm
33. Lerer, Lisa, *Politico*, "Carbon Plan Faces Senate Hurdle," March 25, 2009.
34. Murray, Matthew, *Roll Call*, Union Set Their Sights on Climate Change Bill," July 8, 2009.
35. Palmer, Anna, *Roll Call*, "Farms Groups Split Over Cap-and-Trade," July 29, 2009.
36. Meet the Press Transcript for June 28, 2009. http://www.msnbc.msn.com/id/31584983/ns/meet_the_press/
37. Lerer, Lisa, *Politico*, "Climate Push Gets Personal," July 17, 2009.
38. Lerer, Lisa, *Politico*, "Complete Election Coverage: Energizing the Senate Cap-and-Trade Bill, June 30, 2009.
39. Kowalski, Jason, *The SkyWriter*, "DC Hill Update: the Looming ACES Vote," June 16, 2009. http://www.1sky.org/blog/2009/06/dc-hill-update-the-looming-aces-vote
40. Kane, Paul, *The Washington Post*, "Push and Pull in Senate May Recast Climate Bill," July 7, 2009.
41. Cowan, Richard, *Reuters*, "Obama's Drive for Climate Change Hits Delay," July 9, 2009.
42. Lizza, Ryan, *The New Yorker*, "As the World Burns," October 11, 2010.
43. Dickenson, Tim, *Rolling Stone*, "Climate Bill, R.I.P.," July 21, 2010.
44. Gertz, Emily, change.org, "Breaking: Reid Says climate Bill May Wait Until Next Year," September 15, 2009. http://news.change.org/stories/breaking-reid-says-climate-bill-may-wait-until-2010
45. Lerer, Lisa, *Politico*, "Critics Warm to Boxer's Climate Role," October 27, 2009.
46. Pew Center on Global Climate Change, "Summary of the Clean Energy Jobs and American Power Act (S. 1733) Chairman's Mark," http://www.pewclimate.org/short-summary/clean-energy-jobs-american-power-act-chairmans-mark
47. Lerer, Lisa, *Politico*, "GOP Sens. To Boycott Climate Hearing," November 2, 2009.
48. Senate Committee Agriculture, Nutrition and Forestry New, "Ranking Republicans Seek Satisfactory Analysis of EPA Climate Bill," November 2, 2009. http://216.40.253.202/~usscanf/index.php?option=com_content&task=view&id=1959&Itemid=2
49. Cowan, Richard, *Reuters*, "Senate Panel Approves Democratic Climate Bill," November 5, 2009.
50. Lomax, Simon, *Bloomberg*, "Senate Democrats Pass Carbon Plan Over GOP Boycott (Update2)," November 5, 2009.
51. Snyder, Jim, *The Hill*, "Cantwell-Collins Bill Attracts Support from Some, Loses Others," December 14, 2009.

52. Lerer, Lisa, *Politico*, "Jim Webb Bails on Cap-and-Trade," November 11, 2009.
53. Lerer, Lisa, *Politico*, "Details of Climate Bill Trickle Out," March 24, 2010.
54. About Senator Graham Blog, "Letter on Energy Independence," April 26, 2010. http://lgraham.senate.gov/public/index.cfm?FuseAction=AboutSenatorGraham.Blog&ContentRecord_id=3ae9d334-802a-23ad-46e6-aeda268372be
55. CBS News, "Reid: I'll Do Climate Bill Before Immigration," April 27, 2010.
56. Palmer, Anna, *Roll Call*, "Kerry, Lieberman Gather Allies for Climate Bill," May 13, 2010.
57. Samuelsohn, Darren, and Coral Davenport, *Politico*, "Dems Pull Plug on Climate Bill," July 22, 2010.
58. Obama Campaign Documents, "Energy and Environment Team, Briefing Summary, July 7 and 8, 2008."
59. Personal Conversation with Jason Grumet, March 4, 2009.
60. Konceslik, Joe, Ohio Environmental Law Blog, "Climate Update SEC Guidance,EPA and Cap-and-Trade," February 2, 2010.
61. German, Ben and Sam Youngham, *The Hill*, "Cautious Obama Joins Climate Fray," March 10, 2010.
62. Cummings, Jean, *Politico*, "Transcript: Interview with Carol Browner," April 22, 2010.
63. Samuelsohn, Darren, *Politico*, "Lieberman: Pay $1 a Day for Climate," June 15, 2010.
64. Samuelsohn, Darren, *Politico*, "Deadly Silence on Carbon Caps," June 15, 2010.
65. Bolton, Alexander, *The Hill*, "Climate Change Legislation Teetering After Setbacks from Oval Office and Congress," Jume 16, 2010
66. D'Aprile, Shane, *The Hill E2 Wire*, "Browner: Energy Bill Success Still Possible Before End of the Year," August 8, 2010
67. Wenner, Jann S., *Rolling Stone*, "Obama in Command: The Rolling Stone Interview," September 2010.
68. Romm, Joseph, *Grist*, "The Failed Presidency of Barack Obama, Post-Election Edition," November 4, 2010.
69. Lerer, Lisa, *Politico*, "EPA: Global Warming a Health Hazard," April 17, 2009.
70. U.S. Environmental Protection Agency, "EPA: Greenhouse Gases Threaten Public Health and the Environmental/Science Overwhelmingly Shows Greenhouse Gas Concentrations at Unprecedented Levels Due to Human Activity, "December 7, 2009.
71. Georgetown Climate Center, "Issue Brief: What States Should Know About EPA Regulation of Greenhouse Gas Emissions," January 7, 2010.

72. Pierce, Emily, and Steven T. Dennis, *Roll Call*, "Centrists Hit EPA Maneuver," April 22, 2009.
73. Stanton, John, *Roll Call*, "Murkowski Looks to Block EPA Carbon Emissions Limits," December 14, 2009.
74. Shiner, Meredith, *Politico*, "Senate Rejects EPA Carbon Challenge, June 10, 2010.
75. Lerer, Lisa, *Politico*, "EPA Defends Greenhouse Gas Caps, March 8, 2010.
76. Werner, Carol, Environmental and Energy Study Institute, "House Republicans Introduce Resolution to Block EPA Action on Greenhouse Gases," March 8, 2010.
77. Lott, John R. John Lott's Website Blog, "Battle between the Chamber of Commerce and EPA Over Climate Rules," June 21, 2009. http://johnrlott.blogspot.com/2009_06_21_archive.html
78. Samuelsohn, Darren, *Politico*, "EPA Rejects Challenge to Climate Rules," July 29, 2010.
79. United Nations Framework Convention on Climate Change, "Kyoto Protocol," http://unfccc.int/kyoto_protocol/items/2830.php
80. Allen, Mike, *Politico*, "HRC Names Envoy for Climate Change," January 27, 2009.
81. The Washington Post, "Transcript: President Obama Delivers Remarks at G8 Summit," July 9, 2009.
82. America.gov, "White House Press Briefing by Mike Froman and Todd Stern," July 9, 2010. http://www.america.gov/st/texttrans-english/2009/July/20090710101537xjsnommis0.9978144.html
83. Wintour, Patrick, and Larry Elliott, *The Guardian*, "G8 Summit: Brack Obama Says World Can Close the Carbon Emissions Gap," July
84. Alarkton, Walter, and J. Taylor Rush, *The Hill*, "Upper Chamber Bristles at Criticism from Abroad on Climate Change Pace," September 22, 2009.
85. Off the Cuff, "Secretary-General's joint press encounter with U.S. Senators John Kerry, Richard Lugar and Joe Lieberman (unofficial transcript of Secretary-General"s portion only)," November 10, 2009. http://www.un.org/apps/sg/offthecuff.asp?nid=1345
86. Allen, Mike, *Politico*, "Obama: Little Chance of Climate Deal," November 14, 2009.
87. America,gov, "China, United States Urge Comprehensive Climate Change Agreement," November 17, 2009. http://www.america.gov/st/energy-english/2009/November/20091117140130esnamfuak4.710025e-02.html
88. Javers, Eamon, *Politico*, "Green Groups Split on Danish Idea," November 17, 2009.
89. Allen, Mike, *Politico*, "Obama Going to Copenhagen," November 25, 2009.

90. Lerer, Lisa, *Politico*, "W.H. Raises Climate Summit Stakes," December 4, 2009.
91. Stanton, John, *Roll Call*, "GOP Senators Escalate Climate Battle," December 17, 2009.
92. Good, Chris, *The Atlantic*, "Inhofe on Obama's Trip to Copenhagen," November 2009.
93. Thrust, Glenn, *Politico*, "China Tells U.S.: No Deal," December 17, 2009.
94. Gray, Louise, and Rowena Mason, *The Telegraph*, "Copenhagen Climate Conference: Hillary Clinton Attempts to Break Deadlock with $100bn Offer, December 17, 2009.
95. Eilperin, Juliet, and Anthony Faiola, *The Washington Post*, "Climate Deal Falls Short on Key Goals," December 19, 2009.
96. German, Ben, *The Hill*, "Obama Departs Fractious Copenhagen Talks with Limited Pact," December 18, 2009.
97. Lerer, Lisa, *Politico*, "U.N. Chief Scientists Slams 'Climategate,'" December 7, 2009.
98. Hickman, Leo, and James Randerson, *The Guardian*, "Climate Sceptics Claim Leaked Emails are Evidence of Collusions Among Scientists," November 20, 2009.
99. Ball, Jeffery, *The Wall Street Journal*, "Climate Panel Faces Heat," August 31, 2010
100. MacFarquhar, Neil, *The New York Times*, "Review Finds Flaws in U.N. Climate Panel Structure," August 30, 2010.
101. Jervey, Ben, *Good*, "So What Happened at the Cancun Climate Talks Anyway? An Insider's Account," January 12, 2011. http://www.good.is/post/cancun-climate-talks-an-insider-s-account/
102. U.S. Department of State, "Remarks Todd Stern, Briefing on the UN Climate Change Conference in Cancun," December 14, 2010.

Chapter 3. Green Jobs
1. *The New York Times*, "Transcript Barack Obama's Inaugural Address," January, 20, 2009.
2. Pooley, Eric, *The Climate War*, 2010, pg. 311.
3. Garthwaite, Josie, *Clean2Tech,* "Gore Urges Lawmakers to Pass Stimulus, Start Cap-and-Trade," January 28, 2009.
4. Herszenhorn, David M., *The New York Times*, "Recovery Bill Gets Final Approval," February 14, 2009.
5. *The New York Times*, "Times Topics Economic Stimulus (Jobs Bills)," December 15, 2010.
6. Weiss, Daniel J. and Alexandra Kougentakis, The Center for America Progress, "Recovery Plan Captures the Energy Opportunity, February 13, 2009.
7. *The New York Times*, "Transcript President Obama's Address to Congress," February 24, 2009

8. Baker, Peter, *The New York Times*, "Obama Team Has Billions to Spend, but Few Ready to Do It," February 18, 2009.
9. Personal Conversation with Jason Grumet, March 4, 2009.
10. Schatz, Amy, *The Wall Street Journal*, "Some Agencies are Slow in Handing Out Stimulus Grants," March 2, 2009.
11. Westervelt, Amy, Solve Climate News, "Handing out $32 Billion in Cleantech Stimulus Grants a Slow Process for DOE," June 11, 2010.
12. *The New York Times*, "Transcript Obama's Speech on Renewable Energy Policy," October 24, 2009.
13. Office of the Press Secretary, The White House, "Vice President Biden CEA Chair Romer Release New Analysis on Job and Economic Impact of the Recovery Act," July 14, 2010.
14. Office of the Press Secretary, The White House, "President Obama Awards $2.3 Billion for New Clean-Tech Manufacturing Jobs," January 8, 2010.
15. Office of the Press Secretary, The White House, "Remarks by the President on Jobs and Clean Energy," January 8, 2010.
16. *The Los Angeles Times*, "Obama Calls for $5 Billion in Clean Energy Tax Credits," July 9, 2010.
17. Lee, Carol E., *Politico*, "Obama's Clean Energy Kick Continues," July 9, 2010.
18. Avro, Samuel R., *Consumer Energy Report*, Obama: Clean Energy Policy Will Lead to 800,000 Jobs in 2 Years," August 17, 2010.
19. *Environmental News Service*, "Clean Energy Corps Proposed to Create Jobs, Fight Global Warming," March 2, 2009.
20. Prouty, Sally T., Eugene Sofer, Judy Karasik and Sarah Stankorb, The Corps Network, *The Clean Energy Service Corps*, June 2009.
21. Richert, Catharine, politifact.com, "Create Jobs Training Programs for Clean Energy Technologies, January 8, 2010. http://www.politifact.com/truth-o-meter/promises/obameter/promise/467/create-job-training-programs-for-clean-technologie/
22. Jenkins, Leigh, The White House Blog, "Educating the New Generation of Environmental Stewards, September 27, 2010. http://www.whitehouse.gov/blog/2010/09/27/educating-next-generation-environmental-stewards
23. U.S. Department of Labor, "Veterans Workforce Investment Program (VWIP): Factsheet." http://www.dol.gov/vets/programs/vwip/vwip_fs.htm
24. National Coalition for Homeless Veterans, "DOL-VETS FY 2010 Budget Brief," May 11, 2009. http://www.nchv.org/news_article.cfm?id=541
25. The Vice President of the United States, Middle Class Task Force, *Staff Report, Green Jobs: A Pathway to a Strong Middle Class*.
26. Wilson, Reid, *The Hill*, "Biden Hails Green Jobs; Sierra Club Opposes Energy Bill," June 17, 2009.

27. Bureau of Labor Statistics, U.S. Department of Labor, "Measuring Green Jobs." http://www.bls.gov/green/#definition
28. The Vice President of the United States, Middle Class Task Force, *Green Jobs Update*.
29. *The Wall Street Journal*, "Obama and the Left, The Lesson of the Rise and Fall of Van Jones," September 8, 2009.
30. Barbash, Fred and Harry Siegel, *Politico*, Van Jones Resigns Amid Conttroversy, September 6, 2009.
31. Zichal Heather, The White House Blog, "Progress on Green Jobs from the Recovery Act," January 14, 2010. http://www.whitehouse.gov/blog/2010/01/14/progress-green-jobs-recovery-act
32. Hincha-Ownby, Melissa, *Mother Nature Network*, "Obama's Budget Includes Green Jobs Funding," February 2, 2010.
33. *The Economist*, "Green Jobs Debate," March 11, 2010, http://www.economist.com/debate/days/view/481
34. Fletcher, Michael A.., *The Washington Post*, "Retrained for Green Jobs, But Still Waiting on Work," November, 22, 2010.

Chapter 4. Energy Generation

1. Sissine, Fred, Congressional Research Service, The Library of Congress, *Renewable Energy R&D Funding History: A Comparison with Funding for Nuclear Energy, Fossil Energy, and Energy Efficiency R&D*, Order Code RS22858, April 9, 2008.
2. Goldberg, Marshall, Renewable Energy Policy Project, *Federal Subsidies: Not All Technologies are Created Equal*, Research Report No. 11, July 2000.
3. Kammen, Daniel, "Renewable Energy Options for the Emerging Economy: Advances, Opportunities and Obstacles," background paper for The 10-15 Solution: Technologies and Policies for a Low Carbon Future, Pew Center and NCEP Conference, Washington, DC March 25-26, 2004.
4. Office of the President of the United States and Office of the Vice President of the United States, *The Recovery Act: Transforming the American Economy through Innovation*, August 2010.
5. *EERE Network News*, "DOE Requests $2.4 Billion for Renewable Energy, Efficiency in FY 2011, February 3, 2010.
6. U.S. Department of Energy, "Obama Administration Announces Plans to Install New Solar Panels on the White House Residence," October 5, 2010.
7. Broder, John M., *The New York Times*, "White House Going Solar – Again," October 5, 2010.
8. Office of the Vice President of the United States, "Memorandum for the President, Progress Report: The Transformation to a Clean Energy Economy," December 15, 2009.
9. Shiner, Meredith, Politico, "Dems Hit Agency on Energy Plan,"March 4, 2010.

10. PPA Partners Inc., Blog, "Senate Considers Tighter 'Buy American' Rules for Renewable Projects, March 23, 2010. http://ppapartners.com/news/industry-news/senate_buy_american/421174
11. Lombardi, Kristen and John Solomon, The Center for Public Integrity, *Big Pollutors Freed from Environmental Oversight by Stimulus*, November 28, 2010.
12. Goode, Darren, *The Hill*, "Energy Department Watchdog Notes Woes with Managing Stimulus Dollars," August 15, 2010.
13. Walsh, Bryan, Time Blog Ecocentric, "Robbing Renewable Energy to Pay Teachers," August 10, 2010. http://ecocentric.blogs.time.com/2010/08/10/robbing-renewable-energy-to-pay-teachers/
14. Richert, Catharine, politifact.com, "Create Clean Technology Venture Capital Fund," January 7, 2010. http://www.politifact.com/truth-o-meter/promises/obameter/promise/496/create-clean-technology-venture-capital-fund/
15. Lovley, Erika, *Politico*, "Senators, Greens Spar Over Energy Bank," February 13, 2009.
16. Riley, Michael, Riley, *The Denver Post*, "Renewable-Energy Industry Protests Federal Funding Cuts," August 11, 2010.
17. Browner, Carol, and Ron Klain, Larry Summers, The White House, Briefing Memo, "Renewable Energy Loan Guarantees and Grants," October 25, 2010.
18. Bolton, Alexander, The Hill E2 Wire, "White House Backs Green Tax Provisions to Build Liberal Support," December 10, 2010.
19. Hsu, Tiffany, *The Los Angeles Times*, "Congress Extends Federal Treasury Grant Program for Renewable Energy Projects,"
20. Union of Concerned Scientists, "Production Tax Credit for Renewable Energy" April 22, 2009. http://www.ucsusa.org/clean_energy/solutions/big_picture_solutions/production-tax-credit-for.html
21. Roth, Bennett, *Roll Call*, 'Green Groups, Big Oil Conflicted Over Obama Offshore Drilling Switch," March 31, 2009.
22. Office of the Press Secretary, The White House, "Remarks by The President on Energy Security at Andrews Air Base, 3/31/2010," March 3, 2010.
23. Bolton, Alexander, *The Hill*, "Obama's Drilling Proposal Sparks Battle Among Senate Democrats," March 31, 2010.
24. Harder, Amy, *The National Journal*, "Offshore-Drilling Decision Makes Waves," December 1, 2010.
25. Streeter, A.K., treehugger.com, "Obama Defends Clean Coal, Tells Renewable Activist 'Don't Be Stubborn,'" February, 15, 2010. http://www.treehugger.com/files/2010/02/obama-defends-clean-coal.php

26. U.S. Department of Energy, "DOE's Fossil Energy Budget – Fiscal Year 2010,"
http://fossil.energy.gov/aboutus/budget/10/FY_2010_Budget.html
27. U.S. Department of Energy, "DOE's Fossil Energy Budget – Fiscal Year 2011."
http://fossil.energy.gov/aboutus/budget/11/FY_2011_Budget.html
28. U.S. Department of Energy, "President Requests $881.6 Million for Fossil Energy Programs," May 8 2009.
http://fossil.energy.gov/news/techlines/2009/09026-FE_Releases_FY10_Funding_Request.html
29. Bauer, Carl O., U.S. Department of Energy, National Energy Technology Laboratory, "Growing U.S. Investment in Carbon Capture and Storage.
30. *Carbon Capture Journal*, "DOE Invests $408 Million in Two Coal CCS Projects" July 2, 2009.
31. *Green Environmental News*, "Secretary Chu Declares $3 Billion Investment for Carbon Capture and Sequestration' December 4, 2009.
32. *Green Environmental News*, "Secretary Chu Declares Nearly $1 Billion Public-Private Investment in Industrial Carbon Capture and Storage," June 10, 2010.
33. *Carbon Capture Journal*, "NRG Receives DOE Funding for WA Parish Project," March 10, 2010.
34. Geman, Ben, *The New York Times*, "DOE Revives FutureGen, Reversing Bush-Era Decision," June 12, 2009.
35. U.S. Government Accountability Office, *Clean Coal: DOE Should Prepare a Comprehensive Analysis of the Relative Costs, Benefits, and Risks of a Range of Options for FutureGen*, Report No. GAO-09-465T, March 11, 2009.
36. Darling, Brian, redstate.com, "Obama Earmarks $1 Billion in Stimulus Money for Company in Illinois, August 6, 2009.
http://www.redstate.com/brian_d/2010/08/06/obama-earmarks-1-billion-in-stimulus-money-for-company-in-illinois/
37. U.S. Department of Energy, "DOE's Fossil Energy Budget – Fiscal Year 2008,"
http://www.fossil.energy.gov/aboutus/budget/08/FY_2008_Budget.html
38. *Report on the Interagency Task Force on Carbon Capture and Storage*, August 2010.
39. Clayton, Mark, *The Wall Street Journal*, "Obama's Nuclear Power Policy: A Study in Contradictions?," February 4, 2010.
40. Ling, Katherine, *E&E News*, "What Does $36 Billion Buy Demorats," February 9, 2010.
41. Behr, Peter, *The New York Times*, "DOE Delivers on Its First Long-Awaited Loan Guarantee," February 17, 2010.
42. Fehrenbacher, Katie, gigaom.com, "DOE Backs 2nd Nuclear Project with Loan Guarantee, March 21, 2010.

http://gigaom.com/cleantech/president-obama-to-announce-over-8b-in-loan-guarantees-for-nuclear/

Chapter 5. Energy Efficiency
1. Office of the President, "Memorandum for the Secretary of Energy: Appliance Efficiency Standards," February 5, 2009.
2. Davidson, Paul, USA Today, "Obama Wants Home Appliances to be More Energy-Efficient," February 6, 2009.
3. U.S. Department of Energy, "Secretary Chu Announces More Stringent Appliance Standards for Home Water Heaters and Other Heating Products," April 1, 2010.
4. Struglinski, Suzanne and Wesley Warren, National Resources Defense Council, "An Assessment of the Obama Administration's First Year Environmental Record," January, 2010.
5. U.S. Department of Energy, Office of Energy Efficiency and Renewable Energy, *Multi-Year Program Plan – Building Regulatory Programs*, October 2010.
6. Alliance to Save Energy, "The Implementation of National Consensus Appliance Agreement Act (INCAAA or S.3925), http://ase.org/resources/implementation-national-consensus-appliance-agreements-act-incaaa-s3925
7. Nadel, Steven, American Council for an Energy Efficient Economy, "2010 a Year of Mixed Progress on Energy Efficiency", January 6, 2011.
8. Charette, M.R., associatedcontent.com, "Obama's Appliance Rebate: Good Idea or More National Debt." http://www.associatedcontent.com/article/2107521/obamas_appliance_rebate_good_idea_or.html?cat=75
9. Holan, Angie Drobnic, politifact.com, Reduce Energy Consumption in Federal Buildings, March 12, 2009. http://www.politifact.com/truth-o-meter/promises/obameter/promise/464/reduce-energy-consumption-in-federal-buildings/
10. Norris, John K., *Clean Technica*, "Tapping the Energy Efficiency Market within Federal Building Lease Renewals, October 28, 2008. http://cleantechnica.com/2010/10/28/energy-efficiency-market-federal-building-lease-renewals/
11. The White House, Office of the Press Secretary, "President Obama Signs an Executive order Focused on Federal Leadership in Environmental, Energy and Economic Performance," October 5, 2009.
12. Burnham, Michael, *The New York Times*, "Obama Puts Government on Low-Carbon Diet," January 29, 2010.
13. Medici, Andy, Federal Times, "Obama Signs Law to Train 'Green' Building Managers," December 14, 2010.
14. Terry, David, National Association of State Energy Officials, "American Recovery and Reinvestment Act of 2009 Opportunities,"

15. Lorenz, Brandon, *Building Operating Management*, "Stimulus Bill Funds New Energy Grant Programs," April 2009. http://www.facilitiesnet.com/powercommunication/article/Stimulus-Bill-Funds-New-Energy-Grant-Programs--10703
16. ASHRAE, "ASHRAE Encourages States to Meet Current Building Energy Codes," August 17, 2010. http://www.facilitiesnet.com/powercommunication/article/Stimulus-Bill-Funds-New-Energy-Grant-Programs--10703
17. National Association of State Energy Officials, *U.S.State Energy Program under ARRA Briefing Book*, Fall 2010
18. Executive Office of the President of the United States and Vice President of the United States, *Recovery Through Retrofit*, October 2009.
19. Lee, Carol E., *Politico*, "Obama Touts Jobs-Energy Link," March 2, 2010.
20. Samuelson, Tracey D., *The Christian Science Monitor*, "Obama's Homestar Program: Energy Retrofits Could Take a While," March 2, 2010.
21. Sierra Club, "Vice President Biden Announces New Recovery through Retrofit Initiatives," November 12, 2010. http://sierraclub.typepad.com/compass/2010/11/vice-president-biden-announces-new-recovery-through-retrofit-initiatives.html
22. U.S. Department of Energy, "DOE to Fund Up to $454 Million for Retrofit Ramp-Ups in Energy Efficiency," September 14, 2009.
23. Schwartz, Ariel, *Fast Company*, "White House Retrofit Ramp-Up Program Boosts Local Energy Efficiency Projects," April 22, 2010.
24. The White House, "Memorandum for the President, Progress Report, The Transformation to a Clean Energy Economy," December 15, 2009.
25. Climateprogress.org, "GOP Leader Scrooge Boehner Disses, Weatherization Low-Income Homes and Cutting the Deficit," January 18, 2009. http://climateprogress.org/2009/01/18/house-minority-leader-john-boehner-scrooge-disses-low-income-home-weatherization/
26. Conner, Paul, *The Daily Caller*, "Obama's Weatherization Program Makes Little Economic Sense for Taxpayers," June 8, 2010.
27. Lowry, Rich, *Real Clear Politics*, "Obama's Stimulus & the Home Weatherization Lie," March 7, 2010.
28. Climateprogress.org, "Why the NYT's Criticism of DOE's Weatherization Program Misses the Point," February 24, 2010. http://climateprogress.org/2010/02/24/why-the-nyts-criticism-of-does-weatherization-program-misses-the-point/
29. National Center for Appropriate Technology, LIHEAP Funding. http://liheap.ncat.org/Funding/funding.htm
30. Loveley, Erika, *Politico*, "Obama Says Yes to Smart Grid," March 4, 2009.
31. Lerer, Lisa, *Politico*, "Obama Announces Smart Grid Plans," October 27, 2009.

32. The White House, Office of the Press Secretary, "President Obama Announces $3.4 Billion Investment to Spur Transition to Smart Energy Grid," October 27, 2009.
33. Snyder, Jim, *The Hill*, "Energy Unveils $100M Training Program," September 21, 2009.
34. U.S. Department of Energy, "Secretary Chu Announces $620 Million for Smart Grid Demonstration and Energy Storage Projects," November 24, 2009.
35. Executive Office of the President of the United States and Vice President of the United States, *The Recovery Act: Transforming the American Economy through Innovation*, August 2010.

Chapter 6. Clean Air
1. O'Keefe, Ed, *The Washington Post*, "Obama Halts New or Pending Bush Regulations," January, 20, 2009.
2. Bravender, Robin, *E&E News PM*; "Advocacy Groups Send Wish List to Obama Admin"; February 25, 2009.
3. Bravender, Robin, *Greenwire*, Obama Admin Signals Changes in EPA Reviews; February 20, 2009.
4. Bravender, Robin, *E&E News PM*, "EPA Proposes Revoking, Bush-Era 'Aggregation' Rule", March 30, 2010.
5. Bravender, Robin, *Greenwire*, "EPA Crafting Multipollutant Strategy", October 27, 2009.
6. Nelson, Gabriel, *Greenwire*, EPA Unveils Rules on Smog-Forming Emissions from Power Plants, July 6, 2010.
7. Goode, Darren, *The Hill E2 Wire*, "EPA Issues New Rule to Reduce Emissions, July 6, 2010.
8. Samuelson, Darren, *Politico*, "EPA Pushes Air Pollution Regulations", July 6, 2010.
9. Bravender, Robin, *E&E News PM*, "EPA Proposes New Nitrogen Standards", June 29, 2009.
10. Snyder, Jim, *The Hill*, "Clean Air Rule May Sink Ships", October 22, 2009.
11. Rogers, David, *Politico*, "Dems Trump Obama's Green Agenda", October 27, 2009.
12. Geman, Ben, *The Hill E2 Wire*, "EPA Pushes Tougher Air-Quality Rules", January 7, 2010.
13. Geman, Ben, *The Hill E2 Wire*, "EPA Delays, Tougher Air Pollution Rules", December 12, 2010.
14. Restuccia, Andrew, *The Hill E2 Wire*, "EPA Says Environmentalists are Overreacting to Delays in New Air Rules," December 10, 2010
15. Bravender, Robin, *Greenwire*, "EPA Scientists Recommend Tougher Soot Standards," March 12, 2010.
16. Goodman, Sara, *Greenwire*, "EPA Standards Aim to Curb Toxic Emissions from Boilers," Waste Incinerators," April 30, 2010.

17. Bravender, Robin, *Greenwire*, "EPA Proposes Wirhdrawal of Bush-Era Toxic Assessment," October 21, 2009.
18. Nelson, Garbriel, *Greenwire*, "EPA Moves to Clear Toxics, Rules Backlog," October 21, 2010
19. Samuelsohn, Darren, *Greenwire*, "Obama Admin Drops Mercury Petition to Supreme Court," February 6, 2009.
20. Neville, Angela, *PowerMag.com*, "EPA's Mercury Rule: Another Incarnation Coming," November 1, 2010.

Chapter 7. Clean Water
1. Boyle, Katherine, *Greenwire*, "Water Infrastructure, Great Lakes Benefit in Obama Proposal," February 26, 2009.
2. Bravender, Robin and Taryn Luntz, *Environment & Energy Daily*, "Conferees Vote to Increase Agency Funding by 36%," October 28, 2009.
3. Yehle, Emily, *E&E News PM*, "New EPA Policy Focuses on Infrastructure Planning, Funding," October 4, 2010.
4. Plautz, Jason, *Environment & Energy Daily*, "Nearly All Transporation and Infrastructure Funds Spent – Report," December 3, 2010.
5. Bravender, Robin, *Greenwire*, "EPA to Streamline Regs, Tighten Standards for 4 Carcinogens," March 22, 2010
6. Richert, Catherine, politifact.com, "Improve Water Quality-Obama Promise No. 263," September 30, 2009. www.politifact.com/truth-o-meter/promises/promise/263/improve-water-quality/
7. Bolton, Alexander, *The Hill E2 Wire*, "Senators Ask EPA to Act on Report of Carcinogen in DC's Drinking Water," December 21, 2010.
8. Lydersen, Kari, *Washington Post*, "Obama Plan Could Help Woo Michigan," September 17, 2008.
9. http://www.cglg.org/Overview/History.asp
10. *Great Lakes Restoration Initiative Action Plan - Executive Summary*, February 21, 2010, http://greatlakesrestoration.us/action/wp-content/uploads/glri_actionplan.pdf
11. Richert, Catherine, politifact.com, Fully Fund Contributions to the Preservation of the Everglades No. 504, January, 7, 2010. http://politifact.com/truth-o-meter/promises/promise/504/fully-fund-federal-contribution-to-the-preservatio/
12. *Greenwire*, "Judge Threatens Agencies with Contempt over Water Pollution," April 15, 2010.
13. Quinlin, Paul, *Greenwire*," EPA Smacks Fla. With Commands for Cleanup," September 8, 2010.
14. *Greenwire*, Fla. Officials Slam EPA Cleanup Plan, November 5, 2010.
15. Email from Obama campaign staff Lucas Knowles to David Bancroft and Jason Grumet, Subject: Chesapeake Bay Initiative, September 26, 2008.

16. Bancroft, David, *Baltimore Sun*, "Obama Would Dedicate Resources to Help Restore the Bay and Other National Treasures," October 3, 2008, pg. 25.
17. The White House, Office of the Press Secretary, Executive Order, "Chesapeake Bay Protection and Restoration, May 12, 2009. http://www.whitehouse.gov/the_press_office/Executive-Order-Chesapeake-Bay-Protection-and-Restoration/
18. *Federal Strategy for Chesapeake Launches Major Initiatives and Holds Government Accountable for Progress*, May 12, 2010. http://executiveorder.chesapeakebay.net/post/New-Federal-Strategy-for-Chesapeake-Launches-Major-Initiatives-and-Holds-Government-Accountable-for-Progress.aspx
19. Blankenship, Karl, *Bay Journal*, "New Federal Bay Strategy Promises Unprecedented Effort," June 2010. http://www.bayjournal.com/article.cfm?article=3856
20. Eilperin, Juliet, *Washington Post*, EPA Unveils Massive Restoration Plan for Chesapeake Bay, December 29, 2010.
21. Executive Office of the President, Council on Environmental Quality, "Obama Administration Officials Release Roadmap for Gulf Coast Ecosystem Restoration Focused on Resiliency and Sustainability," March 4, 2010. http://www.whitehouse.gov/administration/eop/ceq/Press_Releases/March_4_2010
22. Bolton, Alexander, *The Hill*, "Obama's Drilling Proposal Sparks Battle Among Senate Dems," March 31, 2010.
23. *Guardian*, "BP Oil Spill Timeline," July 22, 2010. http://www.guardian.co.uk/environment/2010/jun/29/bp-oil-spill-timeline-deepwater-horizon
24. Scheyder, Ernest, *Reuters*, "BP Estimates Oil Spill Up to 100,000 Barrels per Day in Document," June 20, 2010.
25. Bendery, Jennifer, Roll Call, "Obama Warms of 'Unprecedented Disaster Along Gulf Coast," May 2, 2010.
26. Gemen, Ben and Sam Youngman, *The Hill*, "Obama Gulf 'Battle Plan'," June 15, 2010.
27. Phillip, Abby and Glenn Thrush, *Politico*, "Green Wary of Sunny Spill Report," August 5, 2010.
28. Zichal, Heather, The White House Blog, "New Report: 74% of Oil in BP Deepwater Horizon Oil Spill has been Contained or Mitigated," August 4, 2010. http://www.whitehouse.gov/blog/2010/08/04/new-report-74-oil-bp-deepwater-horizon-oil-spill-has-been-contained-or-mitigated
29. Richert, Catherine, politifact.com, "Wetlands Protection Get a Boost," December 1, 2009. http://www.politifact.com/truth-o-meter/promises/promise/282/support-wetlands-protection/
30. Sutley, Nancy, The White House Blog, "Milestone Stormwater Guidance from EPA," December 11, 2009.

http://www.whitehouse.gov/blog/2009/12/11/milestone-stormwater-guidance-pa

31. Executive Office of the President, Council on Environmental Quality, "Obama Administration Officials Announce the Final Recommendations of the Ocean Policy Task Force," July 19, 2010. http://www.whitehouse.gov/administration/eop/ceq/Press_Releases/July_19_2010

Chapter 8. Healthy Communities

1. Morrison, Blake, USA Today, "GAO Report Scolds EPA", March 18, 2010/
2. Stephenson, John B., United States Government Accountability Office, "Environmental Health: Opportunities for Greater Focus, Direction, and Top-Level Commitment to Children's Health at EPA:," Testimony before the Committee of Environment and Public Works, U.S. Senate, Report Number GAO-10-545T, March 17, 2010.
3. United States Government Accountability Office "Environmental Health: High-level Strategy and Leadership Needed to Continue Progress toward Protecting Children from Environmental Threats," GAO-10-205, January 28, 2010.
4. Grevatt, Peter, Director of the Office of Children's Health Protection and Environmental Education, U.S. Environmental Protection Agency, Testimony before the Committee on Environment and Public Work, U.S. Senate, March 17, 2010, http://www.epa.gov/ocirpage/hearings/testimony/111_2009_2010/2010_0317_pg.pdf
5. Jackson, Lisa P., Administrator, U.S. Environmental Protection Agency, Testimony before the Committee on Environment and Public Work, U.S. Senate, December 2, 2009, http://www.epa.gov/ocirpage/hearings/testimony/111_2009_2010/2009_1202_lpj.pdf
6. Dooley, Cal, *The Hill*, "The Chemical-Law Formula," July 6, 2010.
7. Hamby, Chris, The Center for Public Integrity Blog Paper Trail, "EPA Toxic Chemical Bill Likely on Hold Until After Election," September 16, 2010, http://www.publicintegrity.org/blog/entry/2413/
8. Sapien, Joaquin, *Politico*, "Vitter Fights for Formaldehyde," April 15, 2010.
9. U.S. Environmental Protection Agency, "EPA Analysis Shows Reduction in 2009 Toxic Chemical Releases/Agency Completes Analysis on Chemical Disposal and Release," December 16, 2010. http://yosemite.epa.gov/opa/admpress.nsf/d0cf6618525a9efb85257359003fb69d/f5b765d526cae068852577fb0058d5ad!OpenDocument
10. Pritchard, Justin, *The Huffington Post*, "Cadmium, Lead Found in Drinking Glasses," November 21, 2010. http://www.huffingtonpost.com/2010/11/21/cadmium-lead-found-in-dri_n_786615.html

11. *International Business Times*, "CPSC Urges Toy Jewelry Industry to Use Accepted Levels of Cadmium in Kid's Jewelry," October 22, 2010. http://www.ibtimes.com/articles/74914/20101022/consumer-product-and-safety-commission-cpsc-mcdonald-s-shrek-glasses-fashion-jewelry-accessories-tra.htm
12. Nichols, Tim, *Rochester Independent Examiner*, "Fed Rethinks Cadmium Limits, Leaves Foxes Guarding the Hen House," October 20, 2010. http://www.examiner.com/independent-in-rochester/fed-rethinks-cadmium-limits-leaves-foxes-guarding-the-hen-house
13. The United States Conference of Mayors, "New Report Shows Brownfield Redevelopment in Cities Leads to More Jobs, Increased Tax Revenue," November 9, 2010. http://www.usmayors.org/pressreleases/uploads/ReleaseBrownfieldsReport2010.pdf
14. Bravender, Robin, Taryn Lutz and Sara Goodman, *Greenwire*, "Obama Proposal Trims Agency Spending by $300M, February 1, 2010.
15. Goodman, Sara, *Greenwire*, "EPA Provides Grants Worth, $79 M to Spur Cleanups," April 19, 2010.
16. Schor, Elana, *E&E News PM*, "EPA Offers $4M for Brownfields Redevelopment," October 15, 2010.
17. Partnership for Sustainable Communities, http://www.whitehouse.gov/sites/default/files/uploads/SCP-Fact-Sheet.pdf
18. Boyle, Katherine, *Greenwire*, "Water Infrastructure, Great Lakes Benefit in Obama Proposal," February 26, 2009
19. Cappiello, Dina, *newsday.com*, "Obama's EPA Plans Fewer Toxic Cleanups," August 10, 2009.
20. Jacobson, Louis, politifact.com, "Restore Superfund Programs So That Polluters Pay for Clean-Ups," December 11, 2009. http://politifact.com/truth-o-meter/promises/obameter/promise/318/restore-superfund-program-so-that-polluters-pay-fo/
21. Schor, Elana, *E&E News PM*, "EPA Sends Draft 'Polluter Pays' Bill to Capitol Hill," June 21, 2010.
22. Bogardus, Kevin, *The Hill*, "Superfund Tax Push Spurs Rush for New Lobbyists," June 22, 2010.
23. *The Washington Post*, "Mountain of Trouble," March 8, 2009.
24. Hawthorne, Michael, *Los Angeles Times*, "Obama Puts Nuclear Waste on Hold," March 9, 2009.
25. Mascaro, Lisa, *Las Vegas Sun*, "Obama to Zero Out Yucca Mountain Funding, Pull License," February 1, 2010.
26. Soraghan, Mike, *Greenwire*, "Salt Domes Better Than Yucca for Long-Term Storage – Chu," March 4, 2010.
27. Rosen, James, *McClatchy Newspapers*, "Obama to Halt Yucca Mountain Nuclear Waste Site Slammed," July 27, 2010.

28. *Greenwire*, "Investigation of NRC Chairman's Yucca Directions Requested," October 14, 2010.
29. Soraghan, Mike, *E&E News PM,* "Jackson, Congressional Black Caucus to Launch Environmental Justice Tour," January 22, 2010.
30. *Greenwire*, "Agency Eyes Enviro Justice Tool," July 27, 2009.
31. Nelson, Gabriel, *Greenwire,* "Agency Directs Employees to Protect Poor, Minorities" July 27, 2010.
32. Nelson, Gabriel, *Greenwire,* "White House Meeting Yields 'Environmental Justice' Pledges" September 22, 2010.
33. U.S. Environmental Protection Agency, "Federal Interagency Working Group on Environmental Justice," September 22, 2010. http://www.epa.gov/environmentaljustice/interagency/index.html

Chapter 9. Land and Wildlife
1. Richert, Catharine, politifact.com, "Increased Funding for National Parks and Forests," November 4, 2009. http://www.politifact.com/truth-o-meter/promises/obameter/promise/269/increase-funding-for-national-parks-and-forests/
2. Kiernan, Tom, *The Huffington Post*, "Obama Promise & America's National Parks: A Source of Green Jobs and Growth," February 24, 2010.
3. National Trust for Historic Preservation, "Analyzing President Obama's FY2011 Budget Request," http://www.preservationnation.org/take-action/advocacy-center/on-the-hill/budget.html
4. Richert, Catharine, politifact.com. "Protect Forest Service Lands from More Roads," January 4, 2010. http://www.politifact.com/truth-o-meter/promises/obameter/promise/281/protect-forest-service-lands-from-more-roads/
5. Heritage Forests Campaign, "Pew Environment Group Statement on the Obama Administration's Support for Roadless Forests," August 14, 2009. http://www.ourforests.org/press/pr2009-8-14.html\
6. Reese, April, National Forest Legal News Blog, "Obama Admin Gears Up for New Planning Rule," April 4, 2010. http://www.nationalforestlawblog.com/apps/blog/entries/show/3355782-new-obama-forest-planning-rule-to-emphasize-climate-change-current-science
7. Heritage Forests Campaign, "Holiday Ad Asks Obama to Protect National Forest," December 15, 2010. http://www.ourforests.org/press/pr15dec2010.html
8. Goad, Ben, *The Press Enterprise*, "Obama Administration Takes on Climate Change in National Forests," December 10, 2010. http://www.pe.com/localnews/politics/stories/PE_News_Local_D_climate21.3e8b1ab.html

9. U.S. Forest Service, Climate Change Performance Scorecard 2010. http://www.fs.fed.us/climatechange/pdf/performance_scorecard_final.pdf
10. Richert, Catharine, politifact.com, "Increase Funding for the Land and Water Conservation Fund," November 4, 2009. http://www.politifact.com/truth-o-meter/promises/obameter/promise/270/increase-funding-for-the-land-and-water-conservati/
11. Rogers, David, *Politico*, "Lands Bill Lassoes Longtime Foes," March 24, 2009.
12. Remarks by the President at Signing of the Omnibus Public Lands Management Act 2009. http://www.whitehouse.gov/the-press-office/remarks-president-signing-omnibus-public-lands-management-act-2009-33009
13. Subbotin, Melissa, Congressional Western Caucus, "GOP-ers Bristle at Feds' Land Plan," May 12, 2010. http://robbishop.house.gov/WesternCaucus/News/Default.aspx?postid=185178
14. Presidential Memorandum – America's Great Outdoors. http://www.whitehouse.gov/the-press-office/presidential-memorandum-americas-great-outdoors
15. Lee, Jesse, The White House Blog, "Creating the 21st Century for America's Outdoors," April 16, 2010. http://www.whitehouse.gov/blog/2010/04/16/creating-a-21st-century-strategy-americas-outdoors
16. Eilperin, Juliet, and Scott Wilson, *The Washington Post*, "Obama Launches America's Great Outdoors Conservation Initiative," April 17, 2010.
17. Maron, Dina Maron, *ClimateWire*, "Environmentalists Press for Funding Stream to Conserve 'Great Outdoors,'" September 13, 2010.
18. Wyatt, Kristen, *The Huffington Post*, "Wilderness Rules: Obama Plans to Reverse Bush-Era Policy," December 23, 2010.
19. Richert, Catharine, politifact.com. "Partner with Landowners to Conserve Private Lands," December 30, 2009. http://politifact.com/truth-o-meter/promises/obameter/promise/271/partner-with-landowners-to-conserve-private-lands/
20. Power, Stephen, *The Wall Street Journal*, "Obama Blocks Bush's Endangered-Species Rule," March 3, 2009.
21. Clark, Jamie Rappaport, *The Washington Post*, "Interior Department's Decision Imperils Wolves, Endangered Species Act," January 1, 2010.
22. Neary, Ben, *Deseret News*, "Federal Judge Rules for Wyoming in Wolf Lawsuit," November 20, 2010. http://www.deseretnews.com/article/700084056/Federal-judge-rules-for-Wyoming-in-wolf-lawsuit.html

23. Office of the Secretary, U.S. Department of the Interior, "Interior to Examine Endangered Species Questions as Part of BP Oil Spill Reviews," May 14, 2010. http://www.doi.gov/news/pressreleases/Interior-to-Examine-Endangered-Species-Questions-as-Part-of-BP-Oil-Spill-Reviews.cfm
24. Repanshek, Kurt, *National Parks Traveler*, "Interior Secretary Sued for Not Following Endangered Species Guidelines in Gulf of Mexico," July 27, 2010.
25. Reis, Patrick, *The New York Times*, "Obama Admin Denies Endangered Species Listing for America Pika," February 5, 2010.
26. Center for Biological Diversity, "Obama Administration Denies Endangered Species Act Protection to 251 Species," November 9, 2010. http://www.biologicaldiversity.org/news/press_releases/2010/251-species-11-09-2010.html
27. Eilperin, Juliet, *The Washington Post*, "Administration Proposes Listing Artic Seals as Threatened," December 3, 2010.
28. Fears, Darryl, *The Washington Post*, "Polar Bears Will Not Continue as 'Threatened,' not 'Endangered,'" December 22, 2010.
29. Daly, Matthew, *The Washington Post*, "Feds Set Aside 'Critical Habitat' for Polar Bear," November 24, 2010.

Chapter 10. Transportation
1. Lee, Carol E. and Victoria McGrane, *Politico*, "Obama Open to State-Run Emissions," January 27, 2009.
2. Allen, Mike and Eamon Javers, *Politico*, "Obama Announces New Fuel Standards," May 18, 2009.
3. Lerer, Lisa, *Politico*, "W.H. Finalizes Strict Fuel Standards," April 1, 2010.
4. Snyder, Jim and Silla Brush, *The Hill*, "Porsche, Other Cars Companies Lobby to Ease New Fuel Efficiency Standards," December 18, 2009.
5. Geman, Ben, *The Hill E2Wire*, "Obama Shifts Energy Narrative Away from Offshore Drilling to Clean-Energy Plans," May 21, 2010.
6. Bravender, Robin, Politico, "EPA Plan Could Cut Truck Emission," October 26, 2010.
7. Baker, Peter, *The New York Times*, "Obama Mandates Rules to Raise Fuel Standards," May 21, 2010.
8. Bolton, Alexander, *The Hill*, "Senate Approves $2 Billion for Cash for clunkers,'" August 6, 2009.
9. Richert, Catharine, politifact.com, "Mandate Flexible Fuel Vehicles by 2012," December 18, 2009. http://www.politifact.com/truth-o-meter/promises/obameter/promise/472/mandate-flexible-fuel-vehicles-by-2012/
10. Automobile Magazine, "Congressional Flex Fuel Mandates Troubles Auto Industry," http://blogs.automobilemag.com/congressional-flexfuel-mandate-troubles-auto-industry-725.html

11. Bravender, Robin, *Politico*, "EPA to OK Higher Ethanol-Gas Blends," October 12, 2010.
12. Szczesny, Joseph R., *Time*, "Adding Up the Auto Bailout: $80 Billion and Growing," May 11, 2009.
13. Richard, Michael Graham, treehugger.com, Ford to Invest $850M to Retool Factories for More Fuel-Efficient Vehicles," October 29, 2010. http://www.treehugger.com/files/2010/10/ford-to-invest-850m-dollars-retool-factories-fuel-efficient-vehicles-michigan.php
14. Richard, Michael Graham, treehugger.com, "Chrysler and GM are Retooling Their Factories for Fuel-Efficient Cars," November 1, 2010. http://www.treehugger.com/files/2010/11/chrysler-and-gm-retooling-factories-for-fuel-efficient-cars.php
15. Kiel, Paul, *ProPublica*, "The $85 Billion Taxpayer Auto Bailout," May 12, 2009. http://www.propublica.org/article/bailout-for-breakfast-512
16. Maynard, Micheline, *The New York Times*, "Downturn Will Test Obama's Vision for an Energy-Efficient Auto Industry," December 21, 2008.
17. Appel, Adrienne, ocnus.net, "Workers Win and Lose in Chrysler Retooling," May 1, 2009. http://www.ocnus.net/artman2/publish/Labour_9/Workers_Win_and_Lose_in_Chrysler_Retooling.shtml
18. Welch, David, *BusinessWeek*, "GM Files for Bankruptcy," June 1, 2009.
19. Christie, Rebecca and Ian Katz, *BusinessWeek*, "GM IPO: A Good for Obama's Auto Bankers," November 24, 2010.
20. The White House, Office of the Press Secretary, "Remarks by the President on General Motors," November 18, 2010. http://www.ocnus.net/artman2/publish/Labour_9/Workers_Win_and_Lose_in_Chrysler_Retooling.shtml
21. Mills, Richard (Rick), *Resource Investor*, "Obama Clean Energy Agenda on Track," August 23, 2010. http://www.resourceinvestor.com/News/2010/8/Pages/Obamas-Clean-Energy-Agenda-on-Track.aspx
22. Clayton, Mark, *The Christian Science Monitor*, "Why Obama is Putting So Much Stock in Battery Technology," July 15, 2010.
23. Lerer, Lisa, *Politico*, "GM Pins Hopes for Recharge on Volt," June 3, 2009.
24. Coppa, Brian, examiner.com, "Stimulus Funding Spurs Advanced Battery R&D for Hybrid Electric Vehicles," March 5, 2010. http://www.examiner.com/green-business-in-phoenix/stimulus-funding-spurs-advanced-battery-r-d-for-hybrid-electric-vehicles?render=print
25. "State and Federal Hybrid Incentives," http://go.ucsusa.org/hybridcenter/incentives.cfm
26. Farley, Robert, politifact.com, "Enact Tax Credit for Consumers for Plug-In Hybrid Cars" March 23, 2009. http://www.politifact.com/truth-o-

meter/promises/obameter/promise/459/enact-tax-credit-for-consumers-for-hybrid-cars/

27. "Chevy Volt Exact Launch Date Will be Mid-November 2010, Tens of Thousands in 2011,": http://gm-volt.com/2009/04/20/chevy-volt-exact-launch-date-will-be-mid-november-2010-tens-of-thousands-in-2011/
28. Costea, Andrei, *AutoEvolution*, "Nissan Leaf Japanese Launch Date Revealed," December 3, 2010. http://www.autoevolution.com/news/nissan-leaf-japanese-launch-date-revealed-27650.html
29. Jacobson, Louis, politifact.com, "Require Plug-In Fleet at the White House," December 16, 2009. http://politifact.com/truth-o-meter/promises/obameter/promise/468/require-hybrid-fleet-at-the-white-house/
30. Murphy, Jarrett, *City Limits*, "White House: Congestion Pricing on the Table," April 16, 2010. http://www.citylimits.org/news/articles/3939/white-house-congestion-pricing-on-the-table
31. Nelson, Gabriel, *The New York Times*, "'Smart Growth' Taking Hold in U.S. Cities, Studys Says," March 24, 2010.
32. Rahim, Saqib, Transportation Equity Network, "Officials Warn Obama's 'Smart Growth' Initiatives May be Hard to Sell," January 17, 2010. http://transportationequity.blogspot.com/2010/01/transportation-officials-warn-obamas.html
33. HUD-DOT-EPA Partnership for Sustainable Communities, "Livability Principles," http://www.epa.gov/dced/partnership/#livabilityprinciples
34. *The Telegraph*, "Obama Administration Spends $1.2 Billion on Cycling and Walking Initiatives," June 16, 2010. http://www.telegraph.co.uk/news/worldnews/northamerica/usa/7834334/Obama-administration-spends-1.2-billion-on-cycling-and-walking-initiatives.html
35. Phillip, Abby, *Politico*, "Green Transit Advocates Seek Gain," September 14, 2009.
36. Freemark, Yonah, *The Transport Politic*, "High-Speed Rail Grants Announced; California, Florida and Illinois are Lucky Recipients," January 28, 2010. http://www.telegraph.co.uk/news/worldnews/northamerica/usa/7834334/Obama-administration-spends-1.2-billion-on-cycling-and-walking-initiatives.html
37. Jacobson, Louis, politifact.com. "Require Energy Conservation in Use of Transportation Dollars," December 8, 2009. http://www.politifact.com/truth-o-meter/promises/obameter/promise/488/require-energy-conservation-in-use-of-transportati/

38. Freemark, Yonah, *The Transport Politic*, "TIGER II Grants Emphasize Limited Investment in Small and Mid-Size Communities," October 20, 2010. http://www.thetransportpolitic.com/2010/10/20/tiger-ii-grants-emphasize-limited-investments-in-small-and-mid-size-communities/

Chapter 11. Agriculture
1. Winter, Allison, *Energy & Environment Daily*, "Obama Admin to Defend Oversight of Conservative Programs," October 5, 2009.
2. Environmental Working Group, "News Release - Cutting Conservation Program No Way to Fight Global Warming," May 12, 2009. http://www.ewg.org/Cutting-Conservation-Programs
3. Winter, Allison, *Energy & Environment Daily*, "Vilsack to Defend Cuts to Farm Bill Programs," February 22, 2010.
4. Environmental Working Group, "News Release - Farmers, Labor, Green Groups United to Fight Cuts in Conservation Programs,' March 16, 2009. http://reports.ewg.org/Farmers_Labor_Enviros_Fight_Cuts_to_Conservation_Programs
5. Citizens Campaign for the Environment, CAFOs 101 Factsheet. http://www.citizenscampaign.org/campaigns/farming.asp
6. Citizens Campaign for the Environment, "Letter Signed by CCE and Our Federal Coalition Partners Urging Congress to Close the EQIP Factory Farm Loophole," May 8, 2007. http://www.citizenscampaign.org/PDFs/EQIP_CAFOletter_Senate_8May2007.pdf
7. U.S. Environmental Protection Agency, "New Requirements for Controlling Manure, Wastewater from Large Animal Feeding Operations", October 31, 2008.
8. MacCurdy, Meline, Martin Law. "EPA Issues Guidance for CAFPs on Scope of Clean Water Act Permitting, Plans Further Rulemaking," July 1, 2010.
9. Bottemiller, Helena, *Food Safety News*, "Settlement in CAFO Clean Water Act Case," May 28, 2010.
10. U.S. Environmental Protection Agency, Office of Enforcement and Compliance Assurance, *Clean Water Action Plan*, October 15, 2009.
11. Kirby, David, *The Huffington Post*, "Is Obama Ready to Take on Factory Farming," November 11, 2009. http://www.huffingtonpost.com/david-kirby/is-obama-ready-to-take-on_b_352696.html
12. U.S. Environmental Protection Agency, Office of Water, Office of Wastewater Management, *Implementation Guidance on CAFO Regulations – CAFOs That Discharge or Are Proposing to Discharge*, EPA-833-R-10-006, May 28, 2010.
13. U.S. Department of Agriculture, Business and Cooperative Programs, Rural Energy for America Program Grants/Energy Audit and

Renewable Energy Development Assist (REAP/EA/REDA), http://www.rurdev.usda.gov/rbs/busp/REAPEA.htm
14. U.S. Department of Agriculture, "USDA Observes the Anniversary of an Agreement to Cut Dairy Farm Greenhouse Gas Emissions," December 15, 2010.
15. U.S. Environmental Protection Agency, Office of Transportation and Air Quality, *EISA 2007: Renewable Fuel Standard Program*, March 2009. http://www1.eere.energy.gov/biomass/pdfs/Policy1_Simon.pdf
16. Zeman, Nicholas, *Biodiesel Magazine*, B20: The Best of Both Worlds, November 20, 2009.
17. U.S. Department of Agriculture, President Obama Issues Presidential Directive to USDA to Expand Access to Biofuels, May 9, 2009 http://www.usda.gov/wps/portal/usda/usdahome?contentidonly=true&contentid=2009/05/0145.xml
18. The White House, Office of the Press Secretary, "President Obama Announces Steps to Support Sustainable Energy Options, Departments of Agriculture and Energy, Environmental Protection Agency to Lead Efforts," May 2009.
19. The White House, *Growing America's Fuel An Innovation Approach to Achieving the President's Biofuels Target*, http://www.whitehouse.gov/sites/default/files/rss_viewer/growing_americas_fuels.PDF
20. Geman, Ben, *The Hill*, "EPA Ruling Boosts, Ethanol, After Fierce Lobbying Effort for Corn-Based Fuels," February 3, 2010.
21. Hughes, Siobhan, *The Wall Street Journal*, "Obama Administration Cuts Cellulosic Ethanol Target, November 29, 2010.
22. U.S. Environmental Protection Agency, *EPA Finalizes 2011 Renewable Fuel Standards*, EPA-420-F-10-056, November 2010
23. Bravender, Robin, *Politico*, EPA to OK Higher Ethanol-Gas Blends, October 12, 2010.
24. Drevna, Charles T., *The Hill*, EPA Approval of E15 Hurts Consumers, January 5, 2011.
25. Brasher, Philip, *The DesMoines Register*, "Ethanol Industry Wants Milder Pump Label," January 4, 2011.
26. Loveday, Eric, green.autoblog.com, "President Obama Approves Ethanol, Biodiesel, Plug-In Charger Tax Credit Extension," December 19, 2010.
27. U.S. Department of Energy, Office of Energy Efficiency and Renewable Energy, *Fiscal Year 2010 Budget-in-Brief*, http://www1.eere.energy.gov/ba/pba/pdfs/fy10_budget_brief.pdf
28. Crooks, Tony, USDA Rural Development, *Biorefinery Models and USDA Rural Development Funding*, November 17, 2010. http://www.farmfoundation.org/news/articlefiles/1731-Crooks_Biorefinery_Business_Models%5B1%5D.pdf
29. *Sustainable Business*, "Range Fuels Begins Commercial Cellulosic Operations in Georgia, August 19, 2010.

30. Furlow, Bryant, *American Independent*, "NM: Sapphire Energy Poised to Make 'Super Algae' a Competitive Energy Source," July 26, 2010.
31. Pollack, Andrew, *The New York Times*, "Exploring Algae as Fuel," July 26, 2010.
32. National Sustainable Agriculture Coalition, "Organic Certification Cost Share," http://sustainableagriculture.net/publications/grassrootsguide/organic-production/organic-certification-cost-share/
33. U.S. Department of Agriculture, "National Organic Certification Cost-Share Program – Agriculture Management Assistance," November 24, 2010.
34. Gustafson, Katherine, *Sustainable Food*, "Stop the Repeal of the National Organic Certification Cost-Share Program, http://food.change.org/petitions/view/stop_the_repeal_of_the_national_organic_certification_cost-share_program
35. Burros, Marian, *Politico*, "Obama Ag Policies Sow Confusion," February 11, 2010.
36. National Sustainable Agriculture Coalition, "Obama Administration Caves on Agriculture Reform," January 6, 2010. http://sustainableagriculture.net/blog/obama-administration-caves-on-agriculture-reform/
37. Rose, Caitlan, Down to Earth, "What Will the Healthy, Hunger Free Kids Act Look Like in Action," December 28, 2010.
38. National Sustainable Agriculture Coalition, "President Obams Signs Food Safety Modernization Act into Law," January 7, 2011 http://sustainableagriculture.net/blog/obama-signs-food-safety-bill-2/
39. *Crop Life*, MACA Letter to White House about Organic Garden, March 31, 2009. http://www.croplife.com/news/?storyid=1657
40. Burros, Marian, *Politico*, Grapes of Wrath, June 17, 2009.

Chapter 12. Conclusions
1. Stein, Sam, *The Huffington Post*, "Obama Compares Himself to Reagan, JFK,…But Not Bill Clinton," March 28, 2008.
2. Bateman, Thomas S., *The Washington Post*, "Is President Obama a 'Transformational Leader?,'" March 8, 2010.
3. *The Guardian*, "BP Oil Spill Timeline," July 22, 2010.
4. Matthews, Chris, MSNBC "'Hardball with Chris Matthews' for Thursday, January 6th, 2011," January 6, 2011. http://www.msnbc.msn.com/id/40966860/ns/msnbc_tv-hardball_with_chris_matthews/
5. Lerer, Lisa, *Politico*, "Climate Push Gets Personal," July 17, 2009.
6. Romm, Joseph, *Grist*, "The Failed Presidency of Barack Obama, Part 1," July 22, 2010.
7. Lerer, Lisa, *Politico*, "GOP Senators Seek End to Czars," September 16, 2009.
8. Factcheck.org, "Czar Search," September 25, 2009.

9. Shear, Michael D., and Philip Rucker, *The Washington Post*, "Picks for Key Government Posts Play Long Waiting Game," March 4, 2009.
10. Baker, Peter, *The New York Times*, "Obama Team Has Billions to Spend, But Few Ready to Do It," February 18, 2009.
11. Personal conversation with Jason Grumet, March 4, 2009.
12. Wenner, Jann S., *Rolling Stone*, "Obama in Command: The Rolling Stone Interview," September 28, 2010.
13. Raju, Manu, *Poltico*, "Mitch McConnell Doubles Down Against President Obama," November 3, 2010.
14. *The Washington Post*, May 23, 1997.
15. Rogers, Diane Kim, *The Christian Science Monitor*, "Pelosi Proves It Ain't Over Until the Speaker Lady Sings," March 25, 2010.
16. Romm, Joseph, *Grist*, "The Failed Presidency of Barack Obama, Post-Election Edition," November 4, 2010.
17. Dickenson, Tim, *Rolling Stone*, "Climate Bill, R.I.P.," July 21, 2010.
18. Jackson, David, *USA Today*, "Obama's Approval Ratings Fall in Second Year," January 22, 2011.
19. Tomasky, Michael, *The New York Review of Books*, "The Elections: How Bad for Democrats," October 28, 2010.
20. Obama Campaign Email from Lucas Knowles, November 12, 2008.
21. Warmhoff, Steve, Citizens for Tax Justice, "The Bush Tax Cuts Cost Two and Half Times as Much as the House Democrats' Health Care Proposal," September 8, 2009.
22. Strum, Harvey, and Fred Strum, *Environmental Review*, "American Solar Energy Policy, 1952-1982," Volume 7, No. 2, Summer 1983.
23. Employment Research Associates, U.S. Department of Energy, Great Lakes Regional Biomass Energy Program/Council of Great Lakes Governors, "Biomass Resources: Generating Jobs and Energy, 1985.
24. Obama, Barack, *Real Clear Politics*, "A Choice Between Prosperity and Decline," April 22, 2009.
25. Gruver, William R., *Patriot News*, "The Real Transformational Leader: Obama or Tea Party?," December 16, 2010.
26. Lizza, Ryan, *The New Yorker*, "As the World Burns," October 11, 2010.

ABOUT THE AUTHOR

David B. Bancroft, who has over two decades of experience in the environmental nonprofit community, is the Founder and President of Council on Environmental Affairs (COEA). COEA provides a forum for innovative policy ideas on clean air, clean water, renewable energy, sustainability and climate change. During 2008, he served on the Obama Campaign as a member of the Energy and Environment Work Group

Prior to that, David was President of the environmental partnership organization, the Alliance for the Chesapeake Bay. At the Alliance, his dynamic leadership revitalized the organization, and began a period of programmatic growth addressing agricultural, stormwater and watershed restoration issues. In addition, he devised and performed the *Institutional Governance Analysis: The Role of the Headwaters States in Chesapeake Bay Cleanup*. That study resulted in states of Delaware, New York and West Virginia being invited to play a leadership position in the U.S. Environmental Protection Agency Chesapeake Bay Program, after having been excluded for over 20 years.

As Executive Vice President of the Solar Energy Industries Association, David helped spearhead the creation of the Million Solar Roofs program. That initiative was announced by President Clinton at the United Nations in 1997, as the first U.S. commitment to help fulfill the global climate change goals of the Kyoto Protocol.

Earlier in his career, David spent five years as the Deputy Executive Director of the Council of Great Lakes Governors, a consortium of eight governors and two Canadian premiers focused on the environmental protection and economic development of the Great Lakes Basin. He was instrumental in the success of several multi-state agreements including the implementation the Great Lakes Charter, and the genesis of the Great Lakes Toxic Substances Control Agreement.

While at the Council, David formed a partnership with the U.S. Department of Energy, creating the Great Lakes Regional Biomass Energy Program, an advanced biofuels commercialization program. He fostered the groundbreaking study, *Biomass Resources: Generating Jobs and Energy*, adopted by six Midwestern governors as a green jobs and economic development strategy - twenty years before it became federal policy in the Obama Administration.

He has served as Executive Director of the Environmental Business Action Coalition, and David was the very first Executive Director of the Maryland League of Conservation Voters. In that capacity, David campaigned for the re-election of Parris Glendening as Maryland Governor.

Previously, David had worked on the political campaigns of: Herb Kohl for U.S. Senate; Russ Feingold for U.S. Senate; Tony Earl for U.S. Senate; Tom Loftus for Wisconsin Governor; and Paul Soglin for Mayor of Madison, Wisconsin.

David did graduate work in Political Science at the University of Wisconsin-Madison. He holds a Masters degree in Technology and Policy from Washington University in St. Louis, Missouri and Bachelors in Environmental Science from the University of Wisconsin-Green Bay

David, along with his trusted Basenji dog, Digger, is a resident of the Washington, DC area, but spends as much time as he can in Berkeley Springs, WV over looking the Potomac.

If you have any questions or comments for David, you may reach him at dbancroft@live.com

Made in the USA
San Bernardino, CA
28 January 2017